Redemption or Annihilation?

Studies in European Thought

E. Allen McCormick
General Editor

Vol. 17

PETER LANG
New York · Washington, D.C./Baltimore · Boston · Bern
Frankfurt am Main · Berlin · Brussels · Vienna · Canterbury

John Tietz

Redemption or Annihilation?

Love versus Power in Wagner's *Ring*

PETER LANG
New York • Washington, D.C./Baltimore • Boston • Bern
Frankfurt am Main • Berlin • Brussels • Vienna • Canterbury

Library of Congress Cataloging-in-Publication Data

Tietz, John.
Redemption or annihilation?: love versus
power in Wagner's Ring / John Tietz.
p. cm. — (Studies in European thought; v. 17)
Includes bibliographical references (p.   ) and index.
1. Wagner, Richard, 1813–1883. Ring des Nibelungen. 2. Music—Philosophy and
aesthetics. I. Title. II. Series: Studies in European thought; vol. 17.
ML410.W15T64   782.1—dc21   98-21978
ISBN 0-8204-4148-1
ISSN 1043-5786

Die Deutsche Bibliothek-CIP-Einheitsaufnahme

Tietz, John:
Redemption or annihilation?: love versus
power in Wagner's Ring / John Tietz.
–New York; Washington, D.C./Baltimore; Boston; Bern;
Frankfurt am Main; Berlin; Vienna; Paris: Lang.
(Studies in European thought; Vol. 17)
ISBN 0-8204-4148-1

The paper in this book meets the guidelines for permanence and durability
of the Committee on Production Guidelines for Book Longevity
of the Council of Library Resources.

© 1999 Peter Lang Publishing, Inc., New York

All rights reserved.
Reprint or reproduction, even partially, in all forms such as microfilm,
xerography, microfiche, microcard, and offset strictly prohibited.

Printed in the United States of America

Vernunft fänt wieder an zu sprechen
Und Hoffnung wieder an zu blühn,
Man sehnt sich nach des Lebens Bächen,
Ach, nach des Lebens Quelle hin.

> Goethe, *Faust*
> (line 1200)

For my wife Grace and
our sons John and Christopher

Table of Contents

PREFACE	ix
CHAPTER ONE	
PRELIMINARIES: THE SIGNIFICANCE OF *THE RING*	1
1. Philosophy and Music	5
2. Some Recommended Studies of *The Ring*	7
3. The Plot of *Das Rheingold*	10
4. The Plot of *Die Walküre*	12
5. The Plot of *Siegfried*	15
6. The Plot of *Götterdämmerung*	16
7. The Central Questions	18
8. Music and Meaning: Some Illustrations from *The Ring*	20
CHAPTER TWO	
THE STRUCTURE OF *THE RING*: TRAGEDY OR TRANSCENDENCE?	29
1. The Endings of *The Ring* and the Troubles of Wotan	34
2. Conflict in *The Ring*: Love *versus* Power	41
3. The Endings of the Four Parts of *The Ring*	44
4. Renunciation, Love, and Conflict	53
5. Love and the Ending of *Die Walküre*	58
6. Evil and Tragedy	66
CHAPTER THREE	
THE CONTROVERSY OVER *THE RING*	87
1. Dahlhaus and the Optimistic *Ring*	88
2. Love and Redemption	93
3. Politics and Conflict	96
4. Appearance and Reality: Wotan's Inner-life and Politics	100
5. Adorno's Wagner: The Glorification of Destruction	103
6. Music as Drug	105
7. Adorno's Enlightenment Sonata Ideal	115
8. Art and Morality	122
9. Nietzsche's Wagner	130

CONCLUSION
WHAT DOES *THE RING* MEAN? 141
   1. Redemptive Fire 141
   2. The Metaphysics of *The Ring*: Optimism or Pessimism? 151
   3. The Survivors 155

APPENDIX
PHILOSOPHICAL CONTEXTS AND APPLICATIONS 165
   1. Kant and Hume: the Nineteenth Century Begins 165
   2. Goethe and Hegel: Beyond Enlightenment 170
   3. Schopenhauer and Music 176
   4. Schopenhauer and *Tristan*: Love *versus* Society 184
   5. *Die Meistersinger* and the Art of Illusion 192
   6. Nietzsche's Metaphysical Perspectivism 198
   7. A Nietzschean Reading of *The Ring* 215

BIBLIOGRAPHY 229

MUSICAL REFERENCES 237

INDEX 247

Preface

Another book on Wagner, even another on *The Ring*, no longer needs justification or even apology. Clearly, over a century later, we still find Wagner and his works fascinating, controversial, and relevant. The polarization found even today in Wagner interpretation symbolizes the richness of his creations and the vastly different points of view concerning him and his works. This book supports the reading of *The Ring* first suggested, at least in a systematic way in recent years, by Michael Tanner, although great Wagner scholars such as Deryck Cooke and Ernst Newman have held related if not as rigorously articulated views. I hope my own efforts will be justified by two features: first, I explore many more musical examples than does Tanner in my attempt to support this interpretation. Second, unlike Tanner, who does not like generalization much, I brazenly suggest a "theme" that holds the drama and the music of *The Ring* together, providing a coherence denied by some critics, a theme that can be easily connected to the general nineteenth-century rejection of the Enlightenment's realist conception of truth and value. I try to do this by taking Wagner's conception of Music-Drama literally, looking at several examples of how the music extends/augments/determines the dramatic structure of *The Ring*. What might distinguish my approach lies in the connections I draw between this analysis and the philosophical themes that to some extent stimulated Wagner, and which provide the context for my interpretive framework.

In the course of this book I refer to musical examples in *The Ring*. These so-called "leitmotifs" are for the most part identified by their now standard names (however misleadingly) and are widely available in many accounts of the music of *The Ring*. The Appendix contains most of the leitmotifs I refer to, but there are several examples where reference to the full orchestral score is recommended. Dover has published the scores to all four parts of *The Ring* and these are also by far the least expensive. My Bibliography lists the works I discuss; I also include many of the better studies of *The Ring,* including some more recent works not contained in the extensive bibliographies of *The New Grove Wagner* and *The Wagner Companion,* both of which are by now somewhat dated. I also identify those works with more recent bibliographies. Not surprisingly, there is a CD–ROM containing the Solti performance of *The Ring* with the piano/vocal score, German libretto with English translation, commentary and a database of characters, symbols and leitmotifs. There are even essays by singer/teacher Monte Stone and others. The CD (Intel machines only, unfortunately) is available through Media Café. Web surfers will find dozens of sites for Wagner, some quite bizarre. A good deal of information can be found there. The many recordings of *The Ring* available are widely discussed, sometimes with more heat than light. Discretionary silence will be the better part of my valor in this case. An interesting book could be written on the history and analysis of these recordings, but I am not the one to write it. (Tanner reviews several recordings in "Wagner's *Ring*," *Classical CD,* (November 1990) and discusses some in his book.)

Because it has taken so long to write and to publish this book, a brief note of intellectual biography may be in order: Tanner visited Simon Fraser three times during the late 1960's and early 1970's. I attended his seminars on Wagner and Nietzsche, and enjoyed occasional conversations with him. He has been a major inspiration for me. As I have indicated, some of the claims that I make about Wagner in this book are directly influenced by him and by what he has subsequently published. During a sabbatical year in 1976–7, I was a Visiting Fellow at Princeton University and studied with Richard Rorty. His important views about the contingency of society and personhood find their source in the nineteenth century and my understanding of Nietzsche and Wagner in my discussion of "illusion" derives in part from Rorty's account of the origins of pragmatism in the nineteenth-century's critique of foundationalism.

Eventually, I put these ideas together with my interest in music. Although I believe that I give a pretty clear presentation of the intellectual themes in *The Ring*, I wish I had the training and skill to describe the music with more of the detail and subtlety it deserves. I readily admit to the primitiveness that characterizes my discussion of the music of *The Ring*. But perhaps simply identifying signficant examples from *The Ring* as I do, asking that they be considered in the light of what I say about them in the context of my theme about power and love as the unifying dichotomy of *The Ring,* may be sufficient to get my point across.

The Work/Study program of the Province of British Columbia supplied me with three grants to hire students to do some editorial work and to help produce the examples in my musical references. Simon Fraser University also awarded me a grant to help with the publication of the book at Peter Lang. My friend Lief Carter and my wife Grace steadfastly encouraged me to carry on when discouraged. I finally want to thank the referee for Peter Lang who made several constructive suggestions that helped me to organize my discussion more efficiently. This referee brought to my attention the quote from Emil Staiger's book that appears in Chapter 2, kindly translating it for me, also suggesting some specific points about Goethe's *Faust* that I use in the Appendix.

John Tietz, Simon Fraser University
September, 1998

Chapter One

Preliminaries:
The Significance of *The Ring*

> We have created the world that possesses values! Knowing this, we know too, that reverence for truth is already the consequence of an illusion....
>
> ...[T]he destruction of an illusion does not produce truth but only one more piece of ignorance, an extension of our empty space, an increase of our desert.
>
> Friedrich Nietzsche: *The Will To Power* (#602/3)

In this passage, typically dense and allusive, Nietzsche contemplates a paradoxical relation between truth and illusion. Nietzsche makes a philosophical point but, in his unique way, not *qua* philosopher in the academic sense, a tradition firmly established by this time in nineteenth-century Germany. As a young lecturer on philology and Greek civilization at the University of Basel,[1] his studies convinced him that the concepts of Truth, Reality, Knowledge, and Value could not be understood through abstract academic analysis. Value and truth, Nietzsche argued, concern life itself; their natures are not discovered through detached, academic contemplation. In ordinary life, we 'create' values, and seek the truth. Nietzsche contends that our "reverence for truth" is the "consequence" of an illusion in the sense that, since Plato, we associate at least large truths, truth in general, with universality. But if we revere the universal, is not truth the opposite of illusion? If so, why does the "destruction of an illusion" lead only to another illusion? How can truth *depend* on illusion? Is not "illusion" synonymous with "deception"? Why does Nietzsche refer to human life as "our empty space" and "our desert"? Does not truth take us *out* of the desert, *out* of Plato's cave? If the truth lies beyond our illusions, why can we not eliminate illusion in favor of truth?

Richard Wagner was one of Nietzsche's earliest intellectual and emotional influences. Indeed, all of Wagner's music-dramas raise many of the same 'questions' (figuratively speaking) about reality, value, and selfhood that Nietzsche so desperately pursued during his rational life (my quote from *The Will to Power* coming near the end of his sanity). Wagner himself explores the concept of Illusion with insight and subtlety in *Die Meistersinger*. I will try to show how *The Ring of the Nibelungs*, Wagner's longest, most discussed and most puzzling work, provides a key expression of the dramatic changes to the concept of Truth taking place in the nineteenth century, changes that have shaped the ways we now think about ourselves, about society and value, and even the nature of reality. Some of these changes were philosophical, some aesthetic, some political. The many causes of the cultural sea-changes of the nineteenth century include the French Revolution, the works of Kant, the poetry of Schiller and Goethe, the music of Beethoven, Napoleon, the industrialization of northern Europe and Great Britain, and the political changes in Germany and the revolutions that followed. All of these and more.

The Ring contains themes of great intellectual importance and, like all great works of art, it can be interpreted many ways. My bibliography lists several books and articles expressing many different, opposing, and vigorously argued interpretations of this complex work ranging from political readings (George Bernard Shaw's *The Perfect Wagnerite* (1898)) to Jungian psychological readings (Robert Donington's *Wagner's Ring and its Symbols*) to feminist deconstruction (Sandra Corse's *Wagner and the New Consciousness*). *The Ring* expresses complex views concerning the relationship between value, reality, personhood, and society. It is one of the first works of art to address our 'modernity', the unique condition of our time as we look back on our cultural traditions and wonder about their origins and meaning. Nineteenth-century German philosophers and—at least through their work—artists were often preoccupied with the problematic relationship between illusion and reality: On what universal truths does our society and its values rest? *Can* our values be justified *or* are they arbitrary, relative to historical circumstance, sustained only through tradition? These modern questions, it is important to note, are not about what truths there are but about the nature of truth itself.[2]

The Ring tells a story, quite a moving story, about the demythologization of tradition, about the "death of God," as Nietzsche described it. For the young Nietzsche, it was the myth to end all myths, comparable to the tragedies of Sophocles. I will occasionally turn to Nietzsche for help in describing the metaphysics of *The Ring*. Although he broke off all contact with Wagner not long after his first major publication, *The Birth of Tragedy*, and tried to write his own myth about the death of God (*Thus Spoke Zarathustra*, begun in 1883), Wagner was never far from his thoughts throughout the rest of his life. The complex relationship between them tells a love/hate story about the collision of gigantic egos but it also revolves around great ideas expressing tensions still representative of our age. *The Ring* portrays what has become in the twentieth century a familiar story about the loss of authority as a foundation for value and the effect of that loss on our conception of ourselves. These are also recurring themes in Nietzsche's works.

I organize my discussion as follows: in this chapter I raise the general questions and issues I want to address in the course of this book. I summarize the plot of *The Ring*, and introduce some of the musical materials significant in understanding it. In Chapter 2 I turn more specifically to the structure of *The Ring* and to my theme—that the apparent opposition between love and power that underlies every moment of the work actually comprises a single phenomenon rather than two opposing forces. I will discuss several examples from *The Ring* to support this view but I will concentrate in more detail on love and power in *Die Walküre,* the pivotal work in the cycle. 'Conflict', that typically nineteenth-century concept, would be one way to describe the dialectical core of *The Ring*, based on the underlying interdependence of love and power. My point will be that conflict, for Wagner, centers on the creative/destructive potential of *both* love and power.

Nietzsche's intellectual attraction to Wagner, at least as he saw it, arose from the philosophical rebirth of tragedy in *The Ring*. In this grand event Nietzsche saw the union of art and philosophy as a new way to understand truth and value. The late eighteenth and early nineteenth centuries contain many similar and related precursor views of art: Kant thought of art as a concrete expression of the nature of reality unavailable to scientific analysis. Schelling and Hegel described the act of creation as essentially self-creation, something shared between creative artistic genius and God. They also believed that "life is art," a principle advocated throughout Nietzsche's works. In my Appendix of philosophical background material, I discuss Nietzsche's "perspectivism" as one way in which we might see Wagner's own approach to the relation between power and love. I outline my thesis about this at the beginning of Chapter 2.

In Chapter 3 I summarize the predominant theories about *The Ring*, and discuss one of Wagner's most important critics, Theodor Adorno. I try not so much to defend Wagner but to ask for more context, to understand him more broadly in his relation to the other intellectual developments of his time. Indeed, Adorno attacks not only Wagner but also the social effect of Wagner as a "totalitarian" artist. Philosophically, Adorno wanted to find a cultural basis in Marxism for artistic freedom at a time when Soviet and Eastern European communism approached the intellectually stultifying extremes of the Nazis. He saw Wagner's music-dramas as repressive rather than liberating, doctrinaire, even religious, rather than edifying. The fact that the Nazis appropriated Wagner as a cultural icon did not help of course. But it is now quite clear that Hitler's Nazis dreaded the Bayreuth "experience" and, if I am right about the content of Wagner's music-dramas, his "message" about art and morality seems to be completely alien to that historical aberration.

In the Conclusion, I discuss the ending of *The Ring* and try to draw some implications relevant to our own understanding of Western civilization. While this particular story concentrates on destruction, we ultimately see that creation and destruction are not so very different when we understand their common motivation, thus returning us to the unifying element of power and love that I called "conflict." Although Wagner does not have a name for it, this unity of opposites was also something grandly seen by the nineteenth-century antipodes of Schopenhauer and Hegel, and by Nietzsche himself especially in his greatest work, *The Genealogy of Morals*. Nietzsche's term was "the will to power," derived from Schopenhauer's conception of the Will, who intended it to rival Hegel's *Geist* or Spirit. All of these sought something metaphysically constitutive, a general process or force lying at the basis of civilization. Wagner's mature works—*The Ring, Tristan, Die Meistersinger,* and *Parsifal*—similarly incorporate these large themes but do so in a very personal way. In my view, the general sustains the personal in these music-dramas, but it is the personal that brings the metaphysical to life.

In the Appendix I summarize and discuss some of the philosophical background I believe to be important for understanding *The Ring* in its contemporary relevance, at least for "intellectuals" such as myself. In defense of this approach, it should be remembered that Wagner himself consistently thought of his work in philosophical terms. It helps to understand his music-dramas, I think, if we keep this intellectual background in mind. I first summarize the late eighteenth-century revolution of meaning that began with Hume and Kant. The relevance of this intellectual debate centers on the rejection of metaphysical realism and the hope of an objective justification or foundation for morality. Next, I summarize the early nineteenth-century attempts by Goethe and Hegel at inventing a vocabulary to describe a universe in which "God is dead" and where value can only be found in the emergence of human consciousness. Third, because it played such an important role in Wagner's rethinking of *The Ring*, I discuss Schopenhauer's pessimistic rejection of Hegel's historical dialectic. In Section 4 I briefly discuss Wagner's most Schopenhauerian work, *Tristan und Isolde*, in order to contrast its treatment of love with that of *The Ring,* and *Die Meistersinger* in order to illustrate Wagner's conceptions of individuality and creativity. (Both *Tristan* and *Die Meistersinger*, written between acts 2 and 3 of *Siegfried*, also deal specifically with illusion.) Although it has now become a standard approach to discuss all of Wagner's later works as a group, I hope that I have something new to add.

Finally, as I said above, I discuss Nietzsche's "perspectivist" metaphysics, showing how value arises not from an objective description of reality but from a response to alienation. In this, I think he very nearly expresses the central theme of Wagner's mature music-dramas: How can we find something to live for in a universe that does not respond to our needs? Contrary to interpretations of *The*

Ring that see it as an attempt to reintroduce a more "spiritual" view of self and society, Michael Tanner's account, and those of Morse Peckham and Robert Raphael, both of whom earlier pointed in this direction, rest on the thesis of Wagner's "refusal to transcend," on his rejection of what Peckham calls "transcendental authority." This was also an important theme for Nietzsche and it will be the context for my own view of *The Ring*. In the last section of the Appendix, I apply some of my discussion of Nietzsche directly to *The Ring* in an attempt to show that Nietzsche and Wagner were not so far apart. As Tanner says, one learns very little about Wagner from the early Nietzsche's infatuated gushiness in *The Birth of Tragedy* and *Richard Wagner in Bayreuth*, whereas there is often quite a bit of truth in his attempts at devastating, demolishing criticism in *Nietzsche Contra Wagner* and *The Case of Wagner* (toned down several decibels). In Nietzsche's mature works, I will also contend, one also finds a plausible "philosophical" account of what Wagner tells us through his subtle stories (albeit in grandiose style) and amazing music.

1. Philosophy and Music

Too many discussions of *The Ring* neglect Wagner's music but I will try to describe how the meaning of the work can adequately be understood through its music. Although conceptual studies and musical analysis can help us to understand *The Ring*, few would deny that the meaning of any work of music transcends explanations of its musical structure and its conceptual intersections with philosophy, the history of art, and so on. On the one hand, art is not philosophy; it does not appeal solely to the intellect and repeated experience of the work is obviously essential to its understanding. On the other hand, experience must be directed and focused. I believe that meaning in art (however much tied to the emotions) cannot be grasped without understanding something of the context of the work expressing it.

His background will guide anyone's experience of *The Ring*.[3] Everyone experiences a work of art differently and factors such as education, in the broadest sense, can and do make differences to ones understanding of almost anything. We mature through the accumulation of experience and, one hopes, some constructive reflection in the light of ones inherited tradition of values. But life does not always proceed in linear fashion. It sometimes progresses through sudden jumps; one can mature quickly (overnight sometimes) and later in life we tend to characterize ourselves by what we have done (or not done) rather than in terms of what we hope to do. The German word *Bildung* captures this sense of selfhood as development within a culture. It usually applies to the context of education, and originally concerned the evolution of moral character. It is a very important word in nineteenth-century German philosophy. *The Ring*, I contend, can be an important part of that process not just in personal life but also in our understanding of the relation between the personal and the social, and between both of these and nature. The theme of moral authority, and its essential ambiguity in *The Ring,* intersects with the widening self-understanding of its characters—and its audience. This kind of intellectual progress points to the complexity of and the interconnections between the various facets of our intellect, our feelings, desires, and actions—all are part of our *Bildungsprozess.* For many artists and philosophers during the early nineteenth century, persons were not divided into clearly separated mental faculties responsible for particular functions—faculties of sensation, reason, and will power, for example, arranged in an hierarchy of control with reason at the top—and the Enlightenment distinction between reason and emotion was relentlessly challenged both in philosophy and in art. Sometimes, for example, a rational conclusion can be arrived at only through an emotional journey. In the Appendix, I include a few examples of the philosophical developments during this period that may be helpful in understanding the intellectual background against which Wagner wrote *The Ring.*

Wagner developed an entire theory of art that he thought reflected the intersection between philosophy and aesthetics, in which he specified roles for the individual arts. He wanted to create an all-inclusive art form that brought together the personal and the public, the musical, the visual and the verbal, the cultural and the religious, the philosophical and the aesthetic. His name for this invention was *Gesamtkunstwerk,* literally: total work of art. Following general practice, I will use the term "music-drama" to refer to Wagner's conception of his work. I will also briefly describe what music-drama was envisaged to be because *The Ring* was intended to be the first of Wagner's works produced with this theory. In fact, however, over the long gestation of *The Ring,* he gradually moved away from his earlier, rather rigid and doctrinaire views about what he was doing adapting a more pragmatic, and more effective, approach to his work.

Although Wagner's views on the role of music in music-drama changed considerably (I briefly describe those changes in the next chapter and in the Appendix), and despite the fact that some of Wagner's music can stand alone in the concert hall, it was conceived to act in conjunction with a poetic text and staging. These music-dramas were created to be aesthetically interdependent, hence the invention of his terminology: the *total*, or all-inclusive, artwork. As far as I know, none of Wagner's dramatic texts have been performed without their music (a truly ridiculous prospect); contrariwise, the plays of Shakespeare, when adapted to opera, require drastic simplification (Verdi's *Otello* for example). Wagner's music gives life to his texts, which are far more complex than most operatic *libretti*, and the combination of all of the elements of music-drama, including Wagner's stage directions and his ideas for set design, must be born in mind when addressing questions about the music. Great though some of that music is on its own, it was intended to be of service in a larger context.

In my discussion of Wagner's music, I usually point out references to the plot of the drama of which it is a part. I do not address the general issue in the aesthetics of music about how, or if, music can express ideas, even ideas supplied by a text. On these matters I recommend Deryck Cooke's *The Language of Music* (London: Oxford University Press, 1959) and, a more philosophically sophisticated approach, Peter Kivy's *The Corded Shell* (Princeton: Princeton University Press, 1980).

2. Some Recommended Studies of *The Ring*

Although it is now one of the best known works of art in this century, I will presently review the plot of *The Ring* and then ask the main questions pursued in the rest of this book. There are other, more elaborate accounts of the story and how Wagner wrote it. Ernst Newman's classic *The Wagner Operas* (originally published as *Wagner Nights*) summarizes the plots to all Wagner's music-dramas at more length than I will and includes the major leitmotifs as part of the stories. First published in 1949, it continues to be the best place to start for more detailed study. Newman also discusses the complicated history of *The Ring* but for more particulars about the construction of the text and its Nordic mythological background, *The New Grove Wagner* by John Deathridge and Carl Dahlhaus has a good discussion of the creation of *The Ring*. Curt von Westernhagen's *The Forging of The Ring* also tells the story of its creation in detail for those so interested. Newman's *Wagner as Man and Artist* contains shorter synopses of the music-dramas (still with important musical references included) and also a short biography and good discussion of Wagner's theoretical works. This continues to be one of the best works in the field. Newman also wrote the definitive four-volume *The Life of Richard Wagner*.

Barry Millington's *Wagner*, a popular current overview of Wagner the man and his music, contends that Wagner's anti-Semitism was a fundamental characteristic of his work. However, as Michael Tanner ironically points out in his book, if this is so, why it has taken nearly a century for us to discover, through Millington, how devious and surreptitious Wagner must have been in his hate-filled caricatures?[4] If this is what he did, why should he hide it from us so well? As Bryan Magee points out in *Aspects of Wagner,* there has been a tendency to hold Wagner responsible for later historical developments for which he could not possibly have been the cause (Adorno tends to do this, connecting *uses* of Wagner with Wagner's own *intentions*). While this matter is of course worth discussing, I also realize that to do so in any thorough way would require another book, and I am not the one to write it.

Deryck Cooke, one of the greatest Wagner scholars, was working on a full length study of *The Ring* when he died in 1976. Entitled *I Saw the World End* (a line Brünnhilde uses in next to last version of the ending), the published part of this book includes only *Das Rheingold* and *Die Walküre*, with only a few pages devoted to the crucial third act of *Die Walküre*. Nevertheless, it contains many important insights. Fortunately, Cooke published other important pieces on Wagner that help me in what follows. As we will see, one of the problems about the meaning of *The Ring* rests on Wagner's continual revision of his music-drama (I review this in Chapter 2, Section 1).

For example, *The Ring* originally ended with the advent of a new order of society based on compassionate humanism of the sort envisaged in Wagner's more or less socialistic view of redemptive love inspired by Ludwig Feuerbach. A more pessimistic, Schopenhauerian version followed later. But the final version says nothing about a new order of society, and the famous motif of Redemption Through Love heard in the violins at the very end of *Götterdämmerung* takes on a highly ambiguous meaning. Some commentators, such as Carl Dahlhaus (at least at one point), see here the reemergence of optimism and the rejection of Schopenhauer. Others have seen this ending the victory of Schopenhauer's pessimism and rejection of Feuerbach's social optimism. I agree that Wagner was not a Schopenhauerian pessimist when he finished *The Ring*, but neither did he return to his earlier views about the humanistic redemption of society after the collapse of divine authority. The final version of this work projects a complexity of vision simply not present in its earlier versions.

William Cord's *An Introduction to Richard Wagner's der Ring des Nibelungen* provides a fact-oriented introduction (originally written in 1983, it was revised a few years ago).[5] An interesting but idiosyncratic background study showing how Wagner's work epitomizes the aesthetic and philosophical revolutions of the nineteenth century, Morse Peckham's *Beyond the Tragic Vision* has gone out of print but is worth tracking down. Robert Raphael's *Richard Wagner* takes a similar approach although both Peckham and Raphael seriously neglect Wagner's music, treating him like a Germanic Ibsen (to use Thomas Mann's comparison). Robert Donnington's *Wagner's Ring and its Symbols* still stands as the classic psychological/Jungian interpretation and, while undoubtedly somewhat unfashionable now days, it contains many important insights. Along with Shaw's *The Perfect Wagnerite,* Donnington's continues to be a great book to argue about.

As I mentioned earlier, Michael Tanner has elaborated Peckham and Raphael's thesis about Wagner's "refusal to transcend." Tanner's "The Total Work of Art" in *The Wagner Companion*, edited by Peter Burbidge and Richard Sutton, first presents these views. (This 1979 collection contains several other essential essays (including an important one by Deryck Cooke)). His more recent book, *Wagner* (1996), rearticulates his views at more length and in connection with recent literature. Tanner's book and article, and the seminars I attended when he visited at my university, have very much influenced my own views. I do believe, however, that my approach, although intended to be complementary, does have some important differences. First, I take a more philosophically general approach in my thesis about the conflict between and interdependence of power and love as the motivating force in *The Ring*; second, although Tanner does discuss the importance of Wagner's music, I add several more examples that perhaps more systematically point up the significance of its role in the meaning of the cycle.

Barry Millington has also edited *The Wagner Companion: A Guide to Wagner's Life and Music*, one of the more recent collections of essays. To suggest one particular standout amongst the hundreds of articles about Wagner in professional journals, Warren Darcy's "The Pessimism of *The Ring*," in *Opera Quarterly*, 1986 helpfully analyses Brünnhilde's last moments in *Götterdämmerung* and comes to conclusions similar to mine about *The Ring* as a whole. I will refer to other studies in endnotes throughout the course of this book. Thomas Grey's *Wagner's Musical Prose: Texts and Contexts* is perhaps the most thorough of recent attempts to connect discussions of Wagner's music with his theory of music-drama. At once erudite and entertaining, this interesting book should be sought out. It also contains an up-to-date bibliography on music-drama.

Because *The Ring* is a work of art, it can be interpreted endlessly—indeed it almost has been. Finding the "right" way to experience a work of art leads not only to inconsistency (a denial of the maxim that many are the ways of art) but also to boredom. There are many levels to *The Ring*. Its rich symbolism projects an 'open-ended' effect. It is one of those works that can be returned to again and again. As Deryck Cooke says in discussing Shaw's political and Donington's Jungian account of *The Ring*, advocating pluralism in opposition to reductionism:

> The truth is that many of the symbols in *The Ring* work on all levels at once, and to interpret them on one level only is to impoverish them; on the other hand, one here and there does work on one level only, and if that is not the level the interpreter is examining, his attempt to transfer it to that level can only make nonsense of it. Shaw reduces all that he can to social abstractions, and rejects the rest; Donington tries to reduce absolutely everything—including such manifest social element as the castle-building giants—to Jungian psychological abstractions. Nor can it be said that the two interpretations are complementary, since they contradict each other in a way that admits of no reconciliation and they both ignore the existential and metaphysical levels.[6]

3. The Plot of *Das Rheingold*

The first section of *The Ring*, its 'prelude' *Das Rheingold,* opens with its now famous pedal point in the bases and French horns (very hard to sustain) and rises into the tumultuous Rhine river (the mythologically rich easterly parts of the river with its falls and gorges).[7] Alberich, a shrunken, twisted and dark loner, a member of the race of Nibelungs, scrambles along the river in search of opportunity. This race of dwarves lives in Nibelheim, a place of mist and obscurity, and from which Alberich clearly wants to escape. Alberich encounters the Rhinemaidens, who taunt and tease him to distraction with intimations of sexual favors. Alberich eventually sees the Rhinegold glimmering beneath the surface of the water and steals the gold after learning that by renouncing love and fashioning a ring from the gold, he can become master of the world. The Rhinemaidens helplessly cry out for their gold, for the sustaining force of nature, while Alberich, now freed of his libidinal drives by sublimating it into a fantasy of social domination, sets off to become lord of the underworld kingdom of the Nibelungs, enslaving its dwarfish race to refine the gold and create the ring of power—this obscure, hostile nobody wants to rule the world.

While these events take place, Wagner highlights them with his so-called "leitmotifs." Composers have used this technique throughout most of the history of European music (late medieval music is filled with musical symbolism as are Bach's Cantatas and Passions, and Mozart's operas, for example) but Wagner took it to a much higher level of complexity. (We should not, however, become obsessed with the analysis of these motifs and we should not listen to his music-dramas as if they need to be decoded.) A great deal of Wagner's music depends on the occurrences of motifs as signs of dramatic development. I will show in several examples how later *versus* earlier occurrences of a motif take on added significance relative to what happens to the characters. In order to discuss the meaning of *The Ring* I will have to refer to these motifs in order to understand the essential role of the music to the drama (when I do so, I will refer to them by their standard names and most of my references are quoted in the Appendix as well as in Newman's book (and many others)). It helps to realize, for example, that at the end the first scene of *Das Rheingold*, the motif of Renunciation accompanies Alberich as he sets off on his destructive mission. This motif was heard in Scene 1 when the Rhinemaiden Woglinde tells him about the power of the ring (it becomes one of the most important motifs in *The Ring*). The Renunciation motif always, at least indirectly, refers back to the incident between Alberich and the Rhinemaidens, and in so doing it also connects that seminal moment with other instances of renunciation in *The Ring*. Between Scenes 1 and 2, the orchestra brings together several of the motifs that have already been introduced: the wonderfully flowing motif of the Rhine, that of Renunciation, the Gold, and finally a new motif: the solid-sounding, reassuring motif of Valhalla emerging, significantly, out of, indeed a version of, the motif of the Ring itself. Wagner intimates here that the gods need power, but power, as we have already seen with Alberich, always involves renunciation.

The scene shifts from the dark underworld, into which Alberich descends at the end of the first scene, to the recently completed paradise of Valhalla and its contrasting world of light, new home of the gods led by Wotan and wife Fricka. As a sign of his office, Wotan carries a spear on which he has carved the laws of his world, evidently an enlightened aristocracy since he vows not to use force to settle disputes. To build Valhalla (a symbol of his power and control over nature), he made a bargain with two giants, Fasolt and Fafner: in exchange for their labor, they may have Freia the goddess who sustains the gods with the apples she grows. (The connection between Freia and nature becomes more obvious when we realize that her motif supplies the music for the many love motifs that appear throughout *The Ring*.) Why would Wotan bargain away the life force of the gods? Obviously insecure of his control, he has no intention of keeping his part of the deal and awaits the half-human, half-god Loge, whose lawyer-like guile he hopes will extricate him from the contractual mess he has created. Loge has heard the story of Alberich and his domination of the Nibelungs. Thinking their salvation might lie there, Loge and Wotan prepare to visit the underworld to inspect Alberich's financial holdings.

The Renunciation motif forms the basis for the second Interlude depicting the descent to Nibelhiem. Also appearing are the Gold motif, the second part of Freia's motif (symbolizing the need for compassionate love (see Chapter 2, Section 5)), and the seventeen anvils Wagner used to portray the horrors of industrialization (especially noteworthy for its socialist zeal, George Bernard Shaw's account of this part of *Das Rheingold* in *The Perfect Wagnerite*, captures the political/economic 'critique' of the cycle). Since he left the Rhinemaidens, Alberich has now successfully enslaved the Nibelungs (the important motif of Servitude first appears here and in the Interlude) and has bullied his brother Mime, a goldsmith, to fashion for him the fateful ring, giving its possessor the power to create and to destroy. Mime has also created a "tarnhelm" that can magically change the form of its wearer and make him invisible (*tarnen* means to make invisible), but Alberich manages to get control of this too. Loge and Wotan confront Alberich and eventually take 'his' gold (possession being all points of the law down there) while encouraging him to show off his magic helmet. After simulating a dragon, he foolishly transforms himself into a toad and Wotan captures him.

The dwarves take the gold up to the surface where Wotan convinces the giants to take it instead of Freia, but it must be such a huge amount that a wall built of the ingots blocks off all sight of her. After buildingthe wall, however, Fasolt and Fafner can still see her through a crack between the bricks of gold. Loge says that he promised to give the ring back to the Rhinemaidens but

Wotan throws on this remaining bit of gold as well as the tarnhelm onto the pile to cut off the giant's last glimpse of love and beauty, of a world they cannot inhabit. Wotan thus breaks two promises: his own not to use force (in giving away Freia, thus destroying her autonomy, and in taking the gold from Alberich) and Loge's to return the ring to the Rhinemaidens. But Alberich has put a curse on the ring (symbolized by a dramatic motif in the trombones) that immediately begins to extend its destructive influence as the giants quarrel over whether to take the Gold or to keep Freia.

Meanwhile, the passive but forward-looking goddess of the earth and symbol of nature, Erda, mysteriously appears to Wotan to tell him that everything he has built will pass away and that he should give up the ring. Her rising motif resembles that of Nature in Scene 1. It remains significantly unclear whether giving it back to the Rhinemaidens will actually prevent Valhalla's destruction. In fact, Erda says that everything will pass away, Valhalla will fade *whatever* happens. At that point the motif of the Twilight of the Gods first appears, essentially and significantly a reversal of the Nature motif: decline *versus* growth. Even by returning the ring, he cannot escape change and destruction. Alberich's curse begins to take effect when Fafner kills Fasolt, packs up the gold and leaves. Fafner later uses the tarnhelm to transform himself into a dragon to guard the gold, thereby making it and himself socially useless (capital without responsibility, as Shaw points out). Fricka becomes impatient to occupy her new palace and in a grand but ironic scene Donner creates a rainbow bridge and the gods enter Valhalla. The wonders of the scene are underscored by the motif of the Power of the Ring; against this Wotan conceives of the idea of a hero who will save him from the (understandably) vengeful Alberich (and symbolized by the first occurrence of the Sword motif just before Fricka asks Wotan why he named the castle "Valhalla").[8] But the dissonant laments of the Rhinemaidens, and the Rhinegold motif, undercut the pompous music of their entry: Valhalla rests on moral compromise and it will collapse.

4. The Plot of *Die Walküre*

Die Walküre opens a generation later. Alberich's vengeance has now entangled Wotan in a terrible war with the armies of his nemesis and he badly needs a hero to work wonders on the field of combat. Siegmund, Wotan's own son born of a mortal woman, has been created to be that hero. We first encounter him as he enters a crude forest hut fleeing enemies. Sieglinde, the mistress of the place but also a child of Wotan and in fact Siegmund's twin sister, discovers him trying to warm himself by her fire. Sieglinde, married to Hunding, a primitive but honorable warrior evidently and perhaps unknowingly allied with the forces opposing Wotan, offers him the traditional hospitality of shelter, but they are soon attracted to each other. The Prelude to *Die Walküre* depicts the storm surrounding this encounter and shows the presence of Wotan in the bass ostinato derived from his Spear motif, the symbol of his besieged authority. (We should now see the Spear in a different light because of Wotan's double-dealing in *Das Rheingold*.) The love music of the first act, as Siegmund and Sieglinde quickly become involved, entirely derives from the two parts of Freia's motif in *Das Rheingold,* as will the various motifs associated with Brünnhilde. Hunding arrives home after a hard day to find his wife visibly attracted to their guest (he also notices that they bear a striking resemblance to each other). After listening to Siegmund's story about defending a helpless woman from rape and death, Hunding tells Siegmund that the next day he must be prepared to defend himself for killing some of Hunding's kinsmen. He cannot deny Siegmund the ritual hospitality of warriors but he is obviously the one Hunding has spent the day trying to hunt down.

During the next scene, Siegmund discovers a sword embedded in the trunk of a huge tree forming part of Hunding's house (the phallic symbolism of the sword (its masculine, heroic potential and rival to Wotan's spear) and the significance of Siegmund's ability to control it are, of course, obvious)). No one has been able to take it out of that tree. After professing their love to each other in some of Wagner's best music (anticipating *Tristan*, only three years away) they too realize their resemblance to each other (we hear the Valhalla motif at this moment symbolizing their relation to Wotan and to his reason for creating them). Siegmund is a Volsung, the noble family of warriors in whom Wotan has placed the defense of the world governed by his laws. Indeed, unknown to Siegmund, Wotan is the head of the clan. He takes the sword from the tree while singing the Renunciation motif, thus apparently fulfilling Wotan's dream but, in reality, ensuring the fulfillment of Alberich's curse (in Chapter 2, Section 4 I discuss the puzzling occurrence of the Renunciation motif at this point in *The Ring*). He names the sword "Notung" ("need") and it is indeed a symbol of his own immediate needs as well as Wotan's hope of redemption through Siegmund.

The Prelude to Act II indicates immediately that things are about to go fatally wrong for Siegmund and Sieglinde—and Wotan. The poignancy of this moment also shows Wagner at his best, musically depicting how the redemptive love forming so much a part of *The Ring* will also change the world. The Prelude immediately places the private world of the lovers within the larger drama where their love will have a disasterous effect for them and for others. Wotan orders his daughter Brünnhilde (Erda is her mother) to protect Siegmund in his battle with Hunding. (Brünnhilde is one of the Walküre, maiden warriors, all daughters of Wotan.) As the first scene opens, enter Fricka, not only Wotan's wife but goddess of marriage and the laws of the household, who immediately confronts him. After a domestic quarrel of Teutonic proportions, she demands that he enforce his own law against incest. Siegmund must die, he cannot go unpunished for making love to his sister or violating the marriage contract between Sieglinde and Hunding.

In the monologue following this scene, Wotan plunges into painful self-examination and tells Brünnhilde his story. We are reminded of important connections by the recurrence of various motifs as Wotan remembers the events leading up to his crisis. The moment of Wotan's greatest distress, at the beginning of Scene 2, and a good example of Wagner's complex use of music to create layers of implication and significance, brings together several motifs including Alberich's curse, the Power of the Ring, Renunciation, Freia II (the second part of Freia's motif). Entrapped by his own laws, he realizes that he cannot create a being free from his influence. He cannot command freedom by manipulating the lives of others and so resolves to let Siegmund die, commanding Brünnhilde to make sure he does.

In Act IIiv, the so-called Annunciation of Death scene (almost entirely based on an important motif denoted by that name and derived from the Fate motif), Brünnhilde appears before Siegmund to tell him that he must prepare to die.[9] However, she tells him that the glories and pleasures of Valhalla will more than compensate for the inconvenience of heroic death. Siegmund rejects these delights proclaiming his love for Sieglinde to be by far more important to him. Throughout this scene, Brünnhilde experiences nothing less than a change of personality in her realization of the importance of love. She sees in Siegmund's refusal to leave Sieglinde how love is even more than immortality. Her fidelity to Wotan's authority wanes as she empathizes with the lovers. This creates an obvious tension between her compassion for the lovers, on the one hand and the universal demands of law and society (Wotan's command), on the other, that ultimately leads her to side with vulnerable humanity—and then forces Wotan into his actions at the end of *Die Walküre*.

The battle takes place after the Annunciation scene. When Brünnhilde fails in her duty, Wotan appears and smashes Siegmund's sword, Notung, into pieces; Hunding kills Siegmund, only to be immediately dispatched by Wotan, who contemplates from a distance the conflicting demands of law and love. Brünnhilde has failed to do as Wotan ordered and must be punished. Act III begins with the famous Ride of the Walküre but Brünnhilde, no longer the Amazon warrior princess depicted by fragments of that music when she first appears in Act II, tries to save Sieglinde from Wotan. Sieglinde is pregnant with Siegfried and during this scene we hear the misleadingly misnamed "Redemption Through Love" motif as Brünnhilde sings of the hope symbolized by Sieglinde's unborn child.

When Wotan and Brünnhilde finally meet in the moving final scene of reconciliation, he decides not to kill her but to put her into a deep sleep to be awakened only by a hero brave enough to penetrate the magic fire Loge will place around her. Wotan has now completely renounced his power and control. In trying to defend Siegmund and in protecting Sieglinde, Brünnhilde has in fact already defied Wotan's will. She in fact becomes Wotan's redemptive force. When she reawakens, Brünnhilde will be free of Wotan's laws. She will be "at war with the gods." *Die Walküre* ends with the Magic Fire music, the motif of Siegfried—and the Fate motif softly repeated.

5. The Plot of *Siegfried*

Siegfried begins another generation later: Sieglinde has died giving birth to Siegfried, who has been raised by Alberich's brother Mime. He has grown into a strapping, fearless youth wise in the ways of the forest. In Act II he wonders about his mother (all the animals of the forest have mothers, who was his?). The last part of this scene presents a good example of Wagner's kaleidoscopic musical/dramatic symbolism as he brings together Siegfried's yearning for love, the compassionate second part of the Freia motif, and the Volsung motif (Siegfried's identity). Later, in Scene 3, another important example occurs when Mime tries to teach the fearless Siegfried about fear. We hear the motif of the sleeping Brünnhilde as the future source of that fear. He also warns Siegfried about Fafner (the connection between Brünnhilde, fear, and Fafner as a symbol of libidinal sexuality, as Thomas Mann points out, anticipates Freud). Wotan, having renounced the direct use of power, now wanders the world keeping abreast of his fate. He encounters Mime and Alberich; Wotan tells Mime that only a fearless hero will be able to reforge Siegmund's sword Notung and Alberich that the hoard of gold will soon be liberated from Fafner, presumably to help protect and rebuild his society.

In Scene 3 Siegfried does reforge Notung in a stirring and difficult "aria" (for lack of a better word, since Wagner wanted to avoid writing a traditional opera) based on an upward leap in the basses and a downward run in the brass (an augmented reference to Wotan's Spear (a similar upward leap occurs in Brünnhilde's "War es so schmählich":"Was it so shameful" at the beginning of *Die Walküre* IIIiii also symbolizing Brünnhilde's opposition to Wotan)). Siegfried soon kills Fafner and, drenched in the dragon's blood, now understands the birds of the forest—one of whom tells him about the significance of the tarnhelm and the ring (it will make him lord of the world, although Siegfried does not care about that). Siegfried kills Mime when he attempts to poison him (Alberich's curse continues to work). The wood bird then relates to Siegfried a legend about a fabulous maiden cast into a spell on an obscure mountain and protected by impenetrable flames. She can be freed only by one unafraid of such dangers—Siegfried immediately sees that he is just the one for this task.

Act III begins with an amazing Prelude packed with references and based on the Wanderer motif (associated with the music of Brünnhilde's Magic Sleep). This was the point where Wagner returned to *The Ring* after more than ten years, during which he composed *Tristan* and *Die Meistersinger*. One immediately senses not only his renewed energy but also a very different view of the role of music in the work only hinted at in the earlier *Ring*. Its texture now becomes far richer and more complex, telling us much more than it did before. Erda and Wotan meet again and he confides to her that he has "willed the end" of the gods but the "deed that will free our world" from the threat of domination (Siegfried's heroism) is underscored by an unresolved cadence: What will really happen? In an irony filled confrontation, Siegfried meets Wotan for the first and last time, smashing his spear (this being the next of Siegfried's tests in freeing Brünnhilde). The Prelude to Scene 3 provides us with another densely packed tone picture of Siegfried's assent of Brünnhilde's mountain (the sexual symbolism of Siegfried's ascent is obvious and typically direct but can only be appreciated by paying attention to the music and its use of the motif of sexual love derived from Freia's music). The scene of Brünnhilde's awakening follows as Siegfried at last experiences both fear and love at the same time. He also seems to have completely forgotten about the ring and the tarnhelm. The lovers resolve to "die to the world" and live only for each other: love, not politics, will be the center of their lives and the salvation of the world. The fairy tale world of *Siegfried* and the idealized, magical character of love soon encounter the real world.

6. The Plot of *Götterdämmerung*

Götterdämmerung begins with the music of Brünnhilde's awakening, now dark and ambiguous as it points toward the decline of the gods. The Norns, the weavers of destiny, try to foresee what will happen but cannot. The rope of history they weave breaks at that point. They retell the story once more. Many find parts of *The Ring* redundant and repetitive, but in such a huge work we do occasionally need to be reminded of its many events and the music portrays their significance for the specific character doing the retelling as well as for the audience. Wagner also began writing the text of *The Ring* backwards, beginning with what became *Götterdämmerung* and then adding the earlier parts as he went along and perhaps this explains some of the repetitiveness. However, these recapitulations are often interesting and even essential because of their use of musical symbolism. They are recapitulations from specific points of view: from Wotan's, from the Norns', from Siegfried's, and so on, so that we see the story kaleidoscopically through the narrative of their beliefs.

Brünnhilde and Siegfried awaken to a glorious dawn (the same dawn of the gloomy Norns' scene), the optimism of the music of this scene in complete con-

Preliminaries: The Significance of *The Ring*   17

trast to that of the previous Norn's Prolog. He bids farewell to Brünnhilde as he sets off to do great deeds as a heroic expression of his love (not with the intention of saving Wotan's world). He leaves the ring with her as a symbol of their love (but takes the tarnhelm). Siegfried's Rhine Journey, with its depiction of his heroic motifs, ironically leads Siegfried directly to Alberich's son Hagen, who psychologically controls the House of Gibichung and its lord and mistress, Gunter and Gutrune. Everyone has heard of the great hero Siegfried and his encounter with Fafner, of course, and about the gold and the ring.

    When Hagen greets Siegfried, at the beginning of Scene 2, we cannot fail to hear Alberich's Curse. Siegfried swears "blood-brotherhood" with Gunter after Hagen administers a potion to him obliterating his memory. He is immediately attracted to Gutrune, the first woman he sees under the spell of the potion, resolving to help Gunter win Brünnhilde by disguising himself as Gunter and once again braving the fires of Brünnhilde's mountain. Meanwhile Brünnhilde's Walküre sister Waltraute arrives imploring her to return the ring to the Rhinemaidens and to prevent the collapse of their world. For Brünnhilde, however, the ring has becomes a symbol of her renunciation of Wotan's world and of her love for Siegfried. She will not give it up. Siegfried soon arrives and, disguised as Gunter, subdues Brünnhilde, puts on the ring and takes her back to the hall of the Gibichungs.

    Act II begins with Alberich, ever intent on his original goal, imploring the sleeping Hagen to "hate the good." Hagen, however, mutters that he will swear allegiance only to himself. The disturbing Prelude to Scene 2, Hagen's Dawn, follows. Siegfried appears with the conquered Brünnhilde and the wedding between her and Gunter, and Siegfried and Gutrune, is arranged. But Brünnhilde, seeing the ring on Siegfried's hand, accuses Siegfried of treachery, that he took the ring from her by force, raping her and thereby dishonoring Gunter (who clearly could not have done this on his own). In Scene 5 Brünnhilde, Hagen, and Gunter swear to kill Siegfried. She tells Hagen that, while she has protected Siegfried from harm during battle through a magic spell, his back remains vulnerable (what hero would turn away from a fight?).

    Act III begins in the wild countryside, a celebratory boar hunt for the double wedding has been arranged to lure Siegfried into complaisance. He meets the Rhinemaidens and begins to remember something of his past as Hagen's potion begins to lose its power. Hagen morally wounds Siegfried by spearing him in the back in Scene 2 and we hear Brünnhilde's Awakening music for a third time as Siegfried's memory fully returns as he dies. The great Funeral March begins, ending in at the Hall of the Gibichungs at the beginning of Scene 3. Brünnhilde recovers from her rage, to see that she was blinded by a perversion of love that made Siegfried into a symbol of her escape from Wotan's world. She lost sight of him as a lover, she lost sight of the love that Siegmund expressed when he rejected immortality. Finally, she summons Loge to light Siegfried's funeral pyre made from the dead Ash-Tree from which Wotan made his spear. She returns the ring to the Rhinemaidens, claiming that the fire that destroys her will cleanse the curse from the ring. Hagen pursues the Rhinemaidens and drowns. The fire slowly engulfs the forest and eventually we see Valhalla ablaze in the distance as the motif of Redemption Through Love motif brings the cycle to a close.

7. The Central Questions

The 'meaning' of *The Ring* centers on the confrontation of paradox: the paradox of power, that it can destroy what it protects, and the paradox of love, that it can destroy the freedom it needs to be love. These are paradoxes of value: we desire some kind of assurance that we are right in what we do, but the greatest value in life proves to be the realization of the impossibility of absolutes of the kind that will solve our problems by giving clear, univocal definitions to our most important words. These paradoxes raise questions about the operative concepts underlying the plot of *The Ring*: What is redemption? What is love? What is power? Are they opposed to each other,? If so, how? What does the Redemption Through Love motif mean if we accept the paradoxical nature of love in *The Ring*? Details are important in grappling with these important questions: Wagner never called this motif "Redemption through Love," indeed he discouraged naming the motifs at all, generally characterizing it instead as a "glorification of Brünnhilde." But what does it glorify? If the optimistic interpretation of the ending of *Götterdämmerung* raises the possibility of a new form of society, how can that society avoid the paradoxes I have just described? Does Brünnhilde's concluding insight mean that love inevitably triumphs over power—in personal as well as in social relationships? Does Wotan's downfall symbolize the end of the era seeking transcendental foundations for value and society? If so, does it not also symbolize the beginning of a new age of humanity based on values designed by and for us? Or does it point to a deeper level of *The Ring* concerning the search for value? If we reject the optimistic interpretation, does *The Ring* then tell only a very pessimistic story about the inescapable *destructiveness* contained in the lust for power and the power of love?

Briefly, anticipating my longer answers to these questions, although the ring is returned to the Rhinemaidens, love does not triumph over power in *The Ring*. Indeed we discover how love constitutes an even more pervasive form of power and we realize that Wotan's arbitrary use of power in *Das Rheingold* and *Die Walküre* originally stemmed from his recognition of the importance of social stability. Yes, Wotan's downfall symbolizes an end to the search for transcendent values, for a society justified and protected by universal truths; but the age of humanity invoked by Brünnhilde cannot supply a permanent foundation for value either. Redemption, what Wotan desires for his society (redemption from primitive aggressive instincts), even more than he desires it for himself, must also be seen to be an ongoing, dangerous process and not the elimination of the uncertainties and moral insufficiency of life. We are then redeemed from our destructiveness not by finding an unchanging, permanent system of values, or an "objective" view of reality unclouded by impermanent human desires, but rather by understanding the contingency of life itself, the presence of both creation and destruction in it, and by finding value within that flux and changeability. In his conception of redemption Wagner "refuses to transcend." He does not advocate a higher, more stable form of perception, understanding, or civilization enabling us to leave the messy details, the politics of life behind. We cannot get beyond our inability to justify our social and moral creations absolutely; but it also seems unlikely that we can eliminate our fascination with transcendence, the desire to get things right once and for all. *The Ring* shows how these ideals can be destructive, but it also shows us that the only human response will be to have new ones—to continue the process of *Bildung*.

One might think that Wotan's society could not have been preserved even if he had lived up to his other contracts, that it still would have collapsed because he gave away Freia. Wotan bargained with another person's life, treating her as a means and not an end in herself. If Wotan's social authority allowed him to sustain it by force (which it did), it would be a society none of us could accept today. Even if he did not want to use force, appealing instead to principles of responsibility and social role, these were the very principles under threat from both outside and inside from Wotan himself. The larger point concerns the concept of Freedom. Does love free us from the manipulativeness inherent in politics? How can we be ends in ourselves, independently valuable beings, if we depend on each other so much, if the *means* of community is essential to the *end* of autonomy?

At the end of the eighteenth century, Kant proposed that, morally speaking, human beings must transcend the empirical world because moral concepts cannot be described scientifically, and therefore neither can persons, since moral categories apply uniquely to them. However, if we think of ourselves as transcending spirits, we are also physical beings, existing at a time, in a place, with personalities, individual likes and dislikes, but at least partly dependent on social conditioning. On the one hand, we find the metaphysical problem of reconciling the relationship between the freedom required for moral responsibility and the deterministic accounts of the universe in science and in religion (in doctrines of predestination, for example). On the other hand, setting aside metaphysical issues, personal freedom obviously cannot be unlimited even if, as Kant argued, we should see it as a necessary characteristic of morality.

The nineteenth century tended to see morality and social/political freedom interdependently. This was as true of Marx as it was of Mill. Nietzsche saw all politics, all society, as expressions of morality. The Enlightenment also provides an historical background of still pertinent questions in the nineteenth century: Do the responsibilities of citizenship entail certain 'rights' for individuals? What are these universal rights? On what are they based? The important point concerns not just Wotan bargaining away Freia, treating her as a means and not as an end, but the basis on which he does so, the willfulness of his actions driven by his desire to protect his world—an imperative taking us all the way back to Agammemnon as he sacrificed his daughter to get his fleet underway to attack Troy and rescue his brother's wife. We all want a safe world, but at what cost to liberty? It no longer seems that the traditional foundations of society based on religion or on the appeal to the universal theories of human nature that characterized the Enlightenment are available to us in the ways they were in the past. Since the nineteenth century, freedom, human nature, and society are now not understood to be the sorts of things we thought they were. *The Ring* rejects the idea that we can find truth and value by constructing utopian Valhallas. Just as Wotan's effort to construct such a world ruled by law rather than willfulness failed, so *The Ring* warns us of the inevitability of change in political as well as personal life. All of these issues are implied by the story of *The Ring*, but they are not explicitly part of the plot. Yet, note how easily philosophical questions arise when we think about the events of the drama.

8. Music and Meaning: Some Illustrations from *The Ring*

To conclude this chapter I present three examples of how Wagner uses music to portray the forces of change and conflict in *The Ring*. These examples indicate the kind of analysis I will undertake in the chapters that follow by showing how the metaphysical themes I have been discussing form part of the structure of the work. The significance of the events of the drama is shown by the leimotifs, pointing back to earlier events, or identifying and characterizing what happens in the present, and even forecasting the future. Amazingly, Wagner's subtle and complex technique of dramatic contextualization rarely interferes with our experience of the work: we do not feel we are doing some kind of conceptual or psychological or intellectual analysis. In fact, the music facilitates the drama, sometimes simplifying, sometimes projecting deeper meanings.

One example of Wagner's use of music to show the larger significance of particular moments in *The Ring* occurs early on when Fasolt and Fafner are given the choice between Freia and the gold as payment for building Valhalla in Scene 2 of *Das Rheingold*. Besides her own motif—the basis of the love music in the work as a whole as we will see—Freia is also characterized by the motif of the Golden Apples (the source of the immortality of the gods). This descending motif often characterizes the long-term interests of the gods. After Fafner says: "Trust me, more than Freia/we can gain from the gold:/eternal youth can be ours,/when we lay our hands on that gold":"Glaub mir, mehr als Freia/frommt das gleissende Gold:/auch ew'ge Jugend erjagt,/wer durch Goldes Zauber sie zwingt," we hear the Golden Apple motif, and then quickly the rising motif of the Gold. These two 'ideas' dissonantly clash with each other in the rather simple mind of Fafner with the Gold winning out—followed immediately by the faint drumroll that symbolizes death (see Golden Apples and Ring in the Musical References). This single moment, early in the cycle, ingeniously crafted to take us from Fafner's narrow self-interested view to the larger drama, contains the story of *The Ring* in a nutshell. In the larger context, love and power are indeed in conflict, but they are also interdependent. Neither can remain autonomous.

The gold that Alberich took from the Rhinemaidens, through the ring Mime made from it, supposedly gives its possessor great powers. But exactly what powers? In Scene 1 of *Das Rheingold* Wellgunde says that "the world's wealth" can be won by whoever fashions a ring out of the Rhinegold: "That ring makes him lord of the world." Alberich transforms the potential of the gold into a means of control and the denial of freedom. But Wotan already is "lord of the world," before the creation of the ring by Alberich, and no one who possesses the ring ever actually gains control of the world (it symbolizes the fantasy of absolute control rather than control itself). Yet Wotan wants to prevent his overthrow by anyone possessing the ring. In the Interlude between the first and second scenes of *Das Rheingold*, the music of the Rhine, this time troubled and tempestuous, underlies an orchestral restatement of the Renunciation motif in the woodwinds, horns, and brass. As I mentioned in my summary of the plot, at the end of the Interlude, the motif of Valhalla emerges out of the motif of the *Ring* and establishing a clear connection between them: despite its illusions of freedom and justice, Valhalla rests on power. But what is power? Wotan used it creatively at first, but then he became destructive and broke his own rules: Why? If she thinks power corrupts, Brünnhilde rejects it but her love becomes destructive.

Like Hegel's master and slave (see Appendix, Section 2 for a summary), Wotan discovers that becoming the absolute ruler of society changes his conception of himself. The motif of Alberich's Curse is based on an inversion of the Ring motif, as if the ring has become associated with the darker, destructive side of power. However, as we see in the Interlude between Scenes 1 and 2, Wotan's image of the nobility of his society has already been tainted by the ambiguity of his own power symbolized in the relation between the Valhalla theme and the Ring motif. Wotan soon gets possession of the ring through devious means but has to give it up almost immediately to add to the giants' hoard of gold. After this, the motifs of Alberich's Curse and the Power of the Ring follow him everywhere. Valhalla cannot be purely good since its very construction was based on manipulation and lies. How reliable are Wotan's laws? Even pre-Valhalla society was tainted by his destruction of the World Ash Tree, the natural icon from which he fashioned his spear as the symbol of his laws. Once Wotan destroys it, he is no longer able to tell the difference between what he *wants* and what is *right* (also symbolized by his partial blindness), and at the end of *Götterdämmerung*, Brünnhilde uses the limbs of the dead tree to burn down Valhalla.

One of the most important motifs in *The Ring* is the so-called Fate motif. This motif occurs many times in the cycle and, whether Wagner was conscious of this or not, it clearly resembles Beethoven's "metaphysical" question of his op. 135 String Quartet—Beethoven wrote above the passage in his manuscript: "Must it Be?":"Muss es Sein?" In *The Ring* we usually hear it along with a little drumroll on the timpani that gradually comes to signify death. The association between the Fate motif and death occurs when Brünnhilde announces to Siegmund (in *Die Walküre* IIiv) that she appears only to those who are about to die.[10] In its earlier occurrences, this motif has an indeterminate reference, but it becomes completely clear in Siegfried's funeral music in *Götterdämmerung* what the fate of Siegfried and Brünnhilde will be.

The Fate motif appears again at the very end of *Die Walküre* when Wotan puts Brünnhilde into suspended animation to await the next redemptive hero. Wotan has Loge cast a spell of magic fire around her sleeping form and we hear the motifs of the Sleeping Brünnhilde, Fate, and Siegfried. Brünnhilde's fate has now been firmly connected to Wotan's hope of redemption and the fate of his society. An equally significant occurrence of the motif connects the relation between Siegmund and Sieglinde's son Siegfried to Brünnhilde, already established at the end of *Die Walküre*. In *Siegfried* IIIii, reversing the events of *Die Walküre* II when Wotan destroys Siegmund's sword, Siegfried uses the reforged Notung to shatter Wotan's spear (underscored by the Fate motif) and, during the Interlude between Scenes 2 and 3, he climbs to the top of the mountain where Brünnhilde has lain unconscious for decades, since the end of *Die Walküre*. The Fate motif occurs in the music of Brünnhilde's awakening, thereby bringing these two characters together as the redeeming (but destructive) force of Wotan's dream. This ideal of heroic redemption requires a source of justfication for his actions. Why is Siegfried worthy of such an accomplishment? *The Ring* challenges that connection: What is the basis of Siegfried's redeeming power? The mere fact that he has grown up outside of, unaffected by, Wotan's society? Does he have that power; can his naturalness, his ignorance of the ways of society, accomplish the goal? He is also Wotan's grandson. Like (grand)father, like (grand)son? Wagner's music often indicates Siegfried's moral ambiguity: What exactly is his role?

Preliminaries: The Significance of *The Ring*   23

At moments like this we can see the main point of *The Ring*: Siegfried and Siegmund both first see Brünnhilde in the context of the Fate music; they will both die and she will be involved in their deaths. Erda's prophecy indicates Fate: change and destruction are the fate of all things. What happens to Siegfried, Siegmund, and Sieglinde will happen to Wotan too, and finally to Brünnhilde. Nature should not be characterized by the bliss of the Rhinemaidens, a world free of conflict but, as Nietzsche understood it, as the potential for both creation and destruction. Nature is change, change through conflict affecting both individuals and society. Indeed, under Wagner's assimilation and then transposition of Ludwig Feuerbach's social optimism, a major early inspiration for *The Ring*, creation and destruction are part of the same fundamental force of the universe. In anticipation of the transforming power of her own love, Brünnhilde actually sings the Fate motif at the very end of *Siegfried* when she implores Siegfried: "O Siegfried!/Laughing youth!/Love yourself,/and leave me in peace; destroy not this maid who is yours!":"Liebe dich/und lasse von mir; vernichte dein Eigen nicht!" Indeed, destruction is their fate. Through that reference to Fate we see the larger significance of Brünnhilde's second thoughts about her relation to Siegfried. Here the private world of their love confronts the larger context of the fate symbolized by Wotan's world.

This general contrast between the personal and the public appears again at the beginning of *Götterdämmerung* when the music of Brünnhilde's Awakening in *Siegfried* IIIiii, with its imbedded Fate motif, reappears at the beginning of the Prolog. The Awakening music recurs here almost in its entirety, a half-step lower, in different orchestration and with a very different implication from the joyful awakening scene of *Siegfried* IIIiii—the Fate motif now clearly connects Brünnhilde and Siegfried to the larger problem of redemption. Can their love redeem them from the effects of power? The Awakening music prepares us for the fate implicit in Alberich's renunciation of love and Wotan's renunciation of power.[11] The music of Brünnhilde's Awakening occurs a third time, at Siegfried's death in *Götterdämmerung* IIIii when their redemptive love has indeed caused the decline of the gods. When the Awakening music occurs for the last time, we also see the significance of the Fate motif in Brünnhilde's plea for Siegfried to leave her in peace—she too will be destroyed.

The ascending motif of Erda closely resembles that of Nature, of which Erda symbolizes guardianship. They are minor/major versions of essentially the same music, forming the basis for others. *Die Walküre* IIiv, the scene of Brünnhilde's "annunciation of death" to Siegmund, derives from this family of motifs, as does Brünnhilde's "Walküre" motif (Cooke points this out in his *Introduction to Wagner's Ring*). The upward motion of Siegfried's motif exemplifies the "natural man," driven by the forces of nature, who will defeat Wotan. But there are also more sinister connections: the motif of Alberich's Curse, for example, resembles Erda's, and perhaps most significantly of all, the descending motif of the Twilight (or Decline) of the Gods is essentially the rising Erda/Nature motif turned around: Growth and Decline; Creation and Destruction. Nature has two faces, as Erda clearly indicates in her revelation to Wotan at the end of *Das Rheingold*.

Because of its importance in *The Ring*, the Fate motif will play a central role in my discussion its dramatic and musical levels of *The Ring*. I suggested earlier that this motif first occurs in the form of a vague premonition, an open question, just as it does in Beethoven's quartet. But as the cycle progresses the motif increasingly binds the love of Siegfried and Brünnhilde (as well as that of Siegmund and Sieglinde) to Wotan's problems with authority and value, projecting the drama between the individual characters into its broader social and metaphysical levels. We have just seen the transformation of the Fate motif from the Awakening music for Brünnhilde and Siegfried's great scene in *Siegfried* III-iii into its ironic reversals in the Prolog to *Götterdämmerung* and in Act III. Through musical transformations and connections like this, love does not to overcome power, love and power are really part of the same force in human life and experience. The transformation of the Nature motif into that of Erda, and then into its inversion in the Twilight of the Gods is another important example, recurring throughout the cycle.

Another developmental use of a motif that does not change very much in its basic musical form concerns the soft drumroll on the timpani that, as I noted above, sometimes accompanies Fate. This quiet little motif first appears in *Das Rheingold* when Fasolt and Fafner take Freia away (the gods thus losing their life-sustaining force), and again when Fafner kills Fasolt. It finally emerges as the powerful and sinister Death motif in Siegfried's funeral music near the end of *Götterdämmerung*, the last outcome towards which the Fate motif points. We then see the object of its earlier, almost subliminal, premonitions. I will try to show how the fates of Brünnhilde and Wotan are interconnected through the musical transformation of the Fate, Love, and Death motifs into the moment of realization and truth.

The effect of these musical interconnections transforms the love of Brünnhilde and Siegfried, based on their renunciation of the world of power, projecting it into the larger social and metaphysical drama unfolding around them. We move from the inner to the outer, from the beliefs and perceptions of individuals to their confrontations with others, and in so doing we move from the personal and private to the social, but also to the universal and metaphysical. The love of Siegfried and Brünnhilde forms their private world, a world that rejects Wotan's society and its problems, but they are thrust back into that larger political world where their love plays a destructive role. The ironic contrast between the awakening of Brünnhilde and the opening of *Götterdämmerung* clearly draws together the personal and social levels within the larger metaphysical context as the tension between the personal and the social becomes clearer. They cannot be kept apart: our inner-lives have social implications and society affects our inner-lives, our beliefs, hopes, and fears. Like Hegel's master and slave, they cannot be separated from each other without losing their identities, yet the tension between them cannot be fully resolved.

An key instance of this tension can be heard in the contrast between the completely opposite view of the same dawn music at the beginning of *Götterdämmerung*. The opening Norn scene with its minor transposition of the music of Brünnhilde's Awakening in *Siegfried* III portrays the darkness of the world, underscored even more by the reappearance of the Annunciation of Death motif (from Brünnhilde's scene with Siegmund in *Die Walküre* IIiv), occurring four times during the Prolog in connection with each Norn's interpretations as they weave together a rope that symbolizes the history of the world (but it breaks—on B–minor, the key of Alberich's curse—as they turn to the future, they cannot anticipate what will happen). The Prolog also contains the falling motif of the Twilight of the Gods: it forms a negative, inverted image of the opening to *Das Rheingold* with its rising Nature motif. Immediately following this dark scene of premonition we are thrust into the optimistic, up-beat dawn of Siegfried and Brünnhilde's new life—as they deceptively see it, the world promises endless possibility, endless responsiveness to their love. But the world awakening around them will be very different from their expectations. Through this contextualization, largely dependent on irony, we can understand the structure and the significance of the conflicts within and between the other levels in *The Ring*.[12]

In these examples, and in others to follow, we can see how Wagner represents the transformation of reality through the contrast between the beliefs of the characters, what they think their world is like, and what really happens. In the light of philosophical themes of which Wagner was quite conscious, the ending of *The Ring* should be seen quite differently from the way it often is—as the redemption of humanity from the ravages of unrestrained power, the death of God and the beginning of the age of humanity. This theme of social redemption, indeed the one Wagner began with when he started *The Ring,* underwent tremendous changes after he read Schopenhauer's *The World as Will and Representation*.

Notes

1 1869-1876, when he stopped teaching, having risen quickly to the rank of Professor (although he did not resign until 1879).

2 Some would say these are 'postmodern' issues. Without going into the vagueness of that term, which I will avoid altogether, I contend that since Kant, at least, our civilization has become increasingly concerned about foundations, including the justification of its beliefs and traditions, and so on. I contend that *The Ring* exemplifies these questions and that Nietzsche actually formulates them. Perhaps postmodernist theories of truth contend that truth does not exist, that there are only conventions and practices into which truth can be 'deconstructed' into something else. The historical period with which I am concerned, however, does not deny that truth has a role to play, although that role is not the one implied by realism.

3 I generally use the pronoun "his" in its gender-neutral sense. "His or her" is too cumbersome while alternating between masculine and feminine seems to me quite often to change the context and even the meaning. "His conception of sex" and "her conception of sex," for example, imply two quite different, gender-related points of view. In any case, since one of the main characters discussed in this book is female, there will be plenty of feminine pronouns.

4 Popular and scholarly literature alike often uncritically perpetuate anti-Wagner dogma. See, for example, William L. Shirer, *The Rise and Fall of the Third Reich* (New York: Simon and Shuster, 1959), Book I, Chapter 4: "The Mind of Hitler and the Roots of the Third Reich." Shirer describes the end of *The Ring* as an "orgy of self-willed annihilation which has always fascinated the German mind and answered some terrible longing in the German soul." As Tanner points out ("The Total Work of Art," in Peter Burbidge and Richard Sutton, eds. *The Wagner Companion* (New York: Cambridge University Press, 1979), p. 174, even J.P. Stern, usually more circumspect in such matters, draws the by now virtually mandatory parallel between Wotan and Hitler in his *Hitler: The Führer and the People.* See Cooke's discussion of the Wotan/Hitler comparison in *I Saw the World End* (New York: Oxford University Press, 1979), pp. 263–266. Much has been made of Wagner's anti-Semitism and its influence on some of the characters in his music-dramas. Some commentators argue that Alberich, Mime and Hagen, and Beckmesser in *Die Meistersinger,* are anti-Semitic caricatures. L.J. Rather discusses Wagner's anti-Semitism at some length in *The*

Dream of Self-Destruction: Wagner's Ring and the Modern World (Baton Rouge, Louisiana and London: Louisiana State University Press, 1979).

Further discussions of Wagner's anti-Semitism: Barry Millington, "Nuremberg Trial: Is There Anti-Semitism in *Die Meistersinger?*" *Cambridge Opera Journal*, III, 3 (Nov. 1991), pp. 246–260, Leon Stein, *The Racial Thinking of Richard Wagner* (New York: Philosophical Library, 1950) and Mark Weiner, *Wagner and the Anti-Semitic Imagination* (Lincoln, Nebraska and London: University of Nebraska, 1995). For Weiner, we cannot understand Wagner's music-dramas *at all* unless we do realize their anti-Semitic intent. See also Michael Tanner's comments on this literature in his *Wagner* (Cambridge: Cambridge University Press, 1996), Index: anti-Semitism.

5 See also J.K. Holman, *Wagner's Ring: A Listener's Companion and Concordance* (Portland, Oregon: Amadeus Press, 1996).

6 Deryck Cooke, *I Saw the World End* (New York: Oxford University Press, 1979), pp. 32–33.

7 Wagner originally conceived of *The Ring* in the form of a Greek tragedy, which traditionally consists of a cycle of three plays. To preserve that form, Wagner called *Das Rheingold* "a preliminary evening for the festival play of *The Ring of the Nibelungs.*"

8 As Cooke notes, *I Saw the World End,* p. 235, the motif of the Sword can only be a symbol of Wotan's willful intentions at this point since he has no actual sword to flourish.

9 I employ the following conventions to refer to acts and scenes together: upper case roman numerals (II) refer to acts, lower case roman numerals (iv) to scenes.

10 For an important discussion of the Fate motif, see Deryck Cooke, "Wagner's Musical Language," in Burbidge and Sutton, *The Wagner Companion*, pp. 227 f. I will refer to the names for the Leitmotifs generally used by Cooke and Donington. I hope that the reader will become familiar with Cooke's far more extensive discussion of the motifs in his *An Introduction to Der Ring des Nibelungen,* prepared for the Solti/Vienna *Ring* on Decca/London (RDN-1), hereafter referred to as *Introduction to Wagner's Ring.*

11 In *I Saw the World End*, Cooke points out the similarities between Wotan and Alberich as renouncers: the former's capacity for love is weakened by power, and the latter's frustration at love results in the destructive use of power through his curse (pp. 268 f., see also p. 159 for a detailed comparison). They are counterbalanced as the light and dark sides of the same force. Alberich gives up compassionate love in order to have the ring (he does not give up sex—otherwise there would be no Hagen in *Götterdämmerung*). What does Wotan give up in his attempt to get the ring back? One could argue that he gives up nothing, that he only takes; but *Die Walküre* clearly shows that he relinquishes whatever power he retains—and he gives up Brünnhilde in his hope of finding a redeemer for his society. The fulfillment of his hope no longer lies within his grasp.

12 Since the concept of Irony will play a special role in what follows, I should briefly indicate the particular meaning I attach to it. As the dictionaries say, irony involves the recognition of the incongruity between expectations and results; irony also implies an emphasis on chance and time, ironic observations convey an implied nonliteral, sometimes opposite meaning. An important discussion of the role of irony in modern literature and philosophy can be found in Richard Rorty, *Contingency, Irony, and Solidarity* (Cambridge: Cambridge University Press, 1989). See especially his Introduction.

Chapter Two

The Structure of *The Ring*: Tragedy or Transcendence?

Wagner rewrote the ending of *The Ring* at least six times between its inception in 1848 and the final version in 1874. During this time his philosophical orientation changed dramatically from that of a left-wing Hegelian and Feuerbachian[1] to that of a Schopenhauerian around 1854 when he began to write the music for *Die Walküre*. He said it was Schopenhauer who initiated his return to *The Ring* with a very different conception of its meaning. To begin with, at least, the great pessimist simply enhanced the evolution towards clarity of his own initially ambiguous ideas. Before reading him, for example, Wagner had already spoken of Wotan "willing his own destruction" in his correspondence with August Röckel.[2] But what did that imply?

Schopenhauer became common ground for Wagner and the young Nietzsche soon after they met in 1868. Even before 1852 Wagner was already moving away from Hegel and Feuerbach, to whom he dedicated *The Artwork of the Future* (1850), as he simultaneously began work on *The Ring* and on *Opera and Drama* (the latter finished in 1851). By the time of his Schopenhauerian essay *Beethoven* (1870), however, Wagner's conception of music-drama had undergone major changes culminating first in *Tristan und Isolde* (completed in 1859) and *Die Meistersinger* (completed in 1867). His new conception of music was then incorporated into *The Ring* beginning with *Siegfried* III (completed in 1871) and *Götterdämmerung* (completed in 1874) with *Parsifal* (finished in 1882) as his self-consciously final masterwork.

In his essay "The Sufferings and Greatness of Richard Wagner" (1933), Thomas Mann describes Wagner as a "dilettante" at both philosophy and music, an unusual description of someone who pursued his goals with such incredible energy and single-mindedness. Wagner did indeed use whatever was at his disposal and had little formal training in anything, but he was no mere eclectic and far from an amateur dabbler. His music was, and still is, dismissed by some as structurally primitive, harmonically static, turgid and too loud (although the latter has usually been the result of conductors failing to pay attention to Wagner's dynamic markings). More recently, this view has become less pervasive, at least partly due to the influence of Deryck Cooke. Most commentators now agree that, musically, Wagner was innovative and imaginative.

Wagner's prose works, however, are another matter. The major theoretical works—*The Artwork of the Future, Opera and Drama,* and *Beethoven*—do contain important, if sometimes derivative, sometimes rather confused, views about politics, history, metaphysics, music, and drama, views that must be seen as part of Wagner's genuinely creative ability at integrating disparate influences. But the value and interest of his theoretical writings ultimately depends on the music they are about. Those who claim that Wagner was one of the greatest 'thinkers' of the nineteenth century show little appreciation for the vast riches of that period. Wagner's theoretical works sometimes border on the bizarre but they are not untypical of the literary and intellectual experimentalism of the nineteenth century. His anti-Semitism, his seriousness about his grand, expensive life-style, his sometime vegetarianism, his confused *Volkishness* (can 'the people' really understand these works?) all point to the supremely neurotic 'genius at work' ambiance surrounding the creation of his works (and he *was* a genius!). Mann points out, for example, that Wagner's doctrine of the *Gesamtkunstwerk*, the integration of music, poetry, painting (set design), and acting into an art-form transcending its individual components, implies that painting or poetry or music, taken alone, are somehow incomplete and incapable of the expressive power of 'the total work of art'. Mann calls this sort of thing the bad part of the nineteenth century in its mechanistic approach to art (why is poetry somehow 'incomplete' without the music it merely implies—and what music might that be?). In any case, the mechanistic doctrines of the *Gesamtkunstwerk* underlying *The Ring* became less constraining as work on the cycle progressed.

Because *The Ring* depended on it, however variously, we should bear Wagner's theory in mind. In *Opera and Drama* Wagner criticizes traditional opera, except for Gluck, whom he sees as a precursor, for demoting music to the merely supportive role of accompaniment. In the worst case, it plays no role in the dramatic structure. Although many counterexamples to this view were of course known to Wagner (Mozart? Haydn? *Fidelio*?), he generally disparages the state of modern opera as mere entertainment (no better than today's "Three Tenors" pop concerts of greatest hit-arias wrenched out of their contexts). For Wagner, the drama should dominate, as it did in Greek tragedy (which also included music). The commonality of poetry and music lies in their approximation of an underlying concept. The greatest poets try to "tune words" into harmony, but music must be true to that goal too: "when the absolute musician attempts to paint, he brings about neither music nor a painting; but if he wanted to accompany with his music the inspection of an actual painting, then he might be quite sure that no one would understand the painting or the music."[3]

What Wagner envisaged in *Opera and Drama* was a unification of poetry and music: music ought to bring out the meaning of the drama. It should further the dramatic content. Beethoven's *Ninth Symphony* provided Wagner with an example of how that should be done. The music of the fourth movement breaks into words, the bass soloist singing the music first played by the cellos, and in Part I of *Opera and Drama* Wagner describes Beethoven as becoming "fully human"—that is, Man conceived as a social being, the unification of man and woman, symbolized by the relation between words and music. In Part III, Wagner continues this metaphor of unification: "On this new voyage we shall see the poet become the selfsame man as the musician upon his own new journey across the other half of the earth [poets explore one part of the earth, musicians another], traced out for him by the poet [and the priority of drama]; so that we now may look on both these journeys as one and the same thing" (I modify Ellis's translation). Wagner also writes that the metaphysical point of the confluence of words and music lies in its challenge to the separation of intellect and emotion:

> At a performance of a dramatic work of art, nothing should remain for the synthesizing intellect to search for: everything presented in it should be so conclusive as to set our feeling at rest about it: for in this setting at rest of feeling, after it has been aroused to the highest pitch in the act of sympathetic response, resides that very repose which leads us towards an instinctive understanding of life. In drama, we must become *knowers* through *feeling*.[4]

Although this last sentiment vaguely describes Wagner's later views too, in both theory and in practice, he radically and pragmatically changed his theory about the nature of music partly because of the influence of Schopenhauer. In *Opera and Drama*, Wagner maintained that music was an abstract expression of the underlying mood of the dramatic text. Under this earlier view, musical expression depends on a preestablished conceptual context for its direction and content, subordinating music to the ideas of the text and the action of the drama.[5] *Das Rheingold* remains the one remaining part of *The Ring* that most closely adheres to this doctrine, the music articulating the dramatic structure through cross-references determined by the meaning of the text.

Adapting Schopenhauer's theory of the Will, however, Wagner began what was to become a complete reversal of this theory of music. This new and different theory was finally summarized in *Beethoven*, but by then Wagner had already established his modified views in practice midway through *The Ring*. Music became "the essence of the world itself," an essence incapable of adequate conceptual representation even through the imagery of the other arts (although poetry could come close—because of its musical essence). Music should not be subordinated to any larger whole (as he had held in *Opera and Drama*)—it *is* the larger whole and the visible actions of drama and its language are but the phenomenal counterparts of music. Like the essence of nature, it cannot be exhaustively described and can only be communicated directly. The music supersedes the concepts of the text and the visual images of the stage settings as they emerge out of the musical 'Will', to use the Schopenhauerian terminology Wagner adopted. But this does not mean that the words or the voices of a music-drama are insignificant to the symphonic whole: the musical subsumes the vocal and together they become part of a larger phenomenon in the "emotionalization of the intellect" as Wagner called it.

One important element in Wagner's theory of music-drama concerns his view on the relations between his characters. In traditional opera, characters interact; theater and music may be correlated but are not interdependent. While the action concerns the external world and the drama depends on spectacle, costume, and the events of the plot, the relation of these to the music sometimes seems *ad hoc* or contrived. For Wagner, however, like Greek tragedy, music-drama concentrates on what happens inside characters, on how they view the world and others. The music explores their hopes and fears. We see an example of this in *Die Walküre* II, in Wotan's monologue, where the music refers back to the events of *Das Rheingold* and projects Wotan's hopes into the future, giving us his view of the world. As Brian Magee puts it: "music-drama would be the reverse of traditional opera, for in traditional opera the drama was merely a framework on which to hang the music—drama was the means, music the end—whereas the object of music-drama was the presentation of archetypal situations *as experienced by the participants,* and to this dramatic end music was a means, albeit a uniquely expressive one."[6] Later in *The Ring,* especially in *Götterdämmerung,* the music becomes the end and not the means, but not in the traditional manner of opera. The drama becomes essentially musical.

With his theory of leitmotifs, Wagner was able to integrate stage action and music. The music referred in specific ways to characterize objects and events in the visible drama by giving them musical characterizations. The musical *interrelations* between the motifs also creates a deeper level of drama, its "essence," what he thought, rather confusedly, to be pure emotion (which seems more like sensation than emotion, which requires an object). Nevertheless, Wagner wanted to create the "symphonic" foundation of the visible drama in which music does not simply exemplify or comment but becomes integral to the drama itself. Trying to explain Wagner's concept of Music-Drama, Nietzsche describes the relation between music and stage in *The Birth of Tragedy* (Section 16), while the concepts of the drama are universals *post rem* (what we experience as a result of the drama), music consists of universals *ante rem* (prior to the events). Music exists as the independent metaphysical essence of the stage events and does not follow from them. Nietzsche goes on to discuss how the orchestra should be placed to best represent its role. Wagner, at Bayreuth, hid the orchestra completely away *under* the stage, the fact of its invisibility symbolizing its universality.

The Structure of *The Ring*: Tragedy or Transcendence?

One final preliminary: music, as Wagner describes it in *Opera and Drama*, acts as an expressive medium, giving the emotional essence of the drama itself. This raises a fundamental problem, aptly described by Emil Staiger: Wagner uses music to exemplify and elucidate the drama psychologically, and even philosophically. But:

> With this intent he develops his leitmotif device, which permits him to follow every turn of the poetic phrase, to allude to mythical or psychical circumstances.... The more Wagner's music deals with such details of the text, the more he is in danger of losing the larger line. Indeed, the *Ring* cycle, and even separate parts or acts of it, cannot really be apprehended as a unit except by intellectual reflection of the ideational structure. The great single span is missing in this musical epic.[7]

Because intellectual reflection is necessary to understand the significance of individual musical/textual conjunctions, one of the essential features of music— its continuous flow—can be lost. While reflecting on a particular moment, the next one cannot be experienced and the temporal flow stagnates. Furthermore, because there are so many motifs, how can they be held "in mind" with their textual, dramatic referents as we listen to the work? This would be like trying to carry on a conversation in a foreign language while constantly looking up words in a dictionary.

Granting the vagueness inherent in Wagner's theory over its several articulations, as well as the uneasy relation between intellectual analysis and emotional responsiveness, I hope to show that for the most part Staiger's worry does not apply to *The Ring*. For one thing, Wagner ingeniously establishes his fundamental musical-dramatic referents so that they are clearly recognizable at key moments and, especially in *Götterdämmerung*, the recapitulation of motifs helps to hold the significant features of the drama before us. A striking instance of this occurs at the end of the cycle, beginning with Siegfried's Funeral March, where all of the important motifs begin to reappear, bringing together the conflicts between the characters and the "idea of their world" as Wagner described it in *Beethoven*. In *Götterdämmerung*, and at the beginning of the third act of *Siegfried*, music becomes less of a supporting agent as the cycle takes on an explicitly "symphonic" character, as Wagner described it (I say more about his later view of music in the Appendix, Section 3). Nevertheless, this is a work that cannot possibly be understood at once. It may well be the case that the problem Staiger describes can be overcome only through continuing experience of *The Ring*. (This certainly holds true of all great art, does it not?) Sometimes one may have to 'analyze' moments of *The Ring* with score in hand. But, however advisable and even necessary such study may be, learning the details about the structure of the work cannot be the paradigm of ones experience of it. Indeed, while granting that sometimes Wagner has trouble holding his vast invention together (something he does better in his other works of this period), contrary to Staiger, with effort and time, one can experience at least something approaching "the great single span" of *The Ring* in large part because the music eventually became its center.

1. The Endings of *The Ring* and the Troubles of Wotan

It has been pointed out by many commentators—and by Wagner himself—that Ludwig Feuerbach influenced the earlier versions of *The Ring*. These early drafts end with an optimistic prophecy of rebirth and redemption through the creation of a society based on collective compassion and a healthy naturalistic view of human life that, like Siegmund, rejects the divine, inhuman world. Perhaps this socially oriented vision of redemption was inspired by Wagner's revolutionary hopes during the Dresden uprising of 1849. In this almost archetypal revolution (because it was so widely discussed and became a case study for would-be revolutionaries) social philosophers such as Feuerbach argued that humanism would become the successor to religion through our historically progressive demythologization of divine forms of authority. In Western civilization in particular, the transfer of authority from the transcendent God of the Christian era to humanity reorients the source of value in the universe from outside to inside. For Feuerbach, sexual love, not divine authority, symbolized the central force in this naturalistic transformation of society. Love unites mankind through the natural biology of human sexual attraction, value radiating outward from humanity and forming a new basis for social and moral value from inside the human species itself. Both Feuerbach and Wagner understood our erotic existence to be the primary impulse of life and the source of social redemption. Although his view of the relation between value and society in *The Ring* was to change, Wagner maintained this naturalism even in his later Schopenhauerian period, and in part this explains his crucial difference from Schopenhauer.

The love of Siegmund and Sieglinde in *Die Walküre* was, as Feuerbach described all love, "self love"—all the more because they were brother and sister who saw themselves in each other. Wagner put Wotan's divinely ordained society in opposition to his two children (as a joint symbol of himself), hoping that biological instinct would lead to a more secure foundation for society. But where Feuerbach saw this demythologization of divine authority as an objective foundation for society, Wagner saw power and love more in a complex, interconnected way. Love does not redeem society from the power of divinity because love establishes its own kind of power, focused on the self-reflexivity of human value.

In *Opera and Drama,* the urge for social reconstruction in the image of human rather than divine values first takes the form of destruction: one must "annul the state," the impersonal, in order to free the individual for creative moral innovation (Wagner describes the actions of Antigone as an example of this contrast). As with Feuerbach, the state in its monolithic detachment embodies the "otherness" or oppression symbolized in the religious appeal to transcendent, nonhuman authority. Justification for values in the human world lay beyond, in the divine command itself, administered by the acolytes of absolute truth (what Nietzsche later called the "priestly caste"). Feuerbach claimed that humanity can overcome its alienation from the source of authority within this kind of society only through a radical reconception of the concept of Value exemplifying the natural, evolutionary process of human development. This Feuerbachian naturalism, the transformation of religion into sociology, as he put it, pervades *Opera and Drama* and we can still see it at work in the final version of *The Ring.* But Wagner eventually had a different idea about the nature of authority.

The difference between Feuerbach and Wagner lies in the concept of the Self. The increasing domination of mankind over nature raises serious problems with both the romantic and Enlightenment conceptions of the Self as well as with the idea of social redemption implicit in Feuerbach's (and later Marx's) evolutionary view of society.[8] For Wagner, unlike Feuerbach, a fully humanized society can be just as problematic as the divine one it replaces because 'the human' has no univocal definition and contains contradictory qualities (the point of his later works *Die Meistersinger* and *Parsifal* with their emphasis on the control of illusion). Beyond 'love', and perhaps elemental striving, no fundamental list of essentially human values emerges from Wagner's works. Indeed, traditional virtues such as loyalty and courage lead to disastrous situations in *The Ring.* But what is love? One never finds in Wagner a Feuerbachian or Rousseauian appeal to the intrinsic *benevolence* of human nature as the origin of society. Wagner's humans are nasty as well as nice. His view of the self had become too complex for the romantic moral psychology that characterized the later Enlightenment and the early nineteenth century. Human love in *Die Walküre* I, for example, should be seen through its antiauthoritarian results in the rest of *The Ring* but also as the violation of Wotan's own social rules as *they* exemplify another (perfectly human) desire—the desire for control. Hence Wotan is not so 'alien' after all. Love involves control—but was social control *universalized* in the ascendance of humanity, as Feuerbach claimed? If so, it exemplified the same form as divine authority (the universal over the individual), and this Wagner rejected. Universalized human values can be just as arbitrary as their divine counterparts. These complications in the relation between individuality and collective responsibility should also be understood within the rule-breaking context of Siegmund and Sieglinde's incestual attraction (applying just as much to Siegfried and Brünnhilde, since she is his aunt).

We can see how Wagner abandons Feuerbach's humanistic redemptiveness by looking at the character of Wotan. As the principal architect of social value in *The Ring,* the problem facing Wotan at the end of *Das Rheingold* concerns the revitalization of a society suddenly compromised at its moral foundation through his own actions. He must somehow get compassion and freedom back into a world beginning to disintegrate because his confrontation with Alberich has led Wotan to violate his own principles. By Act II of *Die Walküre,* the freedom of virtually everyone in Wotan's society has been threatened by his attempts at reestablishing his power, yet his authority seems to have no foundation beyond his own will. What exactly does Wotan want? Because of his manipulativeness, the contrived encounter between Siegmund and Sieglinde, his treatment of Freia, Fasolt and Fafner, and his murder of Siegmund, Wotan does not have much dignity left by *Die Walküre* II. He seems to have acted from pure self-interest in his desire to control the world and in his attempt to acquire Alberich's ring, yet he expresses social concerns beyond his personal interests.

At this point in the drama, the ring symbolizes power, the control of others *via* the means of production, as the Marxists and Shavians would put it (and as Alberich has actually been using it). Since Alberich has sworn enmity and revenge towards Wotan's society, Wotan sees nothing wrong in deceiving him to get control of his ring. But he later realizes that he must himself break the laws he established for his society in order to save it. Does the end justify the means? Or is it simply another example of the politics of divine oppression Feuerbach described? Can love simply be contrasted with power? Brünnhilde herself, motivated solely by love also becomes fatally oppressive in *Götterdämmerung.* Wotan's Spear motif symbolizes his will, his desire for lawful world domination, as Cooke describes it (*Introduction to Wagner's Ring*, p. 16) while Alberich's ring and its motif symbolize Alberich's will towards unlawful, uncontrolled world domination. This 'Light/Dark' dichotomy reappears many times in *The Ring,* and Wotan himself sees it clearly in his own self-characterization.

Aside from the moral compromise of Wotan's deception of Alberich, and his treatment of the giants and Freia, he sees in his monologue of Act II of *Die Walküre* that the ring, now hidden in Fafner's cave, cannot be used to enforce his laws. He must, yet again, be prepared to use force to get what he wants. He must break his own rules. But he finally sees, in his monologue, that if he breaks them, his laws have no value as an extension of his dream of value and social dignity. Wotan's society forms (at least to him) an enlightened monarchy of responsible individuals within a hierarchy of roles and responsibilities governed by well-understood traditional social classes and a sense of mutual respect for those divisions—an idealized society based on accepted aristocratic virtues such as courage, resourcefulness, honor, rank, and loyalty. But during *Das Rheingold,* after violating his own principles of justice and fair dealing, Wotan's society begins to revert to the primitive state of nature from which he created it through his laws, symbolically inscribed on his spear. In part of the Norse legend Wagner does not include in *The Ring,* Wotan cut off a branch from the World Ash Tree to make his spear, destroying this symbol of natural harmony in order to form his society. To do this, he paid the price of losing one of his eyes to drink from the Well of Wisdom in order to determine the best laws to inscribe onto his spear (the political implications of this phallic symbolism I only need to note). This loss, symbolized in *The Ring* by an eye patch, implies Wotan's shortsightedness about the effects of those laws and even of the impersonal nature of law itself. As the first of its effects, the World Ash Tree died symbolizing, perhaps, the Rousseauian contrast between idyllic nature and the destructiveness of society, an opposition also implicit in the Power/Love axis.[9]

Now, although Wotan and Valhalla symbolize divine, and therefore nonhuman power, Wotan also strikingly resembles we humans in his struggle for order: Valhalla can be seen as symbolic of human society itself. For Wagner, it seems to me, power and love are the same in divine *or* human contexts. So Wagner does not simply dismiss theology as an inhuman and arbitrary symbol of power; in fact, even in the early versions of *The Ring,* there are obvious and important similarities between Wotan's divinity and his (quite human) desire for social order. But even under an overtly political/economic interpretation, and despite his egoism and his willfulness, Wotan cannot accurately be described as the ruthlessly materialistic captain of industry portrayed in *The Perfect Wagnerite.* For one thing, he clearly understands the necessity for freedom in his society; he even has Feuerbachian ideals, but that is why he is so tormented in his monologue. Wotan wants control but he also wants others to freely grant him that control. Although not an egalitarian society, he wants others to have the same dignity in their roles that he desires for himself in his. He supports fundamental principles of justice and respect and wants everyone to share them, whatever their status and role in his society. Nevertheless, Wotan disastrously manipulates Siegmund and Sieglinde, denying their freedom. And, later, he does the same to Brünnhilde.

Wotan finally realizes in his soul-searching monologue that his society cannot be a pure extension of his will if it is to be based on the same freedom for its members that he wants for himself. He realizes that he and Alberich are "brothers." Wotan describes himself as "light Alberich" in his lust for power and control. His manipulation of Siegmund and Sieglinde shows how evil emerges from his desire for good. How can Wotan's position as ruler be sustained in such an atmosphere of moral compromise? This resembles what Feuerbach said about God: if there are to be rational beings in the universe, it would be morally wrong for them to be under the control of values and interests not their own—as Siegmund and Sieglinde are under the control of Wotan.

The tension between Wotan's willfulness and his desire for freedom in his society lies at the center of *The Ring* and exemplifies Hegel's Master/Slave analogy. Indeed, Hegel's little story gives us an insight into the interdependence between Wotan and his society (again, I discuss this in Chapter 3, Section 3 and in the Appendix, Section 2). Except for the goddess of the earth, Erda, the major characters perceive the world as malleable through their desires and actions. Nevertheless, from another point of view, their world is governed by a fate not even the gods can escape—the inevitability of change, as Hegel's two characters would discover in achieving self-consciousness (if they get that far). Indeed, because the contrast between perception and reality plays such a central role in later versions of *The Ring*, Wagner moved away from Feuerbach and towards Schopenhauer in his emphasis on the illusion of social redemption. Erda announces the principle of this fate for the modern world: things change, more radically than Wotan (and we) can imagine. Everything he builds will pass away; even his own self-imagery undergoes radical change. But change and conflict are also the ultimate conditions for establishing values and maintaining their stability.

From this point on, it is apparent how little freedom Wotan really has in the light of Erda's warning that he had better give back the ring (although he does not have it, it was taken by giant Fafner). Otherwise, as Erda says in the early drafts: "A dark day dawns for the gods; your noble race will surely die if you do not give back the ring." Under this version Wotan *can* save his society *if* he returns the ring. The final version, however, reads: "All things that are, perish. An evil day Dawns for the immortals: I warn you, yield up the ring!"[10] In the final version, however, it seems that the gods will perish whether or not Wotan renounces power and the dream of total control—but with no clear connection implied between giving back the ring and saving himself. Giving back the ring could simply be Wotan's recognition of his powerlessness in the face of change and a way of allowing that change to proceed—Schopenhauer's denial of the Will in its form of human individuality.

In the first version of Erda's prophecy, the pursuit of power as a means of dominating others leads to destruction. To save us from destruction, this desire must be transformed into love, leading to a society wherein value arises internally through the actions of its members rather than by external or transcendent imposition. This version adheres closely to Feuerbach's own views on social redemption: the clash between love and power is the real center of Hegel's dialectic. Brünnhilde accomplishes the humanization of value by replacing power with love through her destruction of Valhalla. Human love then becomes the new source of value in society. Through her efforts, the world of human benevolence replaces the world of divine authority, just as in Feuerbach's account.

But human love also resists domination by the institutions of society in a union of love and spirit having less to do with politics than Feuerbach doubtlessly would have wished.

In Wagner's final version, however, it seems that whatever happens, "All things that are, perish" despite Wotan's own attempt to redeem society by renouncing his arbitrary use of power. Eventually love itself becomes a *destructive* power for Brünnhilde as she renounces Wotan's society and his struggle for order. Her love also distorts her view of Siegfried and even involves her in plotting his death with Hagen. In this, Wagner leaves Feuerbachian *eros* far behind: yes, love is politics; but it also represents the nature of all reality in its dialectic of control. Power is also a form of love: the desire to control, to dominate, implies attraction. Feuerbach envisaged a particular image of humanity to stand at the center of his story of redemption. For Wagner, humanist though he was, that *persona* in the story of Western civilization, "humanity," has become profoundly ambiguous.

Does this ambiguity in the concept of Love simply reflect an unintentional inconsistency resulting from combining of early Feuerbachian and later Schopenhauerian versions? In *Opera and Drama*, Wagner had spoken of love in Feuerbachian terms as the longing for physical reality, the desire for an object that can be grasped by the senses. Perhaps the gold symbolizes this object in *The Ring*; but he also spoke of sacrifice, especially on the part of women. Brünnhilde's self-sacrifice seems to reflect Wagner's view of female love: the complete submission of oneself to accomplish a higher goal—in Brünnhilde's case, her compassionate self-sacrifice and compassion achieves the goal of a new society founded on love.[11] In the final version of *The Ring,* however, Brünnhilde does not remain passive but neither does she rise above, leave behind Wotan's society for something better through humanistic benevolence and compassion. She undertakes actions that actually destroy Siegfried and the civilized world along with Wotan, Siegfried and herself. The survivors have to start all over again. But on what principle? If love requires freedom, in this case it is the freedom to destroy—even the freedom to be self-destructive—can it be contrasted with power?

After reading Schopenhauer in 1854, Wagner substituted an ending (in 1856) more explicitly pessimistic than the second version of Erda's warning.[12] In this ending Brünnhilde departs from Valhalla and flees the "open gates of eternal Becoming" and the illusory phenomenal world. As a Buddhist 'see-er' she renounces her phenomenal individuality for a kind of absolute selfhood because she now grasps the destructiveness of the Will at work in the world of society and persons, the world characterized by Schopenhauer as the "Veil of Maya." Here, as Wagner explained in one of his letters to August Röckel, we see love "asserting itself as fundamentally destructive." She sings:

If I now fare no more
to Valhalla's fortress,
do you know whither I go?
From the land of desire I depart,
the land of illusion I flee for ever;
the open gates
of eternal becoming
I close behind me:
to the desire-free land,
the goal of world-wandering,
redeemed from rebirth,
she who understands now departs.
The blesséd end
of all things eternal,
do you know how I reached it?
Deepest suffering
of grieving love
opened my eyes:
I saw the world end.[13]

In the earlier versions, Brünnhilde addresses a crowd of bystanders and offers them the choice between redemptive rebirth through love (which she predicts for Siegfried) and reincarnations of unhappiness (in the case of Hagen). Yet another version ends with a tableau of Brünnhilde and Siegfried united in the flames, symbolizing the universality of love. In the final version of the ending, Brünnhilde rides off into the flames after returning the ring to the Rhinemaidens. We see her no more and the Rhine River, overflowing its banks destroying Hagen (originally Alberich), purifying the world of the tyranny of the gods, and quenching the fires of Valhalla. This after she has been involved in the plot resulting in Siegfried's death in addition to her becoming the agent of the destruction of Valhalla. Although she now "knows all," she does not convey her vision to us and, after undertaking the destruction of Valhalla, she yearns only to be reunited with Siegfried. The ring has, after all, apparently destroyed Wotan's world, but it has done so through Brünnhilde. The bystanders remain, but what are they (and we) to make of her silence? Wagner maintained (in notes to the staging instructions) that the final version of the ending still carried the force of the one of 1856.[14]

The final version ends like this:

By [Siegfried's] most valiant deed
he fulfilled your desire,
but he was forced
to share in your [Alberich/Wotan's] curse—

> that curse which has doomed your downfall.
> He, truest of all men,
> betrayed me,
> that I in grief might grow wise!
> Now I know what must be.
> All things, all things,
> I know now;
> all to me is revealed![15]

Clearly, the ending of the cycle is extremely important to an understanding of the work as a whole, but in order to appreciate the fullness and complexity of its meaning, we must see how it connects up to the rest of the drama.

2. Conflict in *The Ring*: Love *versus* Power

At the end of Chapter 1 I gave some examples of Wagner's use of music to convey the significance of particular events in *The Ring*. By the time Wagner finished the cycle, poetry augmented by music, could not tell the story Wagner wanted to tell and music became far more integral to the story itself. I want now to look at the music of *The Ring* in more detail to show how it expresses a particular view of reality—a metaphysics—very much in tune with the nineteenth-century attack on metaphysical realism but also in its unique emphasis on individuality and redemption.

To characterize his view, as I suggested earlier, I borrow from Michael Tanner and Morse Peckham the idea of Wagner's "refusal to transcend." Wagner does not encourage us to disparage life or to escape from the conflicts of the natural world through love conceived as sensualized subjectivity (Adorno's claim). Nor does he transform conflict itself into a transcendental, supernatural process unifying Spirit and Nature into something Bigger and Better (based on Hegel's conception of dialectical progress through transcendentalized humanism). Wagner's naturalism, as I will describe it, gradually became the most important respect in which he refused to follow Schopenhauer. Society and persons do, for him, possess an illusory status: change is their essence. But nature in no way diminishes our status as self-generating sources of value and order. The contingency of social value—and even personal identity—does not lead Wagner to Schopenhauer's cynicism about the signficance of humanity. I want to defend and extend these claims by looking at Wagner's use of music in *The Ring* and its implications: not only are these implications richly metaphysical but they are also of significance to our own understanding of human life and value.

If change is the essence of the world in *The Ring*, its changes occurs through conflict. Conflict occurs at four different levels in *The Ring*. It occurs first, between individuals: Wotan and Alberich, Wotan and Fricka, Wotan and Siegmund, Siegfried and Hagen, Brünnhilde and Wotan, and even between Brünnhilde and Siegfried (and there are many other pairings essential to the plot: Siegfried and Fafner; Mime and Siegfried; Brünnhilde and Hagen). Every relationship between the characters is either one of conflict or an attempt to resolve it, but leading to further conflict.

The second level of conflict occurs more generally between individuals and society. In Wotan's attempt to protect his society, he violates his own rules of fair play and justice. Siegmund and Sieglinde violate Wotan's laws; Brünnhilde and Siegfried forsake society for their own personal world. In his desire to overcome Wotan's world, Alberich ruthlessly dominates the society of the Nibelungs, who have become his slaves. Following Alberich, his son Hagen wishes to bring Wotan's society down by creating conflict between Siegfried and Brünnhilde, and so on.

Third, the theme of mankind *versus* nature, sometimes understood as human spirit *versus* nature, also involves conflict. In their scenes with both Alberich and Siegfried at the beginning and end of *The Ring*, the Rhinemaidens are expressions of nature in the form of *eros*. But they too are clearly conflict-oriented: each of their four scenes expresses conflict. The Rhinemaiden's sexual taunting carries the suggestion of libidinal desire in opposition to the constraints of social order. Wotan violated nature in creating his spear, his symbol of power, but in so doing his attempt at creating a permanent society, a utopia, conflicts with the natural principles of change enunciated in the prophecies of Erda, the goddess of nature. The Rhinemaidens express this tension at the conclusion of *Das Rheingold*. In their scene with Siegfried, just before his death at the end of the cycle, they remind him of the evil attached to the ring and implore him to return it to them (since it is made out of 'their' gold). Nature, in the form of the Rhine River, finally quenches the self-destructive fire produced by the collapse of Wotan's civilization, returning the world to a state of potential with the Rhinemaidens emerging through the flood: Potential for what?

Fourth, the hierarchy of conflict ultimately reaches a metaphysical level of opposition between what I have been calling the forces of power and love. They comprise the most pervasive dichotomy in the universe as seen through the beliefs, hopes, fears, and experience of the characters of *The Ring*. Power and love are the archetypal forces of nature that shape human motivation. The opposition between them dominates the concept of redemption, the attempt to resolve conflict. In one way or another, all of the major characters see the universe as the opposition between power and love: Alberich renounces love for power; Wotan renounces power for compassion; Brünnhilde and Wotan believe the powers of evil can be defeated by love; Siegfried and Brünnhilde renounce

The Structure of *The Ring*: Tragedy or Transcendence?

everything for love. Hagen concentrates his destructiveness on those who have or desire love. But *The Ring* shows how power and love are *interdependent* opposites: the one cannot be eliminated by the other.

These four levels of conflict characterize both the dramatic and the musical structures of *The Ring*. The world dominated by the lust for power, the 'dark' world of Alberich (and later Hagen), characteristically opposes the 'light' world of Wotan and his vision of social happiness based on aristocratic principles of merit. Alberich (the Alfred Krupp of German mythology) labors beneath the ground commanding the enslaved Nibelungs and the motif of the Power of the Ring that initially characterizes his lust for domination (not just Alberich's lust, but later Wotan's too, often subconsciously) stands as one of the most suggestive in *The Ring*. Its origin in the Rhinegold motif points to nature as the *potential* for conflict rather than its *resolution*. Wotan's apparently very different world embodies many of the values dear to Western civilization at various stages of its history: justice, mutual respect, aristocratic nobility, and the control of nature through the development of society, the sanctity of social institutions. The brass motif of Valhalla symbolizes this idea of social stability as order resulting from justifiably founded values expressing the power of human civilization.

I have suggested that power and love are only apparent opposites. They are in fact interdependent and I contend that Wagner wrote the music of *The Ring* to show this. For example, the connection I pointed out in Chapter 1, Section 8 between the motifs of the Power of the Ring and Valhalla in the Interlude between Scenes 1 and 2 of *Das Rheingold* both clearly indicate this connection. Another example occurs at the end of *Das Rheingold*: the Valhalla motif appears simultaneously and dissonantly with the Rhinemaidens singing the Rhinegold motif, showing that Wotan's world stands in conflict with nature. Ironically, things turn out the opposite of what they are intended to be. Wotan desires stability but gets change; what appears stable is inherently unstable. The very act of searching for permanence can cause change. Wotan's noble dreams become desperate exercises in manipulation: he firmly renounces force in *Das Rheingold* but permits deception to achieve his own ends as he takes the ring from Alberich himself. As we saw in the last section, in Act II of *Die Walküre*, punctuated by key appearances of the Power of the Ring motif, Wotan realizes that his quest for power has changed him into someone not unlike Alberich himself—his own will the only source of value—and he undertakes to renounce power completely.

Brünnhilde's love for Siegfried leads to his, and to her own, destruction. The realization of what she has done in the name of love, and the terrible loss she experiences, are contained in the concluding scenes of *Götterdämmerung*. By this time, her love has in fact become a destructive power—and the basis for this transition rests on the view of love as a *rejection* of society, as a redemptive impetus of freedom opposed to society and its reliance on power. At the end of

Siegfried, the entire social world resembles Alberich's subterranean realm, a dark world of servitude, cruelty and domination, contrasting starkly with the elusive redemptiveness of love, symbolized by the sunrise witnessed by Brünnhilde and Siegfried in their apparent isolation from Wotan's society. The imagery of the sun, of dawn and the advent of a new society, was first associated with Valhalla at the beginning of Scene 2 *Das Rheingold* but now characterizes Brünnhilde and Siegfried in their new world founded on love. I contend, however, that Wagner sees this image of love—redemption as transcendence of the phenomenal world based on its lust for power—as a *source* of conflict rather than resolution although, contrary to Schopenhauer, Wagner wanted to show how love can be valuable even within that kind of universe.

3. The Endings of the Four Parts of *The Ring*

The leitmotifs play a structural role in *The Ring*. They are not merely referential signposts. Several scenes in *Das Rheingold* and *Die Walküre* are based on a single principal motif undergoing continual variation and representing the dramatic flow of the scene in its larger context. The scene of Brünnhilde's Reproach (*Die Walküre* IIIiii) provides one obvious example; another occurs in Scene 4 in Act II between Brünnhilde and Siegmund (called the "Annunciation of Death"). The most musically complex of the music-dramas, *Götterdämmerung* continuously brings several motifs together in key scenes. Some critics, such as Theodor Adorno (whom I discuss in the next chapter), have denied that Wagner possessed much compositional sophistication and used leitmotifs as clumsy mechanical stimuli calling up predetermined images with the larger purpose of denying listeners freedom of thought by controlling their response. I have already shown how the leitmotifs in fact play a far more sophisticated role and in this section I will be concerned with the way the complex musical and dramatic structure of *The Ring* ties in with the philosophical questions I have introduced.

In Chapter 1, Section 8 I introduced the motif of Fate as a key to understanding *The Ring* and the question of the meaning of the ending of the cycle cannot adequately be addressed unless we take the role of that motif into account. Let us consider that ending in relation to the endings of each of the other parts of the cycle. Robert Bailey reminds us of the overall structure of *The Ring*: *Das Rheingold,* prologue (myth and politics), *Die Walküre,* pathos and romance, *Siegfried,* comedy (in the sense of fantasy or 'fairy tale'), and *Götterdämmerung,* tragedy.[16] Looking at the connections between these works more closely, an interesting symmetry becomes evident: both *Das Rheingold* and *Siegfried* end in serious delusions, both of which play a major role in the decline of the gods. *Das Rheingold* ends with its deliberately pompous and yet

The Structure of *The Ring*: Tragedy or Transcendence? 45

hopeful entry into Valhalla, the symbol of social order and value, noble in its intent but flawed by Wotan's attempt at treating society as an extension of his will in his dealings with Alberich and the giants. *Whatever* Wotan does *must* be good, so his tendency for domination has been present as part of his character from the beginning. Wotan and Valhalla actually symbolize Mankind itself—the rational, willful controller of nature and the engineer of society for the greater good.

But the ending of *Das Rheingold* does not simply contrast capitalistic ruthlessness and Rousseauian natural benevolence (as Shaw describes it). Indeed, the Rhinemaidens do not symbolize the idyllic pacification of nature because nature in *The Ring* obviously contains the potential for conflict. The gold, that symbol of the illusion of control and fateful sexuality, existed as nature first of all, and out of Alberich's lust for power and Wotan's own will to power, based on his need for it to preserve his society, sprang the conflicts of *The Ring*. The ending of *Das Rheingold* depicts the conflict between nature and society, between the will for permanence and the reality of change, and between love and power as motivational forces, unified by the ambiguous natural essence of the gold symbolizing these oppositions.

Siegfried ends with the delusion (the potentiall destructive illusion) of romantic love transcending the forces of power and oppression (Valhalla). The lovers want to create a world of their own, ecstatically exclaiming to each other: "My wealth, my world:/my one and all:/Light of our love,/Laughter in death!":"Erb' und Eigen,/ein und all:/Leuchtende Liebe,/Lachender Tod!" They renounce the world of Wotan's power, they 'die' to that world—now figuratively, later literally. By the beginning of the last scene, Siegfried has broken Wotan's spear, "annulled the state" as Wagner put it, and the future seems open to the hopes of the lovers. The pathos of Siegmund and Sieglinde in *Die Walküre* seems about to be redeemed.[17] But, as I pointed out in Chapter 1, the illusion of love's absolute value appears transformed in the Prolog to *Götterdämmerung* as the music of the awakening Brünnhilde becomes the dawn of the gods' final day. The music of Fate (with its subliminal reference to Beethoven's op. 135 string quartet) also becomes increasingly prominent. Brünnhilde's awakening is musically superimposed over the cloudy but slowly clarifying image of the destructive potential of love as the Fate motif expresses her will. I will show later that the inherent instability of love ultimately destroys Valhalla. Hagen manipulates Siegfried and Brünnhilde, but their love, as the personification of Wotan's hope of redemption, constitutes the central illusion of the permanence of their values.

These references to the central illusions of *The Ring*—that power can be used unambiguously for good if motivated by noble purpose, that love can redeem by overcoming destructiveness—depends on the multilevel matrix I have been describing. These motifs sometimes show the point of view of the characters: How do they see their universe? What does it mean to them? Wotan perceives the world through his attempts at overcoming Fate in trying to save his society. Alberich and Hagen see themselves in opposition to Wotan and his society. Brünnhilde perceives a deeper reality through her transcendence of Wotan's world while Siegfried originally sees the world from the standpoint of nature encountering an incomprehensible humanity. But *we* see these narratives from a different perspective involving our own developing understanding of the interdependence of power and love implicit in the beliefs of the characters. We begin to see a larger pattern, as Brünnhilde does at the end of *Götterdämmerung*.[18]

Wagner's use of contextualization, of placing individual moments within a larger whole, thereby changing their meaning, the microcosm reflecting the macrocosm, achieves a distancing of perception that helps to identify the significance of those moments through the dramatic movement of the work as a whole. For example, all of the major characters achieve ends exactly the opposite of what they intended: the attempt of the lovers to isolate themselves ends in their becoming the main characters in the social drama from which they hoped to escape. Wotan's desire for stability, achieved through his renunciation of power, also points to the instability of love. By means of his self-resignation, he wants to rid society of its (and his) lawless inconsistency, but instead he creates even more conflict. At the center of the dramatic development of *The Ring* stands Wotan's compassionate farewell to Brünnhilde (see Section 5 below for a more detailed discussion). He loves his daughter but must use her as a means to save his society. Wotan's hope does indeed lead to a hero, but one who cannot redeem in the sense he had envisaged at all. Indeed, given his build-up he proves to be remarkably ineffectual. The "homecoming" of Siegfried and Brünnhilde (as Adorno describes it) becomes the occasion for Valhalla's destruction and the ironic endings of *Das Rheingold* and *Siegfried*, with their dangerous illusions of security and permanence produced by either power or love, indicate the deceptiveness of their respective illusions—they are destructive delusions. They *appear* to be conclusive and all-encompassing, but Valhalla will fall, and love will not save the world. It will not provide permanence and value where power failed to do so.

Next, consider the endings of *Die Walküre* and *Götterdämmerung*. Both conclude with fire: when Wotan places Brünnhilde in suspended animation and surrounds her with a barrier of flames created by Loge, and again with the end of Valhalla. After *Das Rheingold*, Loge appears only in these two endings and in both cases the fire he creates is caused by love.[19] At the end of *Götterdämmerung*, Brünnhilde destroys what had once been a symbol of hope but had became a symbol of social will and power. But the symbol of fire is also connected to power: in the first case, at the end of *Die Walküre*, Wotan uses it to protect his dream in his indirect attempt to bring about redemption through

Brünnhilde (does he not still trying to exercise control?). In the second case, the fire, I suggest, symbolizes the destructive power of love itself (for love, as much as power, brings Valhalla to ruin).[20] Significantly, the motifs of Fire and of Brünnhilde's Magic Sleep appear at the end of both *Die Walküre* and *Götterdämmerung*: it's downward motion reminiscent of the Twilight of the Gods and, I argue, the potential for change, the contingency of anything humans (or gods) establish.

Both *Die Walküre* and *Götterdämmerung* conclude with extended orchestral commentaries constructed out of several important motifs. *Die Walküre* concludes against the backdrop of the magic fire and sleep music but includes references to the motifs of Fate, Love, and the rising motif associated with Siegfried (and based rhythmically on the curse motif). Far more complex, of course, with its two great orchestral summaries, the closing moments of *Götterdämmerung* include Brünnhilde's sleep music from the end of *Die Walküre*, references to the motifs of power and the Rheingold, Alberich's Curse, Valhalla, Siegfried, the Twilight of the Gods and, finally, Redemption Through Love (a motif related to Brünnhilde's various motifs, and to the Volsung Destiny motif with its implicit reference to Fate). The final chord of *Götterdämmerung* is D–flat major—as is the final chord of *Das Rheingold*, with some C–minor sevenths thrown in by the Rhinemaidens. The endings of *Das Rheingold* and *Siegfried* are not nearly as musically complex as the endings of the other two music-dramas. They focus instead on the central illusions of permanence comprising Wotan's view of his relation to society, on the one hand, and Siegfried and Brünnhilde's erotic escapism on the other. *Die Walküre* and *Götterdämmerung,* in contrast, end with portrayals of the world-processes of *The Ring,* Wagner's modification of Schopenhauer's Will, depicting the interconnections between power and love underlying the struggle for identity and value.

So we have two pairs of endings: *Das Rheingold* and *Siegfried* are about illusion as *delusion* in the sense of shortened or distorted vision. *Die Walküre* and *Götterdämmerung*, on the other hand, are about truth in the sense of the achievement of a higher level of understanding or perception—even if, as we see in *Die Walküre*, this understanding forms part of a more complex illusion. *Das Rheingold* ends with the subjective presence of Wotan's dream (Valhalla contrasted with the Rhinemaidens' lament at the end of *Das Rheingold*). *Siegfried* ends with Siegfried and Brünnhilde's symbolic (and later literal) death to the social world of power (the Fate and Renunciation motifs play an almost subliminal role at the end of *Siegfried*). The inner-lives of the characters play an important role in these endings: Wotan's vision of society, as an expression of his personal integrity and the nobility of his relations with others, is set against Brünnhilde and Siegfried's dream of love as the only real value in the world. But these views are not only set against each other: *both* involve love in *op-*

position to power, and the end of each work in the second pair reasserts the *interdependence* of power and love.

The endings of *Das Rheingold* and *Siegfried* also bring the inner-lives of the characters, their hopes and fears, into collision with the outer-world. The Fate motif heard beneath the fire music at the end of *Die Walküre* also connects with the music of the Sleeping Brünnhilde, and the ending of *Götterdämmerung* realizes the fate implicit in her redemptive/destructive potential. The fire of change, the fundamental truth of nature, emerges in these two endings as the ultimate symbol for love in *The Ring*. Finally, the Rhine overflows its banks to extinguish Brünnhilde's flames and the Rhinemaidens reclaim the ring. The Rhinemaidens are the first and last characters to appear in the cycle. Wagner uses a basic symbol of romanticism to deny its principle of the unity of Spirit and Nature. Comparing *The Ring* to another huge and dramatically pervasive work from earlier in the nineteenth century, at the end of *Faust*, water symbolizes change and the rainbow the illusory stability of reality, but water, in the form of the sea, also symbolizes the redemptiveness of striving as the ultimate principle of unity. This is the secret of the universe for Goethe, the unity of Spirit and Nature. At the end of *The Ring,* however, the gods are dead and humanity must find within itself the goals of its striving. Striving, however, does not bestow upon humanity the divine source of value, as Feuerbach optimistically hoped, since the point of *The Ring* is that gods and humans are no different when it comes to love and power.

At the end of *Götterdämmerung*, Love's Redemption (or Redemption Through Love) appears along with the music of Valhalla and motif of Siegfried's Destiny. I have not seen any commentator notice that the motif of Love's Redemption almost exactly contains the Fate motif in its first bar! (I do not know if Wagner was aware of this.) There are other such close connections. The famous Walküre theme also bears this similarity. The motif of Siegfried's Destiny resembles the motif of Renunciation: the second bar of Renunciation, in particular, almost exactly parallels the second half of Siegfried's Destiny. The underlying connection between these motifs provides an important example of the musical interdependence between heroism and renunciation. There can be no heroism, of course, without obstacles to be overcome; something must be achieved through great difficulty. But Siegfried's 'mission' has contradictory descriptions: to achieve what Wotan and Alberich have renounced, or establish something new. Through Brünnhilde, Wotan wants his redemptive hero, Siegfried, to bring love back into society, thereby stabilizing it on a value shared by all. Alberich, through Hagen, wants to subvert Siegfried, establishing power for himself by destroying Wotan's hope. Wotan believes he can achieve the redemption of his society through his renunciation of power, opening the way for a hero untainted by the desire to shape society in his own image and who can use his autonomy to reestablish freedom for others. Alberich believes that he can get power by forsaking love, but his own dependence on his antiheroic son Hagen leads to destruction through Hagen's (all too easy) redirection of Brünnhilde's love into the desire for revenge. Alberich achieves what he wishes—the destruction of Wotan's society—but in so doing, neither he nor Hagen can use their new power in any constructive way. They have no positive desires. They are purely destructive because they are loveless. They are powerless *because* they have no illusions. Wotan's love, on the other hand, even though it expressed positive, constructive ideals, and seemed at first to be a renunciation of power, reverts to power in the form of Brünnhilde's destructiveness. I contend that this dialectic indicates how love and the will to control cannot be separated.

Originally, Brünnhilde's actions were creative. She desired to serve her father; she wanted to save Sieglinde and later she believes Siegfried can put everything right again. She symbolizes altruistic compassion but she becomes destructive. By helping to kill Siegfried and burning down Valhalla, she reestablishes the interconnection between power and love only apparently severed through Alberich and Wotan's acts of renunciation. Power and love may be perceived opposites, but each is also transformed into their opposite, sometimes merging together. As I will maintain later, Brünnhilde's perception of this connection, of how her love has been transformed, makes up the essence of her understanding, her self-consciousness, the sense in which she "knows all," returning us again to the problem of knowledge in *The Ring.* Even before Wotan's renunciation of power in *Die Walküre* II, he has already accepted diminished vision (symbolized by the loss of one eye) in order to gain the power to create Valhalla. His utopian dream depends on his short-sightedness. At first he believes he can save his society through willful self-assertion. But, in so doing, he compromises the nobility that motivated his creation of that society in the first place. Wotan violates the responsibilities implied by his status in *Das Rheingold* and again in *Die Walküre* when he tries to use Siegmund and Sieglinde to save his world. He realizes the limitation of his power in *Die Walküre* IIii but then substitutes one utopian dream for another, abdication of control for something purer. By using Brünnhilde to save his society, he still manipulates, although his love for her coincides, even expresses, his social responsibility. But the love that drives Brünnhilde cannot be a principle of social order either, however much it may be a motivation for compassion. In the end, she finally sees the destructiveness of her love.

Taken alone, the ending of *Götterdämmerung* might be understood as the defeat of power and evil with love's redemption promising something better. If we look at the ending in relation to the structure of *The Ring* as a whole, however, this view does not take into account the similarities between power and love that make such a victory impossible. If *The Ring* portrays "opposite things" (as Cooke and Peckham rightly contend), Wagner finally settled on the story of opposition and conflict as its center. The *oppositions* between good and evil, hatred and compassion, love and power, resignation and redemption, are all sources of conflict because there can be no ultimate principle, no absolute standard, establishing their resolution. These oppositions involve both constructive and destructive *illusions* about selfhood, society and value, and they may indeed envision the possibility of a permanent, universal foundation for self-identity, value, and community—what Peckham called a transcendental basis for authority as the grounding of value in an essential truth about the world. But the Schopenhauerian character of the later versions of *The Ring* emphasizes the ironic self-destructiveness implicit in all action based on *the desire for resolution*. Such beliefs ensure that the search for timeless foundations of value, for heroes with authority based on the appeal to universal values, will always fail. They can become destructive *delusions*. Our only redemption, impermanent and of our own creation, must be achieved from inside of our world, through the values we are able to establish through the contingent processes of life. The appeal of Feuerbach's naturalism remained with Wagner throughout *The Ring*. However, such optimistic interpretations do not capture what I have claimed to be the interrelatedness of power and love, resolution and destruction, renunciation and redemption that holds it together dramatically in its final form. Wagner *rejects* Feuerbach's thesis that natural instincts will lead to a more secure foundation for society. If nature replaces the divine, it cannot replace divine permanence, as Feuerbach thought it could.

If *Das Rheingold* and *Siegfried* are devoted to the restriction of understanding, *Die Walküre* and *Götterdämmerung* are about gaining it. References to eyes and sight abound in *Die Walküre* while the struggle to understand, to move beyond mere perception, dominates *Götterdämmerung*. Understanding constitutes a higher form of knowledge than does perception because it arises through the recognition of the larger context, something general rather than particular. Brünnhilde's final state of comprehension before returning the ring to the Rhinemaidens shows that she remains in love even after her participation in the plot to kill Siegfried. She has gained the understanding she has sought throughout *Götterdämmerung* and returns to the truth of *Die Walküre* III: compassion remains for her the only positive value in life. While her self-sacrifice defeats both Alberich and Wotan, it seems implicit in *The Ring* that there can be no final state of pacification, no utopian cessation of those processes of conflict holding power and love together as the essence of humanity. In fact, Brünnhilde's compassion destroys society just as surely as does Wotan's manipulativeness! But perhaps Wotan's motivation was to be compassionate, to find another source of compassion beyond himself. The lesson: *we* achieve a higher comprehension of the nature of love through its role as the primary source of our values.

At the end of *The Ring,* we are left with neither Schopenhauerian renunciation nor Feuerbachian victory but with a better comprehension of the *interdependence* of power and love as they personify creativity *and* destructiveness in the characters. The end of this world fulfills Erda's prophecy that "all things that are, perish." Things fall apart—the center will not hold (how Wagnerian Yeats was!). In fact, Erda prefaces her prophecy with: "All of the past, know I./All things that are,/all things that shall be—/all I know":"Wie alles war, weiss ich;/wie alles wird,/wie alles sein wird,/seh ich auch" and this is recalled at the very end of the cycle with Brünnhilde's: "All things, all things,/all I know now;/all to me is revealed!" Through the course of the cycle we have moved from Erda's implicit understanding to Brünnhilde's (and our) explicit realization of the central reason for the events of *The Ring*.[21] The metaphysics here is almost pre-Socratic, resembling Anaximander, for example: "From what source things arise, to that they return of necessity when they are destroyed; for they suffer punishment and make reparation to one another for their injustice according to the order of time" (to cite the only remark of his to survive). The importance of fire at the end of *Die Walküre* and *Götterdämmerung* symbolizes the truth of change as the essence of the world (the fundamental metaphysical element of Heraclitus). The "circularity" of *The Ring*, the return to beginnings, the symbolism of the very title of the work, does convey an Hegelian sense of increased consciousness, but without the social optimism with which Feuerbach read Hegel—without Hegel's own implication that consciousness can be increased to absoluteness.

Yet another dimension concerns the relation between nature and power. In my view, the restoration of the ring to the Rhinemaidens does not pacify social conflict by setting right the order of nature. That symbolic ring, or rather the *desire* for what it stands for, for power and control, was responsible for the destruction of the gods and was also the occasion for the defeat of Brünnhilde's love in *Götterdämmerung* I, Scenes 2 and 3. In Scene 2, Brünnhilde retains the ring as a symbol of her love for Siegfried when she knows she could save the world by giving it up. In Scene 3, the power of the ring begins to work against her when Siegfried stands in for Gunther and takes the ring away from her (unconsciously recreating Wotan's theft of the ring from Alberich—and Alberich's original theft of the gold)—and thereby figuratively assuming Wotan's guilt. This explains why Brünnhilde became involved in the plot to kill Siegfried. She believed that he took the symbol of her escape from Wotan, transforming it into an icon of power, thus betraying her love for him. Through this betrayal (as Brünnhilde sees it), Siegfried has compromised *her* autonomy, *her* power. If the ring, through its connection with the gold, retains its reference to natural forces, the point of this rupture between Brünnhilde and Siegfried seems to be that humanity cannot control its *own* nature and so we cannot achieve the unity between ourselves and nature idealized by the romantics as the unity between spirit and nature. Spirit does not outstrip nature by expressing its unifying force; indeed, as Nietzsche was to see, identifying ourselves with nature rather than with God will not provide *the* answer to our problems.

The ring's identification with power arises from nature itself, from the gold as it symbolizes Wagner's conception of the Will. Can anyone renounce love for the ring and its power-engendering magic? Conversely, can anyone renounce power for the magic of love? Only if love contains the power of transformation. But this is a false dichotomy: the state of nature at the beginning of *Das Rheingold* contains nothing that could possibly count as 'pure' love in the senses that this concept later assumes, although only fleetingly and as a delusion, with Sieglinde and Siegmund, and with Brünnhilde and Siegfried. Indeed nature *is* change. Unlike Siegfried and Brünnhilde, or Siegmund and Sieglinde, love for Alberich amounted merely to the sexual exploitation of the Rhinemaidens although his renunciation of love was simply frustration sublimated as his dominance of the Nibelungs and his lust for political power.

For Wagner, as a naturalist about love, Alberich's lust remains implicit in the 'higher' forms of love too. At the beginning, power seems to be opposed to love. Indeed, in *Das Rheingold*, both Alberich and Wotan (in his treatment of Freia) seem to be in conflict with love as well as with each other. Only Wotan, however, believes that sexual love might somehow save him from this delusion and this sets into motion the events of *Die Walküre* I. He suspends his hope of redemption through love (as Brünnhilde's compassion) at the end of *Die Walküre* until *both* love and power are returned to their natural potential at the end of *Götterdämmerung*. But nature and the gold are the *source* of tension and conflict, not their amelioration. Nature cannot symbolize pure 'feminine' peace opposed to 'masculine' domination and power (love in opposition to society, Antigone *versus* Creon) because Wagner's depiction of nature always involves reference to the potential for change—as much through destruction as through creation. That potential, as Wagner sees the universe, includes both power and love (the will to power, as Nietzsche describes it). Nature is *both* feminine and masculine. To that extent at least, Wagner was certainly Schopenhauerian rather than Hegelian in rejecting the *rational* nature of reality. At the end of *The Ring*, the world reverts to pure potential for future conflict (the orchestra seen as the Will, to use Peckham's insight). This much is consistent with Hegel's conception of dialectical progress, but where Hegel tended toward synthesis and optimism and Schopenhauer toward alienation and pessimism, Wagner sees self-comprehension as open ended because the self, as naturalized spirit, is never complete. Yes, we do understand more, but what next? In the quest for understanding that characterizes the movement from the dark beginning of *Das Rheingold* to the bright fire at the end of *Götterdämmerung*, the only redemption seems to lie in Brünnhilde's comprehension of the power of love to change oneself. But into what?

4. Renunciation, Love, and Conflict

If conflict provides the dramatic structure of *The Ring*, we have already seen that the source of its conflicts lies in renunciation. Wotan renounces some of his sight to get control of nature; Alberich renounces love to get control over the gold; Wotan renounces power to save his society from Alberich through Brünnhilde's love; Brünnhilde renounces power to escape from Wotan's world with Siegfried but her love becomes what it denies. Hagen renounces "the good." To briefly retrace the opening of *The Ring, Das Rheingold* begins with its pedal-point in the basses and bassoons, and the rising horn motif, slowly transforming itself into the mighty Rhine river, inhabited by the Rhinemaidens and their gold.[22] Alberich soon appears, his stilted, minor, dissonant motif contrasting with the deceptively harmonious natural wonders just depicted. We see immediately the amorality and even cruelty of the Rhinemaidens as they taunt and tease Alberich. They are in part responsible for subsequent events, although Alberich is more than ready to sublimate his sexuality by stealing the gold and in his desire to destroy everything that threatens him. As Shaw sees him, the alienated Alberich already feels the effects of Wotan's repressive society. He cannot find love in any form and resolves instead to become a master like Wotan so he can command love. Pursuing the socio-economic-political level of *The Ring,* Shaw, like Adorno, sees Wotan's power as the fundamental repressive force of capitalism: the desire to find happiness through the control and exploitation of others.[23]

When Woglinde tells Alberich that the gold he sees glimmering at the bottom of the Rhine will give him power, she also tells him that he must "pronounce a curse on love. He must renounce all joys of love before he masters the magic, a ring to forge from the gold":"Nur wer der Minne Macht versagt,/nur wer der Liebe Lust verjagt, nur der erzielt sich den Zauber, zum Reif zu zwingen das Gold." The Renunciation motif appears for the first time, associated with the gold, and again at the end of the scene when Alberich curses love forever. Just prior to this, Alberich realizes that he will not get anywhere with the Rhinemaidens. He expresses his anxiety: "Wehe! Wehe!":"Woe! Woe!" The falling semitone of their lament appears in the second bar of the Renunciation motive, in the various "frustration" motifs, in the motive of the Twilight of the Gods, reincarnated again and again especially in *Götterdämmerung*. This falling motif directly opposes those of Nature and Erda, with their similar rising motion, and together these two fundamental contrary motions form the basis of the entire *Ring*. As I noted in Chapter 1, the Interlude between Scenes 1 and 2 establishes the crucial connection between the Ring and Valhalla motifs, and several other important musical connections are also established in this scene based on the motif of the Rhinegold. For example, the falling two-note phrase provides the basis for the motifs of the Power of the Ring and Servitude or Bondage, and later

Hagen, directly connected back to Alberich's renunciation. The Renunciation motif also connects with the motif of the Power of the Ring as it symbolizes Alberich's desire for absolute, destructive power. One of the most important motifs linking individual events to the larger metaphysical story, the Power of the Ring often appears in conjunction with Fate and with the motif associated with Wotan's frustration in *Die Walküre,* reminding us of the reason for that frustration.

We can see the transforming capacity of the Gold motif as well: a natural substance, the gold holds the potential for power and destruction, a potential made actual once Alberich gets his hands on the ring made from it. In Scene 3, when Wotan and Loge visit Nibelheim to confront Alberich, Wotan asks Alberich what value the gold has since there is nothing to buy in his subterranean kingdom. Alberich replies that the gold will allow him to buy the whole world; he will be able to control the world with the ultimate source of capital. When Alberich mentions this wealth, the motif of the Hoard is heard. This motif is derived from the Gold (the upward movement of that motif later becoming associated with the Dragon Fafner as his sleeping form guards the huge pile of gold Wotan liberated from Alberich to pay the giants). The Hoard and the Gold motifs are later associated with blood (during the giants' quarrel) and subconscious sexuality (the sleeping dragon and the sleeping Brünnhilde) as expressions latent destructive power. Both symbol and source of power, the gold holds supreme value for both Alberich and Wotan (Alberich and Wotan are thus both driven by essentially the same desire). We hear it again in *Die Walküre* I, associated with Siegmund, and with Siegfried and Brünnhilde in the last act of *Siegfried*. The motif of the Gold thereby connects up with the very idea of redemption in *The Ring* as subconscious sexual attraction! The dragon's blood and Brünnhilde's sexuality are important for Siegfried: after killing him, Fafner's blood causes Siegfried to understand the wood bird, who tells him everything he needs to know about the tarnhelm, the ring, and Brünnhilde, what he needs to know in order to save the world. Like Alberich, Siegfried learns that the ring will make him lord of the world, but this is lost on him when he hears about Brünnhilde, asleep on top of her mountain. Siegfried's sexual curiosity transforms his life by giving him a purpose, and he immediately loses interest in the ring and the gold.

In *Die Walküre* Iiii, Siegmund sings the music of Renunciation as he removes the sword Notung from Hunding's tree, when he vows to take Sieglinde as his own. The sword, placed there by Wotan as a test for his redemptive hero, ties the worlds of *Das Rheingold* and *Die Walküre* together as the symbol of Wotan's plan for redeeming Valhalla. When Siegmund sings the Renunciation motif, it expresses the need for love, his hope, but more broadly the hope of humanity for compassion at risk because of Alberich's renunciation and Wotan's selfishness. But while Siegmund certainly needs compassion, Wotan

The Structure of *The Ring*: Tragedy or Transcendence? 55

needs it too. Indeed, because of his enormous responsibility, he thinks he needs it more. Siegmund's very existence depends on renunciation: Wotan created Siegmund to save himself from Alberich (the sword enshrines Wotan's hope and, for Freudians, exemplifies an obvious phallic symbol identifying potential redemptive heroes through their sexual drives). But Wotan soon destroys (temporarily) this symbol of hope with his spear in the vain attempt at establishing the power of his law over nature. He wants order and the sword embodies his idea of heroic redemption, but redemption seemed possible only through the violation of his own law prohibiting incest. Wotan's absolute commands put the interests of society and moral stability over natural freedom and individual desire. He broke his contract with Fasolt and Fafner, the promise to give them Freia, for whom he substitutes Alberich's gold. Freia's sexuality and the gold are equally powerful forces, however. Neither was Wotan's to give in his own more enlightened view of society; but even if Wotan had the right to do what he did (justified as a means of protecting his society), this merely takes the drama another step further into Hegel's Master/Slave analogy. Wotan, through his principles, needs the recognition of his society to possess any authority at all but, as we soon see, through his own stratagems, Wotan becomes more deeply entangled in the struggle for power and the denial of his own principles. He denies through his actions the values he wants others to recognize him for upholding.

Why does the Renunciation music occur in *Die Walküre* I (when Siegmund sings: "Holiest love in highest need":"Heiligster Minne höchste Not")? Cooke discusses this question at some length at the beginning of *I Saw the World End* (pp. 3 f.) and it has been a source of difficulty for even the most celebrated commentators. To take one example from one of the best, Ernst Newman asserts:

> Manifestly there can be no "renunciation" of love [at this point]...rather it is an assertion of love.... [W]hen [this motif] first appears in *Das Rheingold* it should be taken as signifying not so much Alberich's renunciation of love as love itself, universal, omnipotent, which the gnome, in his lust for power, has decided to renounce.[24]

Commenting on this passage, Cooke notes that although the leitmotifs in Wagner's other later works have less specific interpretations than most of those in *The Ring*, it should be absolutely clear that this motif does not symbolize love at all. The musical character of the motif precludes any such reading: How can one hear that music as "love itself"? Other commentators such as Donington and Shaw (both also discussed by Cooke) encounter similar difficulties in trying to explain this moment. Yet the question remains: What does renunciation have to do with love? In fact, we see that love requires renunciation for both Brünnhilde and Wotan: he relinquishes power and she her divinity. But if love is also a power—and therefore potentially destructive—how does that help us to understand it? As I have said, I think we can understand *The Ring* better by looking at a few key moments, such as this one, from the point of view of how they fit into the overall drama. Let us try to find readings of the highest possible inclusive subtlety, readings that enhance the relationships between the various levels of *The Ring*. How can the puzzle of Siegmund's 'renunciation' be fit into the larger context of the hope of redemption?

There are other, similarly puzzling occurrences of Renunciation: in the final scene of *Siegfried*, when Siegfried tells Brünnhilde how her beauty has given him his first experience of fear, he sings: "Since you have bound me/in powerful fetters,/give me my freedom again!":"Den du gebunden/in mächtigen Banded,/birg meinen Mut mir nicht mehr!" The Renunciation motif can be clearly heard here. When connected with Brünnhilde singing the Fate motif just a little later (at "Love yourself, and leave me in peace"), we see how they cannot be left in peace, that their isolated world must eventually collide with the world of Wotan and Alberich. This disturbing juxtaposition of renunciation and redemption points up what becomes ever clearer throughout the course of *The Ring*. Through the expression of the different kinds of love binding them together—Siegmund and Sieglinde; Brünnhilde and Siegfried; Wotan and Brünnhilde; and even, in a more general sense, Wotan and his society—the characters are confronted by forces beyond their comprehension until they begin to realize the origin of their motivation and the true objects of their desires. Siegmund and Sieglinde are clearly part of this larger story when the Renunciation motif makes that connection between Siegmund's "need" for a sword (symbolizing control, sex as power) and Wotan's need for redemption *from* the corrupting forces of power. *The Ring* tells us that renunciation must be seen ironically (not, however, cynically): Wotan's need and Siegmund's are the same, but these natural drives are the origin of power. Siegmund's love exemplifies Wotan's renunciation of power, his willingness to let another save him through love, and thus providing a unifying social principle (Feuerbach's social principle).

The unifying force of love between two people ironically expresses the urge to reproduce *oneself*, to stamp ones individuality on another. As Peckham writes about the power implicit in romantic love:

> ...love in its boundless desire to have complete control over its object, destroys freedom; woman, in her determination to make man submit to biological necessity, destroys his autonomy. And freedom, in its fearless and blind and stupid conviction that it is adequate to the conditions which reality imposes upon man, destroys love; man destroys woman in the effort to maintain his autonomy. To gratify man's free exercise of his

The Structure of *The Ring*: Tragedy or Transcendence?

> power over reality, one woman is a good as another; Gutrune can serve Siegfried's purposes as well as Brünnhilde; to gratify woman's biological drives, only one man will do.[25]

Wotan has also manipulated his own children, Siegmund and Sieglinde: he wants to use them to further establish his own identity with his society by taking it over. They see their resemblance to each other, and they also unknowingly resemble Wotan in their need for love but they are both destroyed through his desire to "gratify [his] power over reality." Does love transcend power, returning us to nature, or is it another form of power, politics at the personal level? This is Peckham's point: politics is always personal and the personal is always political. As we saw, Wagner's reversal of Schopenhauer's view of sex shows how it does not transport us into something universal, transcending particularity. Sex puts us completely *into* the world through our involvement with another person. It does not symbolize the anti-individual Will or the transcendence of the world but the extreme individuality of ones desire. (I discuss Wagner's transformation of Schopenhauer in more detail in the Appendix, Sections 3 and 4.) In this way, *Die Walküre* I shows in detail *how* love cannot escape politics. In *Die Walküre* IIii, we see that for Wotan the renunciation of power does not escape politics either because politics reflects the conflict between individual desires. If we all had the same desire, as Schopenhauer argues we do in universal compassion, there would be no politics and hence no society. That is the basis for Schopenhauer's account of the denial of the Will as a transcendence of society. But that does not happen in *The Ring*: Wotan's desire for "the End," the end of his contradiction-filled life, his own escape from power, later becomes the basis for his hope in a new beginning with Brünnhilde at the end of Act III. Symbolically dying to Wotan's world, she will awaken in another formed by the bond between her and the hyperactive hero who braves the fires surrounding her ovum-like passivity.

This focus on the world, and not on our desire to transcend it, distinguishes *The Ring* from *Tristan,* although the latter might more accurately be considered to be about the *dream* of transcendence rather than its actuality. Peckham suggests that for Wagner, neither society nor love transcends nature because they are both *part of* nature, both forms of control: indeed, nature *is* power. Nietzsche clearly saw this very paradox in Schopenhauer's denial of the Will: it takes an act of will to deny the will. So transcendence, as the denial of the Will for Schopenhauer, contains incoherent desires: the desire not to desire. To renounce love requires loving something else; to renounce power requires the will to change ones world.

The Ring contains many examples of this paradox of renunciation. Another key occurrence of the Renunciation motif, one with a different implication from that of Siegmund's example, happens when Brünnhilde refuses to give back the ring in *Götterdämmerung* Iiii. At this point her own musical line includes Renunciation ("My love shall last while I live,/my ring in life shall not leave me!":"Die Liebe liesse ich nie,/mir nähmen nie sie die Liebe"). This particular instance of the motif indicates the delusiveness of her renunciation of power. In fact she plays the central role in the downfall of the gods and in the death of her lover. The Renunciation music refers, of course, to Wotan and Alberich, connecting them to the drama involving Brünnhilde and Siegfried. It also refers to her own rebellion against Wotan in *Die Walküre* when she tried to help Siegmund and Sieglinde, and to her laughter in the face of death at the end of *Siegfried*. When Siegmund sang the motif in *Die Walküre* I, it pointed to the larger context of renunciation involving Wotan and Alberich, and the need of the gods for redemption. By the end of *Siegfried,* the effects of renunciation have come to include even Brünnhilde's relationship to Siegfried. They consciously stand in opposition to a society based on the acquisition of power. Paralleling this movement from the inner-lives of the individual characters towards the social, at the metaphysical level, the dramatic change in the quality and significance of the Sunrise and Awakening music of *Siegfried* III when it reappears in *Götterdämmerung* shows that the lovers' renunciation of the world of power has actually been *part of* that world as the means for the destruction of the gods and the collapse of a civilization based on the ideal of permanence: political gold.

5. Love and the Ending of *Die Walküre*

While both *Die Walküre* and *Götterdämmerung* end in fire, the symbol of truth as change, love also lies at the center of the endings of these two works. Wotan's love for Brünnhilde leads him to cast her in a spell of many years sleep rather than killing her for disobeying him (when she actually carries out Wotan's subconscious desire for survival in trying to save Siegmund), but this act places Brünnhilde even more centrally in Wotan's hope of redemption. Wotan needs a hero powerful enough to break the spell of her sleep. Such a hero will also be just the one to save him too. It is actually Brünnhilde's love at the end of *Götterdämmerung* that causes the destruction of Valhalla as she gives Siegfried his warrior funeral and then returns the ring, at last, to the Rhinemaidens. Her delusive idealization of love as escape, at the end of *Siegfried*, establishes her destructiveness in the form of her "revenge" on Siegfried (and, ultimately, Wotan).

The power of love in *The Ring* can be seen quite clearly if we turn to the love motifs. The motifs of Alberich's Renunciation and Curse are contrasted with several motifs associated with love that appear prominently in first and third acts of *Die Walküre* as well as the third act of *Siegfried* and parts of *Götterdämmerung*. In his *Introduction to Wagner's Ring*, Cooke shows how this love music, first associated with Siegmund and Sieglinde, derives from both parts of the motif originally associated with Freia in *Das Rheingold* (see the Musical References for this distinction). Freia, as we have seen, symbolizes the living principle of the gods—love in the sense of compassion and responsiveness to the needs of another (or others). Her music (misleadingly called "Flight" by Wolzogen) symbolizes complete love, the unification of *eros* and *agape,* the physical with the spiritual.[26] Cooke points out that the rising first half of her motif symbolizes sexual love. We find this, for example, associated with the "Wunschmädchen" music in *Die Walküre* IIiv when Brünnhilde tells Siegmund of the erotic advantages of the afterlife to be gained through heroic death, and with Siegfried's sexual awakening as he climbs Brünnhilde's mountain retreat in *Siegfried* IIIiii. During that scene, the association between the Freia I music (as I will denote the first part of her motif) and the Fate motif indicates the significance of the relationship between Brünnhilde and Siegfried. Her human sexuality transforms her values, but the twilight of the gods begins to emerge with Siegfried's discovery of Brünnhilde and the awakening of his own sexuality. In a few deft strokes, the microcosm of Brünnhilde and Siegfried—isolated from the world of power and law—becomes part the broader conflict between love and power. I have shown how this connection becomes even more prominent with the minor, darkening transformation of the Awakening music at the beginning of *Götterdämmerung.*

The descending second half of Freia's motif becomes associated with a more universal, not specifically sexual love, but *Mitleid* or compassion: Brünnhilde's compassion for Sieglinde and Siegmund, for example, and "der diese Liebe..." in *Die Walküre* IIIii, and many other places in *Götterdämmerung.* Wagner's modification of Schopenhauer's Will from denial of individuality into sexual assertion of individuality, however, dissociates compassion from the metaphysically transcendent roles it plays for Schopenhauer. Sex always has an object for Wagner, it is not a universal. This part of the motif forms the basis for the music associated with Siegmund and Sieglinde, and with Brünnhilde after her reconciliation with Wotan. One subtle example of the clash between compassionate love and Wotan's power occurs in *Die Walküre* Ii when Sieglinde discovers Siegmund in her house and sings: "Can he have fainted there, or is he dead":"schwanden die Sinne ihm/Wäre er siech?" At that point we hear the rising, motif of sexuality (Freia I) associated with Sieglinde and contrasted with the falling motif of Siegmund related to Wotan's spear. Siegmund was to have carried out Wotan's plan against Alberich. But when Siegmund must die, it is Brünnhilde who rebels and disclaims her destiny as a servant of Wotan's will. She then plays that role in a deeper sense since she fulfills Wotan's dream of redemption in a way totally unexpected by him.

Contrary to its traditional name, the music of Freia II should not be characterized as *flight from* power so much as the *need for* compassion. It plays this role, for example, when it accompanies Wotan and Loge on their journey into Nibelheim. Here the motif is greatly accelerated beneath the motifs of Renunciation and the Gold, finally submerged by the overpowering din of Alberich's anvils as they symbolize economic power. There is even a suggestion of Freia II in Scene 1 when Alberich despairs of winning the Rhinemaidens: "Woe! Woe! Oh shame! Oh, shame! The third one, so dear, betrays me as well.":"Wehe! ach wehe! O Schmerz! O Schmerz! Die dritte, so traut, betrog sie mich auch?" This frustrated, falling motif, as I pointed out earlier, continually expresses the need for love and one of its most significant variants occurs after Wotan's great outburst in *Die Walküre* IIii ("O heilige Schmach!"). After that concatenation of negative, destructive motifs—the Curse, Wotan's Frustration, the Power of the Ring, and Renunciation—we hear an extended, brooding solo on the bass clarinet, based on Freia II, signifying Wotan's desperation, his need for compassion, and the hopelessness of his situation brought about by his dominating desire to control. His soul-searching, self-transforming monologue follows.

The second part of Freia's motif (understood as the need for compassion) becomes the basis for Brünnhilde's reconciliation with Wotan in *Die Walküre* IIIiii ("Was it so shameful what I have done":"War es so schmählich, was ich verbrach"). This motif also undergoes a good deal of variation, as Cooke points out (*I Saw the World End*, p. 53), and often portrays love in difficulty or the absence of love—for example when the giants pursue Freia, or when Siegmund despairs of losing Sieglinde. The need for compassion and love comprises one of the most important dramatic motivational forces in *Die Walküre*, every scene of which depicts the intrusion of the social sphere into the personal relationships of the characters. Throughout *Die Walküre,* the problems of Wotan's world come into conflict with love, giving Freia II a melancholy ambiance even when both compassion and sexuality are present (as in *Die Walküre* I). Part of the conflict implicit in his attempt to establish order in his society rests on the fact that Wotan's laws must be enforced against Siegmund and Sieglinde, who Wotan had gone to so much trouble to bring together to save himself and his society. The social world and the world of love cannot be kept separate.

A key example of Wotan's desire for redemption, the motif of the Need of the Gods, succeeds the motif of Valhalla as Wotan's theme in *Die Walküre.* Characteristically longing and unfulfilled, it occurs many times during Acts II and III of *Die Walküre*, often coupled with Wotan's hope for an autonomous savior. He believes that redemption will be possible only if brought about by someone outside the conflict. This desire for purification lies at the center of the mythology of redemption in *The Ring*. Only someone capable of free choice, someone who lives by the values of forthrightness, honesty, courage, and truthfulness can break the cycle of destruction and achieve justice—an idea owing as much to the Orpheus myth as it does to Christianity. The Need of the Gods and the music associated with Wotan's frustration often attached to it becomes the basis for Brünnhilde's reproach ("War es so schmählich"), which also follows the downward motion of the Spear motif, followed with an upward seventh interval, countering the symbol of Wotan's authority. The reproach motif itself is then inverted in the compassionate resolution between Brünnhilde and Wotan ("Der diese Liebe"). This transposition shows how Brünnhilde in her compassion has become the most redemptive character in *The Ring* by turning frustration and reproach into love! The yearning music of the Need of the Gods can be fulfilled only by love, but Brünnhilde's love yields a very different kind of fulfillment of that need.

The orchestration of the Love music of *Die Walküre* I falls predominately in the strings, especially in divided cellos and violas, scored in an amazingly dense counterpoint that was to profoundly influence Mahler, Schoenberg, and Berg. The music creates its own world, isolated from Wotan's Valhalla motif, and almost completely given over to compassion and love—as Siegfried and Brünnhilde also see their world at the end of *Siegfried*. A related development of this music occurs in association with Siegfried's yearning for love in *Siegfried* Ii, scored in the lower strings and with an obvious resemblance to the Freia II motif and its connection with Sieglinde and Siegmund. In that scene, Siegfried wonders who his mother was, but the music of Sieglinde takes a developmental turn into a very general portrayal of love and Siegfried's desire for it. This ambiguity also subtly appears in *Siegfried* IIIiii where the motifs of Freia II, Fate, and Brünnhilde's Awakening, as well as references to Sieglinde, all characterize Siegfried's search for love, connecting him to his parents and ultimately to Wotan.

Sieglinde's responsiveness to Siegmund was not initially sexual but generally human (although subconsciously sisterly) when she expresses compassion for the distraut man she finds in her home (one might contend that, for Wagner, again inverting Schopenhauer, human compassion is sexual, always particular, never universal). Certainly one of the complexities of *Die Walküre* I lies in the musical associations between the many levels and forms of love implicit in human identity. Wotan's acceptance of incest might be understood as a willingness to see love as a noumenal force lying outside law and convention—perhaps the influence of Schopenhauer's conception of the Will. But, as I suggested in the previous section, it might also be seen as Wotan's attempt to impress *his* individuality even on indirect solutions to his problems. His children resemble him both physically and in their need for love. Siegmund, Sieglinde, and later Brünnhilde and Siegfried (Wotan's grandson) all want at the personal level what Wotan wants at the social. Indeed while Fricka compels Wotan to destroy Siegmund, these conventions are the result of his search for order. And—ironically—the unlawful union of Sieglinde and Siegmund produces another redemptive hero in Siegfried, also outside of Wotan's law, whose role in the drama will be even more destructive to social order. For Wagner, we cannot repress sexuality without these kinds of social effects.

The cause of Wotan's anguished outburst in *Die Walküre* IIii, when he must abandon Siegmund, therefore, does *not* simply signify his realization that he has compromised the value of compassion and principle of freedom. His view has become much broader; he begins to see the *irreversible* process of opposition and conflict in which he has become entangled (as he realizes in his monologue). The music of the Power of the Ring underscores Wotan's psychological turmoil while his words are shaped by the Renunciation music. During the monologue Wotan begins the transformation from his role of Man-in-Power (as Cooke describes him[27]), the manipulative exploiter of *Das Rheingold* and *Die Walküre* prior to Act IIii, into the compassionate father who extends his love for his daughter into a concern for society by placing her at the center of the process of its redemption. But the "good Wotan" at the end of *Die Walküre,* the Wotan who wants others to act freely, fails to see that Brünnhilde in fact fits the description of his redeeming hero. She has already acted independently of Wotan's will in trying to save Siegmund and Sieglinde, and it is she who will be "at war with the gods" (as Wotan characterizes his potential hero). Her independence asserts itself once again in *Götterdämmerung* when she refuses to give back the ring. Without her, Siegfried would be irrelevant to the problem of redeeming society and the fairy tale world of *Siegfried* I and II, along with the world of transcendent love in *Siegfried* III, would never have been connected with the real world of *Götterdämmerung*. In becoming human, Brünnhilde has also become completely preoccupied with love in its compassionate and erotic forms and the music associated with her rests on variants of the love music from both Freia I and II. Ironically, Brünnhilde becomes the agent of the destruction of Wotan's world: love should obviously not be associated with harmony between individuals here but, as Peckam pointed out above, with the destruction of what inhibits desire.

Wotan and Brünnhilde's reconciliation at the end of *Die Walküre* provides an important example of the transposition of a personal relationship into the social, and ultimately metaphysical drama. *Die Walküre* begins and ends with moving portrayals of this relationship. Although different, they are the same in other senses. More generally, Wagner takes the personal level very seriously, so seriously that the relations between the pairs of lovers in *The Ring* are extended into compassion of a different kind from Schopenhauer's concept of *Mitleid,* or universalized sympathy. In *The Ring,* as I have been claiming, the value of human life rests on love between individuals rather than on the transcendence of personhood and society as illusory evils. The self-deceptiveness of human life, metaphysically speaking, does not detract from its value for Wagner, indeed its value *increases* because of our total responsibility for its creation and survival. It is all we have! In *The Ring* we see how the social sphere intrudes into the lives of the individual characters, as well as how the personal relationships between Siegmund and Sieglinde, Siegfried and Brünnhilde, and Wotan and Brünnhilde have far reaching social effects. But the destruction of the social world shows us how they depend on each other even when the characters believe they do not. Society and love are really based on the same impulse.

After Siegfried awakens her, Brünnhilde rejects Wotan's world entirely. As a recurring symbol of this rejection, the love music of Freia II almost continually accompanies her in *Götterdämmerung*, as it had previously Siegmund and Sieglinde—all three completely dominated by love, including sexuality as well as compassionate affection (the only thing of value in the human world, as characterized by Feuerbach). However, the effect of their love leads to an even deeper involvement in society rather than the escape from it dreamt of by all four of these characters. Now Wagner's rejection of his earlier explicitly Buddhist, antisocial ending, I have suggested, depends on the difference between his and Schopenhauer's conceptions of *Mitleid*. For Schopenhauer, compassion transcends individuality, for Wagner, it expresses it. But we should bear in mind that the ending of the final version of the cycle does still carry at least some Schopenhauerian sense of the transcendence of the individual even though Brünnhilde's proclaimed hope is to be reunited with Siegfried. Her hope, however, is to remain *herself* not (like Isolde) to merge with the universe as her "highest desire." Yet her eyes are "forever open" (the all-seeing eye—an image of Hindu and Buddhist mythology).

Her hope remains a kind of dream, a vision of life continuing when one knows it is about to end. For her the poignancy of that dream lies in *our* realization that she does not transcend literally even if, to her, love does seem to have that power. Her 'illusion' is that the personal transcends the social. If the personal remains the only real value (Feuerbach), the ending of *The Ring* still takes us beyond both the social and personal levels into the metaphysical, dominated by its dream of transcendence through love (Schopenhauer). Reality is conflict, with resolution the motivational dream, and the great musical characterization of the Will, as Wagner saw it and personalized it in death of Brünnhilde, escapes Schopenhauer's irony that the personal expresses the universal. For Wagner, it seems to be just the opposite!

When he decides to cast Brünnhilde into a magical sleep, Wotan puts the potential for compassionate love and its vivid hope of redemptive reconciliation into suspension at the end of *Die Walküre*. Despite the compassion of this scene, Wotan nevertheless tries to transform his personal reconciliation with Brünnhilde into another plan of social redemption thereby taking one of the first explicit steps into the metaphysical superstructure of *The Ring*. This scene should not, then, be experienced simply at the level of the personal drama. At that level it is, of course, wonderful. Consider the symbolism of understanding expressed there. He sings: "These radiant, glorious eyes, which, smiling, often I kissed":

"Der Augen leuchtendes Paar, das oft ich lächelnd gekost." When the cellos recapitulate that moving theme against the backdrop of the Sleep music, the effect surely should melt the coldest heart! Here, in one of the few purely lyrical moments in *The Ring*, we have the symbolism of Brünnhilde's eyes—her search for understanding—closed by Wotan's command, to be reopened only by love. Risking everything, he places what is most dear to him dangerously at the center of his search for redemption.

The effectiveness of this scene depends on the confluence of the personal and the social, as Wotan's renunciation of power for love begins to have its impact, but this happens in the context of his hope for redemption through love, through the love he shows Brünnhilde and his world by granting her the freedom she has in fact already exercised in her attempt to save Siegmund. She acted against Wotan's orders, but was she nevertheless still expressing "Wotan's will" (as she describes herself)? Wotan did not really want to kill Siegmund, he was forced to do so by Fricka's hobgoblin of consistency. We hear a reference to Brünnhilde's freedom in the final scene when she says, "I beheld Siegmund": "Siegmund musst' ich sehn." The Annunciation of Death motif reappears, and shortly she refers to the "new emotion" bedazzling her eyes. It is the tension resulting from her love for both Wotan and compassion for Siegmund: freedom against loyalty, the personal against the social, and the premonition of her own death.

At the end of *Götterdämmerung*, however, we see that Brünnhilde has understood the power of love and its destructiveness. At the end of *Die Walküre* Brünnhilde's eyes are closed, not eternally open; she does not yet understand the power she has achieved through her love. But at the end of *Götterdämmerung*, after she has experienced love's creative destructiveness first hand, she knows all, which I have taken to imply that her eyes have been opened to the interdependence of power and love. Brünnhilde's love leads to the destruction of Valhalla, to her denial of the Will in accepting her death; but this should be understood in connection with the final scene of *Die Walküre*. Wotan's act of compassion still projects his hope of redemption; even Brünnhilde's dream of reunion with Siegfried at the end of *Götterdämmerung* can be accomplished only through the destruction of Valhalla. Understood in this context, the simple orchestral recapitulation of Wotan's "Der Augen leuchtendes Paar" connects her sight—her understanding—to Wotan's need for redemption. That need will be fulfilled through Brünnhilde's understanding, but only through the destruction of Wotan's world. The relation between sight and understanding, love and redemption, and renunciation and destruction is thus established in one moving instant, one only possible musically and one of the best examples of the theory of music-drama in practice.

Just before Wotan puts Brünnhilde to sleep, when she says "then one thing more you must grant me":"dies eine musst du erhören," asking for a redemptive hero, we hear the music symbolizing her sleep in the violins and cellos—but accelerated and urgent. It seems to express the need for redemption but, ironically, the falling motif also hints at the decline of the gods. Thus, in the final bars of *Die Walküre,* when we hear the Siegfried motif as Wotan says: "Only the man who braves my spearpoint can pass through this sea of flame":"Wer meines Speeres Spitze fürchtet, durchschreite das Feuer nie!"[28] we know what Wotan does not know: that motif tells us that the hero Wotan hopes for will be Sieglinde's son since we have already heard it in Act IIIi in connection with her realization as Brünnhilde gives her the pieces of Siegmund's sword to save for her son. The impact of both of these scenes lies, once again, in the musical connection established between the personal and the universal: the private moments between Brünnhilde and Sieglinde, and between Brünnhilde and Wotan, have a larger significance. We are reminded of it near the end of Wotan's farewell by the recurrence of the Renunciation motif (at "And sadly the god must depart":"Denn so kehrt der Gott sich dir ab"). At this point the Renunciation, Fate, and Death motifs are heard and, after Wotan kisses Brünnhilde, the Sleep music appears along with it the motif of the Twilight of the Gods. Brünnhilde's sleep and Wotan's decline are linked together.

Besides its integral significance for Wotan's drama, the Fate motif also stands at the beginning of Brünnhilde's own journey of self-discovery as it closes the work. When Wotan kisses Brünnhilde, ("my kiss takes your godhead away!":"so küsst er die Gottheit von dir!") the daughter of Wotan falls asleep, but the larger significance of that act is brought out by the motif of the Twilight of the Gods: Brünnhilde will destroy Wotan. Wotan puts her to sleep, sealing his own fate, the death of his Great Society. Following the musical reference to eyes and sight we hear the Fire music, the symbol of the truth of change, and the music of Siegfried and Fate. Twenty-five bars before the end of the act we hear a last reference to Wotan's love and Brünnhilde's eyes, now closed, her fateful consciousness suspended.

Moving as this personal reconciliation between Wotan and Brünnhilde ought to be for the audience, I have argued that the experience effects us even more deeply when taken in the light of the metaphysical role Brünnhilde begins to play in the opposition of power and love. The musical origins of Brünnhilde's reproach ("Was it so shameful, what I have done...":"War es so schmählich, was ich verbrach...") lie in that Fate motif, with its implicit reference to Beethoven's "Muss es Sein?" In his own discussion of the connection between Fate and op. 135, Cooke points out that the final movement of the quartet answers the metaphysical question about overcoming fate with willful creative activity, optimism, and humor: "It must be!" but so what? *Amor fati* (as Nietzsche was to assert)—if that's all you have got to live for, love your fate: you are your possibilities and nothing more.[29] But in *The Ring* the questioning quality to the Fate motif with its unresolved diminished fourth captures the atmosphere of limited knowledge in Brünnhilde's scene with Siegmund in *Die Walküre* IIiv where, again, he asks who appears before him ("Tell me, who are you who appear before me, so beautiful and grave?":"Wer bist du, sag', die so schön und ernst mir erscheint?" Deryck Cooke's translation, "Wagner's Musical Language," p. 230). The last three words are accompanied by Fate, and her answer is that she appears only to those who are about to die. The Fate motif applies to her as well, as we see at the end of *Die Walküre*, something she cannot perceive at the time. The irony of these expressions of humanity becomes apparent only to us only through the development of the rest of *The Ring*. (It should also be observed that when Brünnhilde mentions death in this scene she is accompanied by that short drumroll on the timpani I described as the motif of death throughout the work and culminating in Siegfried's Funeral March, establishes her connection with Siegfried's death as well as that of Siegmund.) The motif that supplies the melodic line of "War es so schmählich" consists of an initial downward movement followed by an upward interval, a reversal of the Spear motif as I pointed out earlier, symbolizing Brünnhilde's independence from Wotan. She was already free of his power when she tried to help Siegmund, enacting her role as Wotan's will to substitute love for order. Her redemptive act comes from inside the system by reversing one of its symbols.

6. Evil and Tragedy

To conclude this chapter, I will compare *The Ring* to some other works of nineteenth-century art, and to some earlier ones, in order to show how it reintroduces the concept of Tragedy—a view of the world that fascinated philosophers and artists in the nineteenth century but one that they also conscientiously avoided. One of the main characteristics of Western civilization since Plato has been its *anti*tragic orientation towards the universe. Tragedy relies on the optimism of human action and expectation, on the belief that we are doing the right thing but, then again, tragedy tells us that 'right' action may be quite wrong in the long run. In a nontragic universe, we know, in principle at least, how our hopes and fears fit into the ultimate truths of the universe. In tragedy, however, the universe and the gods are not clearly linked to what humans value. In *The Ring,* however, we encounter a more mysterious universe because we encounter a more mysterious selfhood whereas classical tragedy rests on a clearly defined conception of the self.

Like Hegel, Schopenhauer, and Nietzsche, Wagner thought that Greek tragedy contained fundamental insights into the natures of truth and value. All three wrote about the Greeks at length and Wagner conceived the poetry of *The Ring* with the concept of Tragedy in mind. There are some obvious parallels between the characters of Brünnhilde and Antigone, for example, between Siegfried and Oedipus, and between Creon and Wotan. In endnote 20 of this chapter, I briefly discussed Michael Ewans' book as one attempt at exploring these connections. Another, somewhat better, book by L.J. Rather discusses the importance of Sophocles' plays in Wagner's changing conception of *The Ring*, especially the virtually Freudian emphasis on the unconscious.[30] Siegfried's relationship to Wotan, for example, like that between Oedipus and his father Laius, depends on legendary antagonisms indirectly expressing his willingness to accept self-destruction as the price of his domination, to conquer the father-figure who limits erotic desire (to use Donnington's gloss). Similarly, like Antigone, Siegmund and Brünnhilde reject the artificial primacy of the society in their appeal to love as a natural force. The demands of Antigone's ancestral religion run deeper than the laws of Creon's society, which were fashioned against the forces of nature just as Valhalla. With Wagner's lovers, however, the role of divinity in the nature of value recedes to the vanishing point.

The concept of Evil was primarily an invention of Christianity. Evil is contrary to specific moral values in Western civilization conceived in the union between self or society and the divine. Evil causes suffering not only physically but also by intentionally defeating the possibility of happiness. Plato and Aristotle could not conceive of the metaphysical possibility of evil, confining their conceptions of moral failure to the inadequate possession of virtue resulting from ignorance of the truth or poor training. For them, immorality was the result of ignorance or of letting passion carry one away from the path of reason. It was a failure of education in the virtues of that society, although Plato and Aristotle differed on how that education was to be accomplished. Anyone who understands the virtues and controls their passions will be able to live the good life. In early Christianity, evil was understood to be a force contrary to God's will (in the mythology of Satan, for example, or Paul's conception of natural instinct). But the power of evil can be subdued through faith in God's benevolence. Life may be terrible for us, but God knows better.

Like Paul, Augustine characterized evil as imperfection (a Neoplatonic view), due to our inability to clearly understand God's perfection and our role in creation. For these early Christians, we must rise above the flesh, and with God's help in the form of Jesus' passion, overcome our metaphysical limitations. Later, in their attempt at escaping the mystery inherent in such theological accounts of reality, the philosophers of the Enlightenment also understood evil as imperfection while a *scientific* understanding in the control of human nature became the primary source for social and moral reform. Philosophers, scientists, and theologians eradicated the possibility of elemental evil by emphasizing the rationality of God's creation, represented through the benevolence essential to human society. So, in the emerging naturalism of the seventeenth and eighteenth centuries, evil was identified with the insufficient actualization or development of essential human qualities, *not* with their intentional rejection. Theologians during that period overcame this tension by literally identifying God with reason, as the engineer/designer of the universe, and then ascribing it to humans as the point at which Mankind differed from the animals. The Enlightenment's conception of social progress, expressed by Locke and Descartes, and even by the pessimistic Hobbes, rested on the principle of human perfectibility through science. Mankind can change itself for the better by perfecting its rationality, by transcending its limitations through the rationalization of politics.

Sophocles' tragedies contain no characters that could be called evil even in the negative sense of bad or poorly formed character. Terrible things happen to people not because they are possessed by powerful negative forces but because they try to do too much, or because they fail to take account of religious restrictions established by the gods (many of which were impossible to know until they were transgressed). In fact, tragic heroes are *paradigms* of virtue who almost always fail to take human limitation into account, who act beyond their knowledge (as we must always do). But the gods of Homeric Greece did not establish what was good in general—they often disagreed about it amongst themselves and there was no universal good for humans or for gods until Plato. In his early dialogue, the *Euthyphro*, Plato formulated his famous dilemma and put it to the self-righteous Euthyphro, full of certainty as he prosecutes his father for murdering a slave, thus violating a fundamental principle of familial loyalty: Is Euthyphro's action good because the gods approve of it, even though he violates a key virtue, or do the gods approve of what Euthyphro does because it possesses some feature of worthiness independently of the gods' interests? If the former, then values change relative to the notorious changeability of the gods; if the latter, some value transcends the gods and their interests are irrelevant. The tragedians believed in the former alternative: the course of human happiness depends ultimately on the contingency of value; there are few fixed truths in such a universe. Plato devoted his great intellectual energies to showing that such a conception of human nature must be rejected. He grasped the second horn of his dilemma: the gods themselves must appeal to higher standards, fixed in the nature of things. Metaphysically, Christian theology can be seen as bringing together the ancient Hebrew conception of God (just as unpredictable as the Greek pantheon) with Plato's theory of forms. God's goodness became identical with His unchanging nature.

Because they did not have a conception of permanent goodness, the Greeks before Plato simply did not have a concept of Evil upon which the contrast could be established. In his article "Goethe and Tragedy" (to which I refer again in the Appendix), Erich Heller points out that Creon in *Antigone* cannot be an evil man (the Creon/Antigone, Wotan/Brünnhilde relationships are similar in significant ways). He cannot even be a bad man: he may be insensitive to other points of view, he may be single-minded, but when he tries to do what is best as he sees it, he runs up against the religious traditions of his family, traditions at odds with his conception of social value based on human good rather than nature. Aristotle points out in his *Poetics* that tragedy does not happen to bad people—in fact, while the final chorus condemns Creon's arrogance and pride, Sophocles clearly sympathizes with his efforts to enhance human society as the only hope for morality in the face of Antigone's mystery religion. The tragedy of *Antigone*, therefore, lies in the complete absence of a *moral* solution to the conflict between the principles of human society (convention) and the demands of the gods (the source of Antigone's religious convictions). If morality exists only *within* human society, human belief will inevitably conflict with what lies beyond society and beyond human comprehension. This contrast between the human and the divine forms the basis of tragedy. For Heller, tragedies generally ask: "What would happen to the human spirit if all human goodness were of no avail on this earth...? Would the ending be despair..., or a faith beyond despair?" ("Goethe and Tragedy," p. 45).[31]

For Goethe, despite his appreciation of ancient Greece, this kind of impasse could not arise because of his faith in the ultimate *unity* of Spirit and Nature. For Beethoven and Hegel, as for Goethe, striving is everything; only through it—not through passive intuitions of permanent truths—can value be realized. But nothing remains in this universe for human striving to collide with on its way toward ultimate unification with nature—except striving itself in the form of other strivers. For Beethoven, our confrontation with the elemental forces of the universe became a symbol for human aspiration and creativity (as it was for Goethe), but the optimism of this quest can be defeated by an equally forceful striver moving in the opposite direction, or by the complete open-endedness of the quest itself. The redemptive unity at the end of *Faust* and in the finale of the *Ninth Symphony* might begin to look like fantasy rather than hope (as Thomas Mann was to invert the redemptiveness of striving in his *Doctor Faustus,* his Nietzschean antihero *reverses* the *Ninth Symphony,* moving from civilization back to nature).

The kind of unity sought by Goethe and Beethoven could be achieved only in great works of art (and we have to bear in mind that those days are over!). The greatness of these two in particular rests on the tensions and ambiguities in their search for unity. What would establish and end to their search? Not only are humanity and nature irreconcilable, so too are *creativity* and humanity because our creativity makes us *unstable* beings. What kind of 'brotherhood' does the last movement of the *Ninth Symphony* portray? Does it have anything to do with actual human society? Seen on the model of the great artist rejecting social conventions, such a self must create its own world, a world better than the one it confronts. But Beethoven and Goethe's contrast between their vision of creative spirituality and the overwhelming power of nature cannot be tragic since it rejects the insurmountable conflict between human interests and happiness, on the one hand, and the mystery of the universe on the other. The *Ninth Symphony* and *Faust* tell us that no such conflict really exists, except in the eye of the beholder—the conflict can be resolved. Creativity can fathom every mystery but itself. Indeed, unlike Ancient Greece, it was the self that preoccupied the nineteenth century, not God, not nature.

The reconciliation of Spirit with Nature, based on the artistic visions of the early nineteenth century, cannot happen in *Antigone* or in the *Oedipus* trilogy. Humanity may be limited in its understanding of the universe, eternally alienated from the divine, but it possesses its own hard-won dignity, the values of which cannot be universalized for the tragedians. Human spirituality must always be seen *within* its strictly confined social context, not transcending it as we see in Platonism, Christianity, or in the early nineteenth century. The blind Oedipus at the end of that cycle has achieved a self-comprehension he did not have when he could see. He has become noble because his human desire to know now includes his realization that the limits of that knowledge restrict his happiness. He remains content to live out his last days with his children, accepting the frailty of human life and its precious, precarious community. Here again the contrast between goodness and evil simply does not occur.

By contrast, Paul, like Plato, conceives of human nature dualistically. Two forces oppose each other in the human spirit: the universal and the divine pull humanity towards God, but natural desires, particularity "the flesh," pull us downwards, away from God. In his *Letter to the Romans* Chapter, 7: 13–25, Paul writes: the "law of my members" (the reference obviously sexual) is constant war with "the law of my mind and makes me captive to the law of sin which dwells in my members. Wretched man that I am! Who will deliver me from this body of death?" The flesh and our "members" are not merely hindrances to perfection, however, they symbolize a dark antiuniversal force in the universe, a force devoted to the destruction of universality. Indeed, Paul characterizes the created world in opposition to God. Our good lies beyond the world:

> We know that the whole creation has been groaning in travail together until now; and not only the creation but we ourselves, who have the first fruits of the Spirit, groan inwardly as we wait for adoption as sons, the redemption of our bodies. For in this hope we are saved. Now hope that is seen is not hope. For who hopes for what he sees? But if we hope for what we do not see, we wait for it with patience. (*Romans* 8: 22–25. *Revised Standard Version.*)

This contrast between good and evil was notably absent during the German debate about truth and value in the early nineteenth century. The good was translated directly from Enlightenment rationality into the general tendency of striving; but since striving had as its goal unity with nature, it was also, for example, the source of Faust's moral ambiguity. The terrible things done by him in the name of striving undercut conventional moral values because striving stands as the only ultimate value even if it transcends humanity (as it does in Goethe's final scene). Over fifty years before the completion of *Faust*, Mozart portrayed striving as an embodiment of both good and evil in *Don Giovanni* but he concluded this remarkable work with a universal condemnation of deception (an essential aspect of the Don's striving) as the worst possible social defect in an Enlightenment society. Nevertheless, the strongest impression remains of Giovanni's elemental, Faustian creativity: to *do*, to *accomplish*, and to *live* even at the expense of moral stability. This irresistible, even noble villain needs society to provide him with the means of his self-assertion. Unlike Faust, he has no self doubts because he has a clear view of who he is. But Giovanni's condemnation rests on his breaking the bonds of morality. He destroys others but Faust, perhaps more destructive than Giovanni, did so in search of what he hoped would be wisdom through striving, a wisdom that ultimately unified reason and emotion. Giovanni, less self-consciously, strives only for *his* good. Faust does not know *what* he is, that being the point of Goethe's drama.

The distinction between good and evil, still possible in art before *Faust*, nowadays makes Mozart's final condemnation of Giovanni seem unconvincingly *ad hoc* in the light of his character's elemental vigor. Striving can take us beyond good and evil into new visions of value. But if we how react ironically to the reasserting of established mores at the conclusion of *Don Giovanni*, they at least existed in that era as a viable if even then merely traditional social institution. By the 1820's and 30's, after the French Revolution and Napoleon, however, the *moral* power of social institutions had severely declined or had even become part of a negative characterization of value, a source of alienation. Unlike Giovanni, Faust, who falls into this last milieu of alienation, was not condemned for destroying others simply *because* his higher goal had transcendental authority while society did not. The morality of social responsibility that eventually caught up with Don Giovanni no longer existed in *Faust*, its foundation in Enlightenment science and rationalism, or religion, having largely been abandoned. At the beginning of the drama, Faust forsakes science as the—or even one—pathway to truth. Without God as a symbol of that rationalism, society no longer remained strong enough to separate good from evil, opening the way to the unity of Spirit and Nature in a way the morality of the Enlightenment could not comprehend. Faust's exclamation "feeling is everything" summarized this change. Faust was saved and Giovanni condemned because the search for the self, by the time of Goethe, had eclipsed the search for value. (I discuss Goethe in more detail in the Appendix, Section 2.)

In *The Ring,* the concept of Evil certainly reemerges in nineteenth-century art with the characters of Alberich and preeminently Hagen. They represent the destructive aspects of conflict as Wotan (at least in *Die Walküre* IIIiii) and Brünnhilde are associated with the positive—both are aspects of striving. Yet we have seen that even the positive forces of social stability and love can also be also destructive. The good cannot be characterized simply through Brünnhilde's compassionate redemptiveness because *the very hope of redemption can be as destructive as it is creative.* It is the kind of thing that Nietzsche describes as "beyond good and evil." The metaphysical drama of *The Ring* involves not only the moral *opposition* between good and evil but also their *interdependence.* Alberich's malevolence rests on his original intention of gaining control of the world through a power without love, based on exploitation, and driven by revenge. Wotan, in contrast, may have had good intentions in creating Valhalla, and even in wanting to save it, but finds himself to be as obsessed with the consolidation of his power as Alberich is with getting it. One of the most disturbingly manipulative characters in art, the cold and calculating Hagen does not stand "beyond good and evil" in Nietzsche's sense of getting beyond that particular interpretive distinction because, like Alberich, he "hates the good." He wants power as the means for overcoming the established good of Wotan's world, not for establishing something new in any positive sense. Hagen's motivation depends on that distinction.

Nietzsche's conception of the contrast between good and evil helps our understanding of *The Ring.* He took the metaphysics of striving as the source of selfhood and applied it specifically to social value. Values are created but to discover the nature of creativity we must go beyond specific values, beyond good and evil. For Nietzsche, to go beyond good and evil requires the assertiveness to redefine the good through a new vision of social existence, to see in cultural innovation the source of all value through the assertion of "life in all of its complexities." Hagen and Alberich, however, are representatives of what Nietzsche describes as *"ressentiment"* (Essay I in *The Genealogy of Morals*). These people change the content of value by making the considered 'good' (the assertivess of creative individuals, whom Nietzsche calls "masters") into 'evil', by transforming what used to be 'bad' (what hindered the striving of creative innovators) into a new characterization of the good. This is the core of his theory of the "revaluation of values." Nietzsche contends that the values of "the herd" (the greatest good for the greatest number, humility as a virtue, the common good, benevolence, compromise, acquiescence to the will of the majority) stands in opposition to creative individuality (which may seem "selfish" by comparison). The "noble mode of valuation," in contrast, "acts and grows spontaneously, it seeks its opposite only so as to affirm itself more gratefully and triumphantly—its negative concept 'low', 'common', 'bad' is only a subsequently-invented pale, contrasting image in relation to its positive basic concept—filled

The Structure of *The Ring*: Tragedy or Transcendence? 73

with life and passion through and through...." "Good" originally meant "noble," "assertive" and "innovative," but when it later came to mean "utility" or "selflessness" the original meaning has been reversed.

Slave moralities (characterized by the 'masses', the collective good, utilitarianism), Nietzsche argues, are therefore primarily reactive rather than assertive. They are created in opposition to "the good," which becomes revalued as evil. Their entire conception of Good rests on the opposition between them—the masters who oppress them, and their values, are evil. Their conception of Good rests on reaction rather than innovation. "The herd" is thus united by the virtues of opposition rather than invention. For example, the ancient Greek view of the pride as a supreme virtue justified by achievement *versus* the Christian disparagement of worldly accomplishments as irrelevant to salvation: pride exemplifies preoccupation with self rather than God. Reactive characters are intentionally destructive rather than creative. They do not create anything new and their desire for domination remains merely negative. But this is not necessarily a bad thing for Nietzsche because herd values also provide an occasion for revolt and the establishment of new values of individuality. Herd values *are* innovative to the extent that they are successful. Indeed, master morality *always* leads to herd morality, than then to a new revaluation of values. Wotan's intention in creating Valhalla (and the destruction of the World Ash Tree) was based on establishing human values. But he then became reactive, like Alberich himself. This is Wagner's point: the striving of both Wotan/Siegfried and Alberich/Hagen must be seen as two (or four) aspects of the same force, what Nietzsche called the will to power. This connection also opposes Hagen's, and Wotan's, destructiveness to the positive character of Brünnhilde herself at the end of *Götterdämmerung*. Her final actions—her involvement in the plot to kill Siegfried and her destruction of Valhalla—are ostensibly motivated by love, but love has obviously become a *destructive* force.

Because of the dramatic scale of its characters, *The Ring* bears comparison with Shakespeare. Hagen and Iago, for example, resemble each other in their manipulativeness, but Hagen's coldness differentiates him from Iago in his perverse, even detached wickedness. Not *obsessed* in the way Iago or Alberich are, Hagen's evil only nominally involves the injustice of Wotan's taking the ring from Alberich. He controls those whom he sees as his "betters" because he rejects their values and sees Gunther and Gutrune as weak and ineffectual, and therefore useful to him as means. Iago's motivation derives from jealousy of and contempt for Othello (conveyed with a directness in Verdi's *Otello* that transforms Iago into a rather different character). Hagen's destructiveness has a point, but a far broader one than can be expressed by anything so specific as revenge or jealousy. His character must hate the good in a general way, to force the world into the elemental struggle for power concealed by social order, a struggle Hagen knows he will win.[32] For Hagen, reason must always be a slave of the passion for domination. For him, we already know what to desire—the subversion of established mores. The more apt Shakespearean comparison on that point would be the character of Richard III: although Richard *has* power, he uses it to destroy established connections that restrict his desires. Neither Hagen nor Richard are Nietzschean heroes, however, because they have no real vision of *their* good beyond the acquisition of power and the destruction of their enemies: they are nihilists.

In its association of evil with darkness, *The Ring* bears a closer resemblance to *King Lear* than to *Othello*. In *Lear,* the forces of Light (Cordelia and, deceptively, her father) are destroyed along with the forces of Darkness (the evil sisters but ultimately her father again). Like Wotan, Lear has participated in the formative events of the tragedy. And, like *The Ring, Lear* conveys the importance of mutual responsibility: For how much of their troubles are Wotan and Lear themselves responsible through their self-centeredness, self-pity, shortsightedness, and bad judgment? Without these failures, could they have resisted threats? Or, contrary to Plato and the Enlightenment, are these shortcomings inevitable characteristics of human nature? Where Iago's malevolence contrasts starkly with the pride of Othello and the innocence of Desdemona, Lear's and Wotan's own ambiguous values are part of the problems that they both face. Othello's pride leads to his jealousy because he fails to trust, to accept Desdemona's faithfulness but, were it not for Iago, no harm need have come from that pride. Lear's own personality, by contrast, stands as the true source of his problems. He believes himself justified in his treatment of Cordelia when he is not; he continually misreads and misjudges people, he is a monster of self-pity. Both Lear and Othello are deceived, but Lear's failings are (like Wotan's) self-destructive while Othello, through ignorance and pride simply plays into Iago's hands as does Siegfried into Hagen's—both victims of their own short-sightedness. To see this contrast in complexity, try to summarize Lear's relationship with Cordelia, or Wotan's to Brünnhilde, in one (reasonably short) sentence (it can easily be done for Othello and Desdemona). Like Alberich, Iago's evil has a specific goal in the downfall of a single individual. Iago's sociopathic irony threatens at times to turn the 'tragedy' into a comedy. Hagen's evil, and his irony, however, as we have seen, have a far more general purpose. Like Lear, Wotan fails to see the implications of his actions and believes that he will establish the good for all simply by following his own interests. But, like Lear, he does not see that those interests are inconsistent.

Alberich enjoins the sleeping Hagen to "hate the good" in *Götterdämmerung* IIi. This scene and its Prelude concentrate on the descending fourth that characterizes Hagen. Despite the generality of his destructiveness, Hagen is not an abstract expression of evil, (as Mephistopheles often is). Hagen's evil *depends* on his contempt for the so-called nobility and it has a distinct personality. He wants to overcome those *called* good, those who are considered better than him and to defeat the social system that has created this particular stratification of the good life. But we have seen how Wotan's conception of the good is itself flawed. When Alberich describes Siegfried's meeting with Wotan and the smashing of his spear, an almost unrecognizably distorted Valhalla motif occurs ("but now he has been vanquished/by one of his heroes [Siegfried];/to the Wälsung [Volsung] he lost/domination and might":"vom eignen Geschlechte/ward er geschlagen:/an dem Wälsung [Volsung] verlor er/Macht und Gewalt"), and the symbiotic struggle between good and evil brings about the destruction of both Alberich and Hagen as well as Siegfried and Brünnhilde—and through them Wotan. (Those who know their Freud will find much in this scene.) Significantly, Hagen does not swear to Alberich that he will get hold of the ring; he swears allegiance only to himself. Because he has a definite purpose, Hagen *is* as self-sufficient as Siegfried *thought* he was. Interestingly, at the end of his scene with Hagen, Alberich enjoins him to "be true" to him ("sei treu/sei treu") the last iteration being a falling minor second echoing the first notes of the Rhinegold motif and its distorted, dissonant Hagen variation. This important musical reference becomes Hagen's own falling motif based on a diminished fifth and following directly from the falling fifth at the end of Siegfried's horn call. At the beginning of Brünnhilde and Siegfried's dawn in the Prolog to *Götterdämmerung,* the bass clarinet plays the interval A–E against the opening of Siegfried's motif (with its upward leap from B-flat to G) and over the love music in the cellos (including some references to Freia II). These intervals connect the characters of Hagen, Brünnhilde, and Siegfried in the web of fate at the end of the Norn's scene: the motif of Alberich's curse also appears here and itself consists of these very intervals.

In *The Ring,* neither the efforts of the divine Wotan in *Das Rheingold* and *Die Walküre,* nor the human Brünnhilde of *Götterdämmerung* are of any avail in forestalling the inevitability of change. The music of the Dawn of Hagen's Day follows the scene with Alberich and the posthypnotic suggestions Alberich has fed Hagen during his sleep awaken to dominate the rest of *Götterdämmerung.* The canonic development of this interlude in the bass clarinet and horns is a permutation of the Rhine music that begins the entire cycle; this music later becomes the basis for the Gibichung vassals when they sing Hagen's praises as their real leader. The second bar of the motif is related to the descending clarinets of Gutrune's music, symbolizing Siegfried's entanglement in Hagen's plan through the innocent and well-meaning but weak Gunther and Gutrune, and the end of the Hagen's Dawn prelude brings in his falling motif, emphasizing it over and over. The motif, with its characteristic diminished fifth, and its continual variation throughout Act II, encapsulates a kind of recapitulation in miniature of *The Ring* from its other, darker side taking Hagen from the dawn of his hate to the dominance of his power.

Hagen thus stands as the mediating point between the hope-filled reference to Siegfried in *Die Walküre* IIIi and its death-oriented occurrence of his motif in the Funeral March: What has happened to the hope of heroic redemption? The fatal association between Siegfried and death occurs immediately when Hagen greets him right at the beginning of *Götterdämmerung* Iii ("Heil Siegfried, teuerer Held"), the significance of the moment perfectly captured with a crucial occurrence of the Curse motif. Hagen and Siegfried meet, the curse will be fulfilled. This dramatic confrontation was presaged by Fafner: fatally wounded by Siegfried in *Siegfried* IIIi, he says to him, "And who told you to do/what you have done?":"Dein Hirn brütete nicht, was du volbracht?" That moment is packed with several motifs that envisage the fate of Siegfried: the Curse, a reference to the love music, and the hope of heroic redemption (the motif of Siegfried's Destiny). Siegfried himself finally begins to see this just before he dies. Remembering Fafner's symbolism of the unconscious sexual force that awakens Brünnhilde, the juxtaposition of these motifs anticipates the fulfillment of the curse by love: Siegfried's heroism and Brünnhilde's love will be completely subverted by their opposite, Hagen's hatred. Again, the transformation of the Rhinegold motif from its joyful symbolization of nature, as the Rhinemaidens sing it, to the distorted version of perverted nature in Hagen's motif effectively brings this out.

One final example of Hagen's manipulativeness as it is shown through the music occurs in the ironically fervent assertion of Siegfried's and Gunther's "Blood brotherhood" in *Götterdämmerung* Iii. The music of this scene rests on the motif known as Siegfried's Mission but Hagen subverts Siegfried's heroism. Both Siegfried and Gunther are already firmly in the grip of Hagen and begin to act out his plan. The music of Siegfried's and Gunther's pact, overdone to point up the irony of their forthrightness, shows that the larger significance of Siegfried's heroism lies within his lack of direction—his undirected energy soon taken over by Hagen. What is Siegfried's Mission? To become a pawn in Hagen's game? During this scene Hagen does not join the other two saying, "My blood would spoil all your drink;/my blood's not pure/and noble like yours;/stubborn and cold,/slow to stir,/my blood flows slowly and strangely":"Mein Blut verdürb euch den Trank;/nich fliesst mir's echt/und edel wie euch;/störrish und kalt/stockt's in mir;/nich will's die Wange mir röten." He keeps his distance but remains the manipulator. The reference to blood seemingly differentiates Hagen and Siegfried but really brings them together as it implies the latter's death, and the earlier reference to Brünnhilde's blood/sexuality should be recalled in this scene. As Mann notes about his manipulative distance, Hagen assumes a "mythical character-mask" in his watch scene and in his sleep-talking scene with Alberich—"the theater knows nothing nearer to the demonic than these scenes."[33]

To return to tragedy, Sophocles' tragedies never result in a full comprehension of the relation between the self and the universe. Indeed the point is that no such comprehension is possible. In *Faust*, understanding has become the goal; but Faust confuses his dream of knowing enough in order to do right with the attainment of universal power, be it through reason or feeling. As Heller puts it:

> Of these two strivings the [latter] desires the attainment of the superman, the alchemist heightening of all human faculties, whereas the [former] aims at renunciation and resignation to the simple state of man. The first is the native element of Goethe's genius, the second the longing of Goethe's moral existence. ("Goethe and Tragedy," p. 61)

The theme of redemption as the reestablishment of value through striving thus contains a fundamental ambiguity: Does one strive to *be human*, or to transcend one's humanity *for the universal*? What *is* it to 'be human'? Goethe could never reconcile these two opposing moral directions in his desire to unite Spirit and Nature. He envisaged a transcendent form of spirituality that brought together the rational, the Enlightenment universality of Kant's Kingdom of Ends (where all humans are conceived as ends in themselves and never as means to an end), and the ever-elusive emotion of love so desperately sought by Faust. For the Enlightenment, as for Plato and Aristotle, redemption from evil lay in overcoming ignorance—knowledge remained as much the basis of virtue for Kant as it had for Plato. But Goethe's point was that one had to *desire* knowledge and the problem became one of desiring the universal more than the particular. How can one love another *individual* if the only worthwhile thing about humans derives from their *universality*? The problem for Goethe and Beethoven concerned the *object* of this desire: What is it to be human—to be particular or to be universal? Can *any* particular be worth of the kind of love they envisaged? Perhaps this applies to Brünnhilde in *Götterdämmerung* as well.

Tragedy happens when humans try to do their best in a universe that inevitably destroys their achievements, their goodness defined solely by their social context but insufficient to justify their values and protect them against fate. Value was always relative to society. For Sophocles, this was expressed in the inconsistency between humanity and the gods, an unresolvable tension driven by the human desire to excel and exceed within the universe as they saw it. The fundamental problem of tragedy concerned the limits of human value and knowledge: When does our reach exceed our grasp? For Wagner, however, the universe itself became metaphysically as well as morally indeterminate. Fifty years earlier, Goethe and Beethoven could not accept this possibility and tried to find conceptions of Spirit and Nature that reintroduced universality, that gave the universe the structure of their artistic conceptions. But it quickly became clear that Spirit, as the self generalized, was indeterminate too, and I understand the endings of *Faust* and the *Ninth Symphony* to express this. Hegel embraced this indeterminacy but found enough structure in Spirit, conceived as the development of civilization through conflict and resolution, to justify optimism about unifying spirit and nature. In his new conception of Reason, he therefore rejected the central metaphysical point about ancient tragedy—that there are *fundamentally* incommensurable views of the universe, *fundamentally* incommensurable sets of values (the gods' values, the values of humans), with no possible way of uniting them through the dialectic of history. Hegel and Goethe rejected that possibility in their search for unity between Spirit and Nature where Wagner and Nietzsche embraced it. Value and identity have no metaphysical foundation at all.

The Ring reintroduces some of the elements of classical tragedy into art. But Wagner was not Sophocles reborn (as Nietzsche breathlessly characterized him in *The Birth of Tragedy*). Human identity and value undergo genuine transformation in *The Ring* of a kind impossible in ancient tragedy with its fixed conception of the inscrutable division between human and divine values. In tragedy, the collision between the human and the divine forces us to revalue our conception of value and our relation to the gods. Even if we cannot know what the gods want of us, we can show some humility towards values that excell and exceed ours and thereby discover something about ourselves. But no such comparison is possible in *The Ring*. Indeed, Wagner shows how the gods have exactly the same problem as humans in determining the content of the concept of Good. Because of the pervasive presence of the divine in Greek tragedy, and its absence in the nineteenth century, Wotan and Brünnhilde are alone in their world in a way Agamemnon, Oedipus, and Antigone were not in theirs.

Notes

1 The 'Old Hegelians' tried to reconcile Hegel's historicism with Christianity and to interpret *Geist* or Spirit, as the historical realization of God. They eventually became known as "right-wing Hegelians" after David Strauss used the radical/conservative divisions of the French Parliament to characterize interpretations of Hegel. Feuerbach, however, claimed that humanity has become the true subject of theology. He was a 'Young Hegelian' or, to use Strauss's terminology, a left-wing Hegelian.

2 Röckel was a fellow revolutionary along with Wagner and Michael Bakunin in the Dresden uprising of 1849 but, while his two friends were imprisoned,

Wagner escaped to Switzerland and then to England. This is but one example of his amazing luck and uncanny ability to overcome seemingly overwhelming odds. Wagner's long letters to Röckle contain his most extensive comments on *The Ring*. Even if nothing said by an artist about his work can be taken at face value, Wagner's account remains a convincing interpretation in the way it ties together the political and personal drama with the Schopenhauerian essence of the universe as Wagner saw it at that time. See the discussion of the Röckel letters in *I Saw the World End*, Chapters 1 and 2. It seems likely that Bakunin's boisterous anarchistic zeal was an early inspiration for Siegfried.

3   Richard Wagner, *Opera and Drama,* trans. William Ashton Ellis (New York: Broude Brothers, 1960). The prose works of Wagner badly need new translations, the old ones by Ellis are by today's standards mannered and virtually unintelligible in places. The quotation is from Part II of *Opera and Drama,* p. 121.

4   Quoted in Deryck Cooke, *I Saw the World End*, p, 1. See also Michael Tanner, *Wagner*, pp. 9–13.

5   This resembles Hegel's view, in the *Lectures on Aesthetics,* that music "concerns itself only with the undefined movement of the inward spiritual nature, and deals with musical sounds as, so to speak, feeling without thought...." Translation by Bernard Bosanquet, *The Introduction to Hegel's Philosophy of Fine Art* (London: Routledge and Kegan Paul, 1905), reprinted in J. Glenn Gray (ed.), *G.W.F. Hegel: On Art Religion, Philosophy* (New York: Harper and Row, Harper Torchbooks, 1970), p. 54.

6   Brian Magee, *Aspects of Wagner* (New York: Stein and Day, 1968), p. 22.

7   Emil Staiger, *Musik und Dichtung* (Zurich and Freiburg: Atlantis Musikbuch-Verlag, 1947 & 1980), pp. 32–33.

8   See George Windell, "Hegel, Feuerbach, and Wagner's *Ring*," *Central European History,* IX, 1, (March 1976), pp. 27–57. Windell points out the difficulties Wagner had in understanding Hegel (along with many others to this day), but he got what he needed from him with the help of others. One reason the already famous Wagner encouraged the young, unknown Nietzsche's interest in him was to have someone to explain philosophy to him. My point is that Wagner's concepts of Selfhood, Reality, and Value fit right in with the transformation of dialectical thought during the early and

middle nineteenth-century. See also Ronald Gray, "The German Intellectual Background" in Burbidge and Sutton, *The Wagner Companion*.

In the first of his *Theses on Feuerbach*, Marx (for whom Feuerbach was also an early influence) claims that Feuerbach's materialism is conceived physiologically ("only in the form of the *object or perception* [Anschauung], but not as *sensuous human activity, practice* [*praxis*], nor subjectively"). He says that Feuerbach does not "comprehend human activity as *objective*." That is, he does not take *praxis* as the fundamental nature of mankind and remains within the empiricist theory of knowledge as experience rather than action. I think Wagner's modification of Feuerbach embodies the same criticism. See *Writings of the Young Marx on Philosophy and Society*, Loyd Easton and Kurt Guddat (ed.s) (New York: Doubleday and Co., Anchor Books, 1967), pp. 400–402.

9 See Deryck Cooke, *I Saw the World End*, pp. 144–46 for a discussion of the World Ash Tree.

10 Unless otherwise indicated, translations will be from Andrew Porter's translation of *The Ring* (New York: W.W. Norton, 1977). Porter's translation was intended for performances of *The Ring* in English; consequently, rhythm of pronunciation (among other things) sometimes takes precedence over accuracy. This is, however, the most widely available translation of the text.

11 For a discussion of Wagner's views of his female characters, see Sandra Corse, *Wagner and the New Consciousness: Language and Love in The Ring* (London and Toronto: Associated University Presses, 1990), pp. 38–41. But see Thomas S. Grey, *Wagner's Musical Prose: Texts and Contexts* (Cambridge: Cambridge University Press, 1995), Chapter 3, for a very thorough discussion of Wagner's use of feminine metaphors for music and his female characters.

12 The ending of 1853:

> Not goods, not gold
> nor godly pomp;
> nor house, not court,
> nor lordly splendor;
> not shady bargains'
> deceiving bonds,
> nor two-faced customs'

> rigid laws;
> blessèd in joy and grief,
> let there be only—love.
>
> Translation by Cooke, *I Saw the World End*, p. 20.

13 Translation by Cooke, *I Saw the World End*, p. 22.

14 In Chapter 3 I will discuss Carl Dahlhaus' thesis that Schopenhauer confused Wagner and that the final version of *The Ring* really expresses a return to Feuerbach.

15 To quote the passage from one of Wagner's letters to Röckel: "I shaped [the text of *The Ring*] at a time when I had built up in my conceptual thought a Hellenistic-optimistic world, the realization of which I held to be entirely possible, if only men wanted it—though I rather ingeniously pushed away the problem why they actually didn't want it.... But I hardly noticed that, in carrying out my plan—indeed, even in laying it down—I was unconsciously following a quite different, much deeper intuition, and instead of conceiving a phase in the development of the world, I had conceived the essence of the world itself and recognized its nothingness; from which it naturally followed that, since I had been faithful to my intuition and not to my conceptual ideas, something different came to light from what I actually thought." Translation by Cooke, *I Saw the World End*, p. 21.

16 Robert Bailey, "The Structure of *The Ring* and its Evolution," *Nineteenth-Century Music*, I (July 1977), pp. 48–61.

17 See Grey, *Wagner's Musical Prose,* pp. 157–172 for his discussion of the last scene of Siegfried, including a breakdown of its structure and an account of the "allegory" of Brünnhilde and Siegfried and Brünnhilde's representation of music (to follow up one of Wagner's recurring analogies). The contrast rests on the distinction between Woman/Music and Man/Intellect (poetry) that Wagner wanted to unify in his theory of music-drama. Siegfried's ongoing confusion of Brünnhilde with his mother in this scene exemplifies this search for unity. As Siegfried lowers himself to kiss Brünnhilde, she rises. Siegfried has risen to the top of Brünnhilde's mountain, but it is really Brünnhilde who, in the three-fold repetition of the awakening music, rises to the challenge of sexual conquest, the ultimate emasculation

of Wotan. See also Tanner's discussion of "Laughter in Death," *Wagner*, p. 172.

18 See Warren Darcy's comparison of *Das Rheingold* and *Götterdämmerung* shows the structural parallels between them: "The division of the first and final drama into a prologue and three acts reflects the division of the first drama into an introductory scene (the theft of the gold) followed by three main scenes (the story of the gods). The first scene of *Das Rheingold* opens in the key of E–flat major and closes in [D–flat major] as the three Rhinemaidens witness the theft of their gold; the Prologue of *Götterdämmerung* opens in E–flat *minor*, and its first half closes in D–*flat* (or B) minor as the three Norns experience the breaking of their rope. In each case a tragic event of cosmic significance is underscored by the tonal move of a descending third," "The Pessimism of *The Ring*," *Opera Quarterly*, IV, (Summer, 1986) p. 34.

19 As Cooke points out, Loge is not the god of deceit he might appear to be in *Das Rheingold*, but "practically the god of truth, the one character who continually tells Wotan the simple facts that he does not want to face" (*I Saw the World End*, pp. 172, 353). Loge symbolizes "the mind in its demonic aspect," that is, as a source of inspiration and new ideas. Not purely divine like the other gods, Loge's "thoughtfulness" includes his cynicism about absolutes. Cooke argues that Loge symbolizes not intellectual thought but Promethean inspiration—fire symbolizes the mind in its most creative and elusive form—intuitive comprehension rather than rational proof (see pp. 169–175).

20 For a similar view, see Michael Ewans, *Wagner and Aeschylus: The Ring and the Orestia* (London: Faber and Faber, 1982), pp. 249 f. This useful book contrasts Wagner with the Greek tragedians arguing that Wagner does not hold out the hope of an advanced society (as does Aeschylus), but returns everything to nature to begin again. However, in my view Ewans wrongly concludes that the end of *The Ring* signifies the defeat of power. He says: "Wotan and Brünnhilde have at last reached that glory which Sieglinde attained in the one brief, visionary moment when she learnt that she bore Siegfried in her womb. It is the special glory which can be granted by knowing that your life will achieve its purpose..." (p. 252). If Brünnhilde's life has achieved its purpose, how can the moment of her final understanding be compared with Sieglinde's realization that she will bear Siegfried? Brünnhilde's understanding would be that she has made new life possible; but she must also realize, through her own actions, that this life contains

the seeds of destruction as well, something Sieglinde did not realize, although it was true for her too. But then Sieglinde did not conspire against her lover. Unfortunately, Ewans does not pursue the concept of conflict as consistently in his discussion of *The Ring* as he does with *Antigone* or the *Orestia*. Brünnhilde, for example, does not defeat power by overcoming Alberich's Curse, she *fulfills* that curse. It seems to me Ewans' conclusion about restoring the balance of nature ought to be that both power and love are put back into a state of potential for conflict (that is, that society reverts into the state of nature), just as they were at the beginning of *Das Rheingold* or in the form of the sleeping Brünnhilde at the end of *Die Walküre*.

21 In "The Pessimism of *The Ring*," Darcy analyses the last scene of *Götterdämmerung* arguing that redemption and transcendence are intimately linked "so Brünnhilde's love for her dead husband enables her to transcend the essential nullity of human existence." In the final music of *Götterdämmerung,* the rising Nature motif is countered by its inverse, the Twilight of the Gods: the will to live by the denial of the Will. Confronted with the prospect of denial, however, we cannot transcend life without destroying it, as Brünnhilde did herself. I contend, however, that Brünnhilde does not escape "nullity of human existence" for something better (what exactly is that supposed to be?) but, realizing human life to consist of inescapable illusions, ends her life with the illusion most important to her.

22 Wagner claimed that this idea came to him in a (strikingly Goethean) dream about the watery essence of the world, but see John Deathridge's doubts about the truth of Wagner's claim in *The New Grove Wagner*, p. 39.

23 See Cooke's discussion of Shaw, *I Saw the World End,* pp. 14 f. and pp. 269 f.

24 Ernst Newman, *The Wagner Operas* (New York: Harper, 1983), Vol. II, p. 509. Quoted in Cooke, *I Saw the World End,* p. 6.

25 Morse Peckham, *Beyond the Tragic Vision: The Quest for Identity in the Nineteenth Century* (New York: George Braziller, 1962), p. 253. See also the Appendix, Section 4.

26 Baron Hans von Wolzogen invented the term *Leitmotiv* and developed the first systematic attempt at identifying all of them in his *Die Tragödie in Bayreuth und ihr Satyrspiel* in 1877. See Cooke's important discussion and criticism of Wolzogen in *I Saw the World End,* pp. 38–56. A. Lorenz's

mammoth *Das Geheimnis der Form bei Richard Wagner* (4 volumes, 1924) stands as perhaps the most extreme example of the lengths to which Wagner scholars are willing to go for the sake of completeness. There are several more accessible (and briefer!) examples of formalistic treatments of the structure of *The Ring* in *Wagner 1976: A Celebration of the Bayreuth Festival* (London: Wagner Society, 1976). See in particular the articles by Erich Rappl and Marcel Barenko. For a particularly insightful discussion of musical structure of the last scene of *Die Walküre,* see Joseph Kerman, *Listen* (New York: Worth Publishers, 1987).

27 See Cooke's distinction between the "old" and "new" Wotans: "...the old, conservative, power-dominated side responsible for his creation of his authoritarian world with its immutable laws" and the "...new, progressive side, committed to circumventing these laws through his children the Walsungs [Volsungs], since his new side has as yet [in *Die Walküre* II] no real appreciation of the value of love" *I Saw the World End,* p. 324.

28 Porter's translation. Literally, however: "Whosoever *fears* my spear's point, may *he never pass* through the fire."

29 "Wagner's Musical Language," pp. 227 f.

30 L.J. Rather, *The Dream of Self-Destruction: Wagner's Ring and the Modern World* (Baton Rouge, Louisiana and London: Louisiana State University Press, 1979). Along with others, Rather overestimates Wagner's theoretical works. It is an exaggeration, for example, to contend that his prose works reveal his "greatness as a theoretician in the realm of the sociology of knowledge." Most of what he had to say he got from others, creatively adapting it to his aesthetic purposes. Wagner's greatness lies in his music-dramas; everything else merely supports those accomplishments.

31 For a sensitive and persuasive study of the tragedians, see Martha Nussbaum, *The Fragility of Goodness: Luck and Ethics in Greek Tragedy and Philosophy* (New York and Cambridge: Cambridge University Press, 1986). Nussbaum sees the contingency, and irony, of human life as essential for tragedy, and I believe this was also Nietzsche's view.

32 As Rather points out, Wagner's appeal to the interdependence between the forces of life and death anticipate Freud's *Civilization and its Discontents*. Hagen symbolizes the will to self-destruction of Wotan himself: a new society must be founded on the death of the old one. Where Siegfried sym-

bolizes the unconscious natural force of creation, Hagen symbolizes the force of destruction—both aspects of Wotan.

33 Thomas Mann, "Richard Wagner and *The Ring,*" in Thomas Mann, *Essays of Three Decades,* trans. H.T. Lowe-Porter. (New York: Alfred A. Knopf, 1948), pp. 368–9. It should be noted that the sense of mission that accompanies Siegfried expresses a very Germanic sentiment concerning the achievement of cultural and even racial unity extending back to Frederick the Great, to Luther, and beyond to the Teutonic Knights of the fifteenth century. This of course became an extremely volitile and problematic aspect of German politics in the 1920's and 30's.

Chapter Three

The Controversy Over *The Ring*

Of all Wagner's works, *The Ring* has been the most debated: One of the greatest works of art in Western civilization—or the most horrendously overrated/morally corrupting/misleading/etc.? Even more than today, during the late nineteenth century Wagner's music polarized listeners.[1] Even today he remains one of those few who continues to generate extreme reactions. In this chapter I discuss opposing views of *The Ring* by reviewing a very few examples from the vast critical literature surrounding it, but I attempt to do so in a way that leads to a better understanding of *The Ring* itself. I will not engage in debate simply because I disagree with what others have said about Wagner; disagreement, after all, should be put to some positive use. Controversy about art like this *can* be a symptom of its significance: if we can glimpse what that core of controversy might be, it ought to be our guide fully realizing that it *ought* to remain that way.

Both Theodor Adorno and Friedrich Nietzsche accuse Wagner of overwhelming reason through his technology of sound in order to further his romanticist political goals. They see in Wagner and his works an ideology of subjectivity, taking it as their duty to shake us free from the Wagnerian *Rausch* (intoxication), admonishing us to reject what they regard as its irrational quasi-religious sense of conversion. Conversion to what? Is there no more mature, contemplative character to his works? Wagner's music-dramas are about ideas and I have tried to show how they possess a complex intellectual content. Still, I willingly accept the principle that one can get only so much conceptual precision out of a work of art. It is more important for art to be suggestive and edifying, to provide us with new and unexpected ways of looking at the world. Works of art are not logical arguments, nor are they empirical generalizations. If we can judiciously discuss its 'ideas', however, we might become clearer what *The Ring* implies and then address the matter of Wagner's subjectivist ideology. While Adorno and Nietzsche view Wagner pessimistically, they do so against a tradition that sees him as a social optimist. In this Chapter I first deal with the optimistic reading of *The Ring,* taking as my main example the interpretation of the eminent German musicologist Carl Dahlhaus. This will take the next four sections. Then, in Sections 5–8, I turn to Adorno, Wagner's most trenchant twentieth-century critic from the Left. Finally, in Section 9, I have a few brief points to make about Nietzsche's rejection of Wagner.

1. Dahlhaus and the Optimistic *Ring*

For Dahlhaus, the explanation of the inconsistency of the various endings I discussed in Chapter 2, Section 1 must be that Wagner became distracted from his earlier 1853 ending when he abandoned its emphasis on the redemptive triumph of love over power.[2] He argues that the final ending (1856), with its "repudiation of the supremacy of love" (as Cooke puts it), indicates that Wagner had allowed himself to become misled by Schopenhauer in denying the revolutionary potential of redemptive love expressed in the 1853 version. Recall that in the earlier Feuerbachian ending, society was redeemed through Brünnhilde's exemplification of compassionate, humanized love between individuals (rather than divinely oriented transcendent love). In later versions, however, love seems to destroy everything. Dahlhaus claims that neither the earlier Feuerbachian nor the Schopenhauerian ending is clearly implied by the final version (although Wagner said the "I saw the world end" ending *was* implied by final version). Nevertheless Wagner was "deceived as to the meaning of his own work" (p. 140) and the authentic ending should be the earlier social utopian one of 1852: "his first conception was also his last." (In his later *Grove* article Dahlhaus softens this view saying that Wagner leaves the ending of *The Ring* "open to interpretation," p. 84.)

Dahlhaus employs two major arguments:

> A. The overall concept of Love in *Die Walküre* III and in *Siegfried* III places it in opposition to Wotan's world of power and renunciation. The optimism of love envisages reconciliation in a future society. (Dahlhaus might also have pointed to the love of Siegmund and Sieglinde, especially Siegmund's rejection of Valhalla's "paltry charms" in favor of the bond of love with Sieglinde.) As Ronald Gray puts it in a similar interpretation: "What remains in the music is not pure Schopenhauer after all. After the destruction of Valhalla, the audience is left confronting not an awful emptiness, no gaping, terrible Naught, but the Love motif [Redemption Through Love]. But Love implies beings, relationships which Schopenhauer's Naught cannot tolerate." *The Ring* is about the "continuance of love beyond the grave" and not Nirvana—Novalis and not destruction.[3]
>
> B. The famous Redemption Through Love motif that closes the work and foretells the birth of Siegfried in Sieglinde's "O radiant Wonder" in *Die Walküre* IIIi (the first of only two

occurrences of this motif) indicates that love not only opposes power but actually overcomes it. This music was also composed to fit the 1852 ending and was worked back into *Die Walküre* later (Act IIIi). The reoccurrence of the motif at the end of the work clearly shows the triumph of love connected with its earlier occurrence where it symbolizes the hope of a new era of human freedom. Love thus vanquishes power when it expresses "the freedom of human consciousness" (as Wagner wrote in his 1848 sketch).

Dahlhaus contends that Wagner did not explicitly return to the specifics of his early utopian ending because the final ending of 1874 best dichotomized the extremes of resignation and denial, on the one hand, and transcendence and love, on the other. That is, Wagner de-emphasized the political and social theme of *The Ring,* conceived under the influences of Hegel and Feuerbach, to the extent of contrasting his utopian optimism with the metaphysics of Schopenhauer. This allowed him to show the dialectical advance of social redemption over both renunciation and the unbridled appeal to power. (Dahlhaus does not use this terminology, yet if Wagner did indeed revert to his Feuerbachian roots, the language of the Young Hegelians ought to be appropriate.)

There are two major difficulties with these lines of argument: first, as Roger Hollinrake points out, Dahlhaus assumes that Wagner rejected Schopenhauer almost completely and reverted entirely to his original optimistic conception of *The Ring* in the versions spanning 1848–1956.[4] But even if he did reject Schopenhauer's determinism and anti-individualism, Wagner may have remained in partial agreement with Schopenhauer about renunciation and the denial of the will as metaphysical forces—they became forces of creation as well as destruction. In fact, as I try to show in the previous chapter and in the Appendix, Wagner did not in the end completely disagree with Schopenhauer. Wagner's linkages between renunciation and redemption, and between power and love, are due to Schopenhauer's influence. Although he was not the pessimist about personhood that Schopenhauer was, Wagner did see it as a construct rather than a given, and that raises a question about the role of optimism in his work.

Hollinrake rightly questions the inferences drawn by Dahlhaus. For example, Wagner's retreat from the brink of world-renunciation to the early sketch of 1848 was made possible by his "slight modification" of the Will to mean sexual love between man and woman (as he described it in a letter to Mathilde Wesendonk, with whom he at least tried to have an affair, causing the break-up of his marriage). Reemphasizing this Feuerbachian view of love surely led to a major humanization of Schopenhauer's Will, but to see Brünnhilde's love as the basis for universal social redemption from conflict simply does not follow from this. Other interpretations are possible and, I believe, better suited to the complexities of Wagner's insight and to the subtlety of his musical symbolism as the work developed over the next thirty years.

The major change in Wagner's conception of *The Ring,* I contend, involves the enlargement of the context of the work with the result that his earlier political/social drama of social redemption became only one of its levels rather than its whole point. Because of what happens at the other levels, the utopian optimism of the earlier version of the drama fundamentally changes its central point. It has in fact been "overturned" in the sense of being *Aufgehoben*—to use the intentionally ambiguous German philosophical term Hegel depended on so much. *Aufheben* (n., *Aufhebung*) means to raise up (to preserve or keep) but also to annul or cancel (to break up or abolish). Feuerbach's social optimism about the triumph of social responsibility over alienation remains in *The Ring* as the substitution of human love over divine authority, but Wagner seems to have gotten confirmation from Schopenhauer of the possibility that our utopian dreams can lead to destruction. He therefore retained the idea of change along with the story about the origins of human value based on love, but not with the social optimism he had earlier attached to it. Indeed, understanding the problems of *The Ring* as a result of Wotan's failure to compromise, or from Wotan's or Alberich's denial of basic human rights, problems to be overcome by compassion and love and other Enlightenment conceptions of humanity, completely misses the import of Wagner's reconception of the work. Paradoxically, Wagner is an optimist—not about politics, however, or even about love. He is an optimist about energy; he believes that the balance between creation and destruction, however slightly, tips towards creation. But it is always in *precarious* balance, and that insight leads to a very different *Ring* than that implied by its earlier conceptions.

I argue in the Appendix that, like *Faust* and Hegel's *Phenomenology* at the beginning of the century, *The Ring* rejects the Enlightenment's realist conception of human nature as a discoverable, fixed essence. Perhaps this is why this work remains so troubling, for many of our own conceptions of mankind and society still derive from the Enlightenment. Wagner, along with others in the nineteenth century such as Schopenhauer, Nietzsche, Marx, and later, Freud and Heidegger in the twentieth, believed that there are unresolvable tensions within our conception of the self, and within the societies we have created, that prevent us from living in the way Plato or Aristotle, or Jesus, or Locke or Rousseau or Kant, or even Hobbes and Hume had hoped. For Wagner, as for some other of his contemporaries, I suggest, we cannot discover a stable image of humanity that will provide us with absolute, universally exportable social and moral concepts, empowering us to resolve the inevitable conflicts between locally differing views of value and happiness.

The Enlightenment's metaphysical foundations for scientific theories of human nature had become extremely dubious by the mid-nineteenth century. By the twentieth century, the focus human sciences shifted (in the work of Wilhelm Dilthey, Max Weber, and Emil Durkheim, for example) towards describing the *processes* and *structures* of personhood and society rather continuing the search for *essential attributes*. The emerging view, originally Hegel's, was that those processes change us and therefore change the concepts of Value and Happiness on which we operate both individually and socially. The nineteenth-century artists and philosophers I have been discussing suggest that we take contingency seriously, and this applies to developmental views of human nature too. What we might become certainly depends on what we have been and are, but even the bud-blossom-fruit analogy Hegel used in the Preface to the *Phenomenology of Spirit* to describe the birth of ideas and civilizations alike depends on the assumption that we are going somewhere in particular (see Appendix, Section 2). Immediately after Hegel, the question raised by Schopenhauer, Nietzsche, Wagner and others was "Where?" They accepted Hegel's evolutionary analogies (except for Schopenhauer) but questioned his rationalism.

By modifying his conception of *The Ring* from that of a *Grosse Heldenoper* (with its emphasis on Siegfried's redemptive heroism) to that of a *Grosse Welttragödie* (to a work about the tragedy of the universe generally and the destructive power of love) Wagner did something more than show how the evils of power are overcome by love. *The Ring* became a work centering on the problem of renunciation in the characters of Wotan and Brünnhilde, and on the tragic (and even comic) nature of conflict between love and power that finally emerged as the core of the work. As Cooke puts it, "clearly, Wagner began the text of *The Ring* with the intention of making it say one thing only, and gradually completed the whole music-drama so that it went on to say other and opposite things as well" (*I Saw the World End*, p. 23). It became a work about the conflict *between* power and love and not about the *victory* of love (symbolizing humanity) over power (the gods). *The Ring* does indeed center on the *hope* of that victory, but it also emphasizes the tragic implications of that hope in that the very conception of conflict implies the inability to ultimately determine the nature of reality—or human nature.

Wagner perhaps also got from Hegel's conception of *aufheben* the idea that societies develop through higher levels of conflict, but without any single normative ideal achieving absolute victory or permanence: permanent evolution. Conflict constitutes *higher* levels of civilization because on-going resolutions of conflict require higher levels of reason made more and more explicit. For Hegel, in every period of Western civilization, in every story we have told about value and human nature, crises have emerged that have *always* changed the direction of that developmental process. Christianity changed the Hellenic ideal of Athens and Rome (the soul is more important than civilization); the Enlightenment challenged Christianity (reason leads to science and theology had to measure up to its rational standards); and finally the nineteenth century challenged realism.

The Ring shows how these kinds of changes happen through its story of love and power as the formative dichotomy in our civilization. How we handle the relations between them portrays the personality of our civilization.

So, in the destruction of Valhalla, the sense of the 1856 ending ("I saw the world end") carries through into the final version. But if the effect suggests Schopenhauer's Eastern conception of the unity of all things in the Will, it also remains thoroughly Western in its acceptance of the dignity of humanity in the hope of redemption, and its conception of the relation between moral and social theory. While the final version does not show the victory of love over power, it does show their interdependence. The essence of reality has become conflict rather than resolution (as portrayed in the earlier versions) and Wagner's symbolic destruction of the aristocracy became a metaphysical indicator of this deeper point about civilization. The penultimate 'Buddhist' ending faintly lingers to show the idealized hope of transcendent redemption through love, but it dissolves into the universal force of the Will as conflict only momentarily resolved. The point, however, is not to show us the *path* of redemption through transcendent love, and the illusoriness (changeability and contingency) of society, but to underscore the illusory permanence of *both* redemptive heroism and romantic love underlying the social and personal conflicts of *The Ring*.

The second difficulty for Dahlhaus' position, setting aside the issue of relating the different versions, or of establishing Wagner's intentions (which clearly changed often over the years of composing *The Ring*), rests on the obvious fact that the later versions of the work embody a view of the relations between power and love, renunciation and pacification, and hope and destruction clearly inconsistent with the early versions. If Wagner did not simply return to his earlier socialist ideals, how does the last version differ from the Feuerbachian, utopian, humanistic transcendence of capitalism and Christianity? The social interpretation of *The Ring* remains an important aspect of the final version and some of the personal political commentary originally attached to the characters of Wotan and Siegfried also undoubtedly remains.

For example, the cycle can easily be seen to be a symbolic story about the rise and fall of the aristocracy with Wotan as Frederick II of Saxony, whose actions precipitated the revolutionary events of 1848–9 and cost Wagner his position as royal Kapellmeister. In this story, Siegfried can be seen as a Bakunin-like revolutionary overturning the *status quo*. But describing *The Ring* essentially as social drama, and using *The Perfect Wagnerite* as a production guide (as one might well see the Boulez/Chereau Bayreuth productions in the late 1970's), distorts the broader features of the work. The last version extends from the primordial beginnings of presocial existence, to the political-social understanding of value. But it goes beyond this to encompass at least two further levels: the conflict between the personal and the social, and finally a metaphysical level wherein the personal and social aspects of the drama are understood through Wagner's modified Schopenhauerian account of the Will.[5] I therefore agree with Cooke that *The Ring* cannot be understood on a single level (*I Saw the World End,* p. 247), but I want to take this point further. Although the problem of social injustice remains embedded in the work until its last version, in *Götterdämmerung* the overall context of representation and understanding has become metaphysical and not political. Dahlhaus' reading of *The Ring* ignores these crucial aspects.

2. Love and Redemption

The cohesiveness of Wagner's music I tried to describe in the previous two chapters carries through to the so-called motif of Redemption Through Love, or Love's Redemption. It is not, as Dahlhaus suggests, an isolated reference to the transcendence of love in the two places where it occurs. In what I described above as Dahlhaus' second argument, he implies that this music stands alone, essentially unrelated to the other thematic elements of *The Ring*. But even though it was composed later, it clearly and closely resembles the music associated with Brünnhilde's humanity, with the motif Donington calls Brünnhilde's Holy Love, and with the Siegmund/Sieglinde music (and hence Freia II). One can also hear an obviously similar theme associated with Brünnhilde at the beginning of the second dawn of the Prolog of *Götterdämmerung* as Brünnhilde and Siegfried awaken. Redemption Through Love shares the same appogiatura phrase—with its clear reference to the Fate music (as I pointed out in Chapter 2, Section 3 the same modulation of the Fate motif appears in the first phrase of Redemption Through Love). We can also see a connection with the Destiny of the Volsungs and with the motif of the Rhinemaiden's Innocence. "Redemption Through Love" got its name from Wolzogen whereas Wagner himself called it (as I pointed out in Chapter 1) a "glorification of Brünnhilde," a characterization of her role in Wotan's search for redemption. This role, and her love of Siegfried as well as her compassion for Siegmund and Sieglinde, makes *her*, not Siegfried, the primary symbol of redemption in *The Ring*. Her family of motifs projects that symbolism as it connects to Love's Redemption.[6] As Cooke points out, both parts of the Freia motif symbolize love as it grows from sexuality to compassion for humanity (*I Saw the World End,* p. 63). Love's Redemption should be seen as, and can easily be seen as, the culmination of the many variations of Freia I and II as well as a reflection of the Destiny of the Volsung motif.

When Love's Redemption occurs for the last time at the end of *The Ring,* it does not, therefore, simply refer back to Sieglinde's hope (and implicitly to both Wotan's and Brünnhilde's as well). While in Sieglinde's case it anticipates the birth of Siegfried, at the end of *Götterdämmerung* it immediately preceeds the Valhalla and Siegfried motifs and in its final reocurrence follows the Twilight of the Gods. Here the references to Siegfried are retrospective—a memory, even a caricature (given the inadequacy of his actual performance). But the hope of Siegfried's redemptive potential failed in part *because* of the very love it embodied. The motif of Redemption Through Love symbolizes that hope, but it also symbolizes the dream of transcending conflict through *Wotan's* denial of the Will and escape from the evils of power. The referential richness of the final occurrence of the motif lies in its association with the mythology of romantic love. But what role does love play in the cycle? In part, Redemption Through Love links together the love motifs I have just noted showing the development of love from its innocent sexual origins to humanistic altruism growing out of the personal bonds of affection and trust between lovers. What happens to the characters involved in the complexities of love? When the Redemption motif first appears in *Die Walküre,* it foretells Siegfried's birth as the hope embodied in the trust and love of Siegmund and Sieglinde, expressed and culminating in the related love motifs in Act I. But what happens to Siegfried? Does he redeem anything at all in Dahlhaus' sense—or does his 'betrayal' of Brünnhilde simply release the power of destruction within her? Redemption Through Love, I contend, symbolizes the power of love, undoubtedly a power that redeems, but in what sense does it redeem?

As we have seen, the complexities of Wagner's conception of love grew out of the Feuerbachian theory of *eros,* a continuing aspect that carries through to the final version of *The Ring*. But in the final version the redemptive portrayal of love contrasts directly with the renunciation of power. Here love does not merely oppose power; it is an opposition through conflict. Indeed conflict has become essential to the evolution of love from innocent sexuality to compassion. The actual role of love and in the cycle emphasizes its power to change persons and societies. This transforming potential, however, implies something far different than Feuerbach's social optimism and the advent of humanism through the destruction of divine, but alien, authority that we see in the earlier versions of *The Ring*. In the later versions, love does not triumph over evil in the sense of eliminating alien authority by establishing a new form of society based on conflict-free human values because the very the nature of value has become the issue in this work. After witnessing the effects of love on Wotan, Brünnhilde, and Siegfried, the final occurrence of Redemption Through Love at the end of *Götterdämmerung* can no longer invoke the optimism of a new age of humanity based compassion rather than politics. Instead, it involves the realization of the interconnectedness of love and power as the source of change and unity in our own self-image. Love transcends death not by defeating evil but by perpetuating this process of change. Love's Redemption, at the end of *Götterdämmerung*, symbolizes not the escape from that process but its realization.

Optimistic interpretations of *The Ring* fail to see that the implicitness of the Fate motif in the Love music—including Redemption Through Love—rests on this larger story of the interdependence between love and power, something Wagner began to see more clearly after reading Schopenhauer and talking to Nietzsche. Perhaps this is why *Das Rheingold* fits as well as it does with the rest of *The Ring* in spite of its radical change of direction later on. The Feuerbachian, Hegelian origins of the work remained because they were seen to be earlier stages of a yet larger story about the conflict between love and power. This point helps us to understand the connection between culture and belief, mankind and nature, love and freedom in all of Wagner's later works. In the evolution of love from *eros* to *agape*, love remains inescapably sexual and individualized however much it involves the dream of transcendence. For Wagner, we never transcend ourselves because we cannot transcend *eros*. And because *eros* takes many forms, as many as we can invent.

In what sense then *does* love overcome power or evil in *The Ring*? Once again: What, exactly, does Brünnhilde redeem in the final moments of *Götterdämmerung*? *Wotan's* hope for a society free from emasculating contracts? She never expresses such general sentiments. *Her* idea of society based on compassionate love rather than selfish instinct? Love certainly does not overcome evil or power in the sense of the German word *Überwindung* (to subdue or to overcome by beating down or defeating); the right word here, again, should be *aufheben*—being preserved as well as canceled. If love becomes a form of power, it also remains love. *Aufheben* best describes what happens to society and the self through the transformation of the conflict between love and power into higher, more complex stages of cultural development. It suggests that Wagner never did completely give up all of his earlier Hegelianism—indeed, that he relied on one of Hegel's most important insights by making it the central subject of *The Ring*.

Understanding the chief motivation of life and society through the interaction between love and power in *The Ring* also involves a kind of *Aufhebung* on our part. The conflicts of every age abolish something of value, but they also create something new on the basis of old distinctions and traditions. We can appreciate this only by understanding the ambiguity implicit in creation: the new depends on the old. While Wagner's reading of Schopenhauer disabused him of the optimism that characterized the Left Hegelianism of his youth, the final version does not portray the anti-individualism of Schopenhauer's pessimism; it does not conflate Brünnhilde's self-destruction with redemptive *Überwindung*. Neither does the outcome of *The Ring* imply a return to the Hegelian/Feuerbachian resolution of love overcoming unreason, of good overcoming evil and leading to the next, more rational level of civilization. It rather portrays the revitalizing power of contingency. All our resolutions are subject to *aufheben*. The process of holding onto what is dear to us, fraught with struggle, conflict, and change, changes us. This happens to Brünnhilde, and perhaps this is what she sees at the end in her fantasy of rejoining poor Siegfried, who at the point of his own death achieved at best the faintest glimmering of this point.

3. Politics and Conflict

In the next two sections I concentrate on the concept of Conflict by focusing on the character of Wotan. For Dahlhaus, Wotan's self-destruction opens the way for "mankind to attain to consciousness of its freedom."[7] As the original Feuerbach ending has it, humanity will be released from the fear and desperation justly befalling the gods in Erda's prophecy. For Dahlhaus, an outside agency destroys Siegfried and Brünnhilde; their love is overcome by a world "in opposition to it," by Wotan's will to power and its effects. Love nevertheless promises a future society without the corrupting domination of power—the first conception of *The Ring,* and the one reinstated with the music of Redemption Through Love, reasserts this Feuerbachian optimism after the misguided interlude of Wagner's Schopenhauerian pessimism.

Under my interpretation, however, this view leaves out the deeper role of conflict in *The Ring,* one more complex than the visionary dialectic of Feuerbach's redemptive humanism. Dahlhaus infers that Wotan's willing his destruction in *Die Walküre* IIii opens the way to a new kind of society. He hopes for a just society brought about by a hero free from his control who can do what he cannot—act compassionately without being compelled by law or by the will of another agency. He must give up Siegmund as this redemptive hero because of Fricka's demand that he must obey his own laws, and this brings about his monologue in *Die Walküre* IIii. In Act III however, (transformed into what Cooke calls "the new Wotan" because of the compassion achieved through his self-understanding in that monologue) he tries to find another hero through his own renunciation of power. His despair again turns to hope. Wotan steps aside for that hero in *Siegfried* IIIii, hoping that this one has enough autonomy and authority for the job. He thus retires from the scene to let Siegfried accomplish the goal of establishing a new society founded on love as he sets off to awaken Brünnhilde and discover fear.

In his monologue in *Die Walküre* IIii, and its minute, almost Shakespearean depiction of the transformation of his character, Wotan comes to see his problem not simply as the frustration of his will but of the clash between his will and reality: by his treaties he rules, but they enslave him too. Can he be a true source of order without treating his society as an object, manipulated to accord with his desires? As he says in exasperation, realizing his problem in the creation of his society, "I find myself/in everything that my hand has created":"Zum Ekel find ich/ewig nur mich/in allem, was ich erwirke!"(Porter's translation (with performance in mind) might more accurately be rendered: "With disgust I eternally find myself in everything I have created.") Such a society would indeed be the opposite of one built on and sustained by the free choices of its members, a society based on agreements about central values and on the consent of the governed. Wotan in effect wants to establish society in the Enlightenment sense, as a rational act of will, but finds himself in a dilemma: if he continually intervenes to protect it, he manipulates and violates the rules of that society (the drama of Siegmund and Sieglinde) but if he stands back and renounces power, society will collapse because of the external threat of the absolutely unenlightened Alberich. In willing his own destruction, Wotan thus tries to eliminate fear as the motivating foundation of society, leaving the way open for love in the form of Siegfried's protection of Brünnhilde from Alberich. Who would enter into a contract with *him*? But this does not lead, as Dahlhaus suggests, to the final victory of love as a redeeming social force, as the new authority establishing the identity of the self. It leads to the destruction of everything the new Wotan hoped for too. He may be relieved when Siegfried shatters his spear in *Siegfried* IIIii but, given what he has learned, how can he realistically hope that his society will be redeemed? But, of course, hope is often unrealistic.

Under Dahlhaus' reading, Wotan does not will his own destruction as an end in itself but as a means for establishing a society free from fear and oppression. For my reading, he does not achieve his goal because the *love* to which he has appealed becomes destructive when manipulated by Wotan. It destroys the society he dreams of along with those who could achieve it. In effect, perhaps after reading Schopenhauer, Wagner came to see that the Enlightenment conception of harmonious society must be impossible because the Will can never be pacified, stability never achieved. Wotan wants a world without the unpredictable inconveniences of arbitrary power, but such a world proves to be impossible because Wotan can find no limit to power. Even love, by which he tries to redeem himself, cannot limit power but merely give it new expression. Now while Siegmund and Sieglinde are certainly destroyed by outside influences—by Wotan himself enforcing the laws of his society—Brünnhilde directly participates in the destruction of Siegfried. Indeed, her own destruction, in large part, results from what she has done herself, not by what was done to her by Hagen. We see this clearly in her scene with Waltraute in *Götterdämmerung* Iiii when she refuses to give the ring back to the Rhinemaidens just before Siegfried returns disguised as Gunther to capture her. Since she knows the consequences, why does she refuse? After meeting Siegfried, why does the ring mean so much to her?

The Ring does not, therefore, end with a resolution of conflict. Where for Feuerbach and Hegel the universe became increasingly human through conflict (for Hegel, like Wotan, *we* increasingly find ourselves in what we create), Wagner introduced Schopenhauer's emphasis on the unresolvable strangeness and inhumanity of the universe. For Hegel, the tiny campfire of human society started centuries ago will eventually engulf the universe itself in flames of civilization and reason as humanity achieves harmony with nature. For Wagner, civilization can never unlock the mystery of the relation between spirit and nature and its campfire may be extinguished by the most rational, best-intentioned efforts of mankind itself. This vision of the possibility of failure—failure resulting from the optimistic pursuit of our highest ideals—lies at the heart of Wagner's *Aufhebung* of Feuerbach's view of love.

If one were to characterize "the old Wotan's" political theory at the beginning of *The Ring*, it might be something like that of Thomas Hobbes in the *Leviathan*: a mutual relation based on obedience and protection founded on the natural instinct to self-preservation.[8] Hobbes, however, saw power both as the foundation of society and its greatest problem:

> I put for a general inclination of all mankind, a perpetual and restless desire of power after power, that ceaseth only in death. And the cause of it, is not always that a man hopes for a more intensive delight, than he has already attained to; of that he cannot be content with a moderate power: but because he cannot assure the power and means to live well, which he hath present, without the acquisition of more.[9]

Wotan comes to realize exactly this in his Act II monologue. Wagner's revised Hegelianism (conflict, yes; interaction, definitely; progress, up to a point, but not necessarily) holds that all forms of society, all value, are based on conflict because we cannot avoid disagreements about what we all ought to desire. Can our aggressive tendencies *ever* be fully tamed by the social contract? Are those bonds strong enough to hold society together while still preventing self-destructive conflict? Does the contrasting motivation of love provide another, better foundation than the contractual limitation of power?

Wotan's attempts at social engineering rested on his vision (symbolized by Valhalla) and, consequently, on the question of the uses of power. At the beginning of his monologue, Wotan describes his lust for power. He created a new social world, wrenching it out of nature, but yet he acted wrongly. With the help of Loge's legal skills, he built an army of men held in bondage to him that he thought Brünnhilde would lead in defending Valhalla from Alberich, saying to her "you would assemble my army:/the men whom we held/by our laws in bondage,/the mortals, whom we/had curbed in their pride/whom by treacherous treaties,/shameful agreements,/we'd bound in obedience/blindly to serve us": "hiess ich euch Helden mir schaffen;/die herrish wir sonst/in Gesetzen hielten,/die Männer, denen/den Mut wir gewehrt,/die durch trüber Verträge/trügende Bande/zu blindem Gehorsam/wir uns gebunden." How can he so ruthlessly control others *and* require their freely given loyalty? Wotan came to see that his view of society, indeed his conception of himself as its ruler, was a threat to the freedom and autonomy of others when he undertook to preserve his society from Alberich—and even before when he took Alberich's ring. If compassion became the root of the new Wotan's *persona* in his final scene with Brünnhilde in *Die Walküre* IIIiii, he has *not* found a less arbitrary basis for his society in the sense of finding a way to save it from change by grounding it on a more authentic value than that of his own will to power. Indeed, he has *not* stopped willing. That is the point Dahlhaus overlooks. In his identification of the Will with sex, including compassion, Wagner indicates how change and conflict must be inevitable in personhood and so in society itself.

Like Hegel's master, in order to rule Wotan needs the recognition of his society just as Hobbes's atomistic individuals require mutual respect (or at least mutual fear) for their contracts to work, for them to form social molecules. Without that recognition, Wotan lacks authority because his nobility can be reflected only in the actively accepted social principles of justice and freedom. But when Wotan steps outside of these principles in *Das Rheingold*, his nobility vanishes and his society begins to crumble. He protects justice with injustice, freedom with bondage. When the new Wotan withdraws from his society in the hope that an autonomous hero will be able to establish both freedom and order, he believes that he has opened the way for a willful hero free from the desire for domination. But *any willing at all*, even compassion, involves some form of control. As Wotan characterizes himself metaphorically to Siegfried in the Wanderer scene, *Siegfried* IIIii, he wears his hat down over his eyes because "That's how the Wanderer wears it,/when against the wind he must go":"Das ist so des Wand'rers Weise,/wenn dem Wind entgegen er geht." The wind of opposition always blows *against* initiative. But Wotan perceives the flaw of his society: justice and freedom can only be fashioned within society through the efforts of its members, they cannot be imposed by an authority external to it, his original Hobbesian act. He thus stands aside for Siegfried at the end of that scene, his spear broken by Notung. When he reforged the sword in *Siegfried* Iiii, Siegfried was accompanied by an upward interval followed by a downward run in the brass signifying opposition to Wotan's spear, presaging their confrontation in Act IIIii..

The story of Siegfried and Brünnhilde also shows that we misunderstand love if we see it as the transcendence of society, as the rejection of social bonds as contracts for some more authentic connection to each other. Because it exists within society, for Wagner, love is *always* social, it does not *become* social.

The oppositions between power and love, society and freedom, selfish individuality and the greatest good for the greatest number were to have been overcome in the Enlightenment by a clearer view of what humans are, so that society could be reconstructed to enhance the positive attributes of reason, compassion, and self-interest as sources of the good life. With Rousseau and then Kant and Goethe, and later on with Nietzsche, however, the question about whether there actually was a definition of human value that could function as the foundation for social theory became deeply vexed. No recognition of this controversy appears in Dahlhaus' interpretation of the social drama symbolizing the nineteenth-century rejection of the Enlightenment. As I understand it, however, *The Ring* expresses fundamental doubts about the social optimism that inspired its earlier versions.

4. Appearance and Reality: Wotan's Inner-life and Politics

I have mentioned before that the monologues or soliloquies of *The Ring* sometimes seem to hold up the action. But they represent the fears, hopes, and beliefs of the characters and it is through them that we see the interdependence of the inner- and the outer-worlds—one of the chief aspects of Wagner's conception of music-drama. Many critics, including Adorno, point out that these monologues supply verbal accounts of actions accompanied by musically primitive signpost-leitmotifs and during which the minimal musical coherence Wagner achieved grinds to a halt. Near the beginning of Chapter 2, I quoted Emil Staiger's concern about coherence: the complexity of the motifs and their micro-extensions of the text threaten dramatic continuity. Granting that Wagner did indeed sometimes have difficulties with stagnation, and admitting that the coherence of *The Ring* suffers in comparison *Die Meistersinger* or *Parsifal,* these monologues should be seen as narratives rather than chronicles. They are not mere accounts of past actions and events but descriptions of them from the point of view of the narrator, from the point of view of his or her interests. As I pointed out in Chapter 2, the doctrine of *Opera and Drama* holds that the real "drama" occurs inside the minds of the characters, their inner-lives are the reality to be portrayed, and the contrast between those hopes and fears, on the one hand, and the outer-world provide the basic dramatic linchpin for *The Ring*.

The crucial role of Wotan's monologue in *Die Walküre* lays out the moral dilemma of his struggle for power. We experience the conflict between his hopes and recalcitrant outer reality *as it seems to him*. We need to know what a character believes in order to understand this contrast. For example, without Wotan's original Hobbesian willfulness and his dream of social order there would not have been a society at all. His creation of order out of chaos depended on his vision of value in his attempt to stabilize nature, to bring the world under his control. His social commitment comes through in this monologue. In Wotan's mind Valhalla symbolizes a just society created out of his own moral resources, his own hopes and his own moral horizon. This and the other monologues give us representations of the minds of the characters contrasted with the dynamic flow of the world around them (bearing in mind that he took tragedy as a model).

The course of Wotan's self-analysis indicates his growing understanding of the nature of the world defined through conflict. As Windell points out in his discussion of this monologue, the shift Wotan's personality undergoes there resembles Hegel's conception of self-consciousness through the understanding of ones interdependence with others.[10] He has enslaved himself by his treaties but, in realizing this, Wotan passes from the previously limited perception of his relationship to his society to a deeper realization of the corrosive effects of his quest for power on his own values. He begins to understand Erda's warning when he sees how he has become enmeshed in the struggle for control and this leads to his renunciation of direct action; but in Act III we also see Wotan's hope that the opposition between power and love can be turned to his own advantage, with love forming the basis of a new society. He hopes that somehow he can indirectly get compassion and freedom back into the world if his hero, his "friendly enemy," can repossess the ring and take it away from those who would misuse it. Perhaps, Wotan seems to think, the curse will not then apply because he will not be directly involved.

Realizing his own destructiveness, in trying to protect his society from Alberich, Wotan foresees and even welcomes *das Ende* in his monologue. He desires his own destruction as a means to what he hopes will be a society that does not compromise its (and his) nobility. Wotan's end has the sense of the conclusion of his futile attempts to save his society by direct interference (the optimistic interpretations are quite right about this point). He realizes that his 'end' coincides with the end of society as he knows it. His original creative intention, however, leads not to a new society but to a kind of destructiveness he could not imagine, and it is here that the optimistic interpretation goes wrong. He desperately wants to get love and freedom back into his society and does so by changing his own relationship to Brünnhilde. Wotan in essence, as I suggested in the previous chapter, tries to compromise with Erda in the form of a trade-off. By renouncing the direct use of power, he removes himself from the chain of events, but he tries to arrange things so that redemption will result. I tried to show, however, that the catastrophic end of society in *The Ring* does not rest on the failure to compromise, or even on Wotan always trying to get his own way. Wotan's downfall owes as much to his desire for compromise (at least as he sees it) as anything else. The kinds of changes he fears are inevitable, compromise or not.

The musical references in Wotan's monologue are not mere signposts; they depict the world *as Wotan understands it*. Wotan's ambiguities, the inconsistencies of his hopes and fears, the conflict between his dream of control and the world, become fully explicit through the interaction between the orchestra and the stage with motifs such as Alberich's Curse and the Power of the Ring pointing to the larger context of Wotan's frustration, the motif of which occurs frequently in this scene. In the descending bass register of the beginning of the monologue, we are taken into the depths of Wotan's beliefs. As it progresses, the music shows how he begins to realize the inescapability of the effects of power on him and his society. We see his hopes and beliefs against the metaphysical background comprising the conflict between the inner- and outer-worlds. When he realizes that he cannot have both ultimate control and the free participation of his fellow citizens, he begins to conceive of himself as torn between love and power, as if they are mutually exclusive forces. The same vision drives Siegfried and Brünnhilde to renounce the political in their acceptance of love. But love and power are *not* mutually exclusive and the destructive delusions of both Wotan and Brünnhilde rest on that seeming dichotomy. We cannot achieve freedom and compassion simply by renouncing power, they require action too. We see in *Götterdämmerung* how love becomes power, how it was already implicit in Wotan's compassionate farewell to Brünnhilde at the end of *Die Walküre*. Because of Wotan's obsession with redemptive heroism, he envisages Brünnhilde as a source of love and the basis for a better world when she becomes the ultimate test for Siegfried's heroism. (My specialized use of the distinction between illusion and delusion receives more discussion in the Appendix, Section 5.)

The symbolic imagery of the motif of the Sleeping Brünnhilde introduced at the end of *Die Walküre*, also implying the decline of the gods, signifies the potential of redemption seen from the shortened view of Wotan's hopes. From the longer view, the "opposite things" Cooke sees in *The Ring* tell a deeper story about the insurmountable opposition and interdependence between power and love entangling both Wotan and Brünnhilde. Wotan's hope to change the foundation of his society from power to love ironically confronts the impossibility of escaping the will to power. As Nietzsche put it, life in all its forms *is* the will to power. In his attempt to connect the world of action with his visionary project, Wotan ensures only that what will happen in his world will be exactly the opposite of what he hopes for—as that final reference to Fate in *Die Walküre* implies. The sleeping but now human Brünnhilde, when awakened to be driven only by love, symbolizes the potential for destruction. As I tried to show in Chapter 2, Section 5, creation and destruction merge in her character, symbolized in her Magic Sleep music. All of this can easily be seen as a ramification of Master/Slave dialectics—if power and love cannot be disentangled, the Feuerbachian ending cannot be the final one for *The Ring*.

In one of his letters to August Röckel, Wagner describes his changing conception of the relationship between the social and musical levels of *The Ring* as the contrast between phases in the development of the world and the essence of the world itself. The world as it appears to us—including society—is "nothing" in the metaphysical sense because it is the result of a process that cannot be fully understood from the world of appearances alone. He describes this larger process, in his modification of the Will as the "essence of the world itself"—in my terms as the apparent opposition between power and love seen ultimately as their interdependence. I believe that the essence of Wagner's modification of Schopenhauer comes down to his concentration on the phenomenal world as it exemplifies the inscrutability of the Will, the forever indeterminate essence of reality and the self.

5. Adorno's Wagner: The Glorification of Destruction

Although Theodor Adorno's criticisms of Wagner are made from a socialist perspective that Nietzsche rejected, *In Search of Wagner* bears more than a passing resemblance to the latter's almost-too-late realization of Wagner's "decadence." Both saw in Wagner an evil genius manipulating an unsuspecting, but eventually slavish public through the force of sound and a socially subversive ideology of romanticized subjectivism—Klingsor, the diabolical magician from *Parsifal*, masquerading as the socially respectable, but revolutionary in disguise, Hans Sachs. This witches' brew of sound and sensuality substitutes erotic passivity for redemptive social action and achieves transcendence through the denial of humanity. Both Nietzsche and Adorno, however, seriously and often willfully misunderstood Wagner. I do not believe that Wagner was an apologist for antisocial subjectivism and "bourgeois sensuality." In fact, these are the central aspects of Western civilization that he explores with as much critical force as Nietzsche—or Adorno himself—although he does so as an artist with philosophical pretensions. But their vehement rejection of Wagner seems to me to rest on confusion about a false dichotomy between idealized humanistic redemption and decadent, pessimistic renunciation.

For example, in *Nietzsche Contra Wagner,* Nietzsche describes the psychological effect of what can only be the Prelude to *Tristan*:

> Swimming, floating—no longer walking, dancing…. The "infinite melody" seeks deliberately to break all evenness of time and force…. The imitation or domination of such a taste would result in a danger to music which cannot be exaggerated: the complete degeneration of the rhythmic feeling, *chaos* in place of rhythm…. *Espressivo* at any price and music in the

service of, the slavery, of poses—*that is the end.* ("Wagner as a Danger," in Kaufmann, *The Portable Nietzsche,* pp. 666–667)

Adorno was to put it no better. But how much of this describes precisely the effect Wagner intended to achieve in that revolutionary Prelude? How much of Wagner's "attitudinizing" in reality portrays romantic sexual desire in a way never before achieved in music—and for a larger purpose? So much the worse, Nietzsche would say: Wagner *intentionally* corrupts our spirit by championing transcendence of the phenomenal world through sensuality. That is his larger purpose. But the effect of *Tristan*, as I try to show in the Appendix, cannot be an *apology* for subjective transcendence. We should not confuse the pathos of that metaphysics, so powerfully conveyed by Wagner, with his advocacy of a way of life.

Like Nietzsche, Adorno 'argues' (most often by simply asserting) that Wagner's portrayal of love identified redemption with self-destruction. For Adorno, Wagner *believed* the mythology of *Tristan* about the transcendence of the individual through the denial of social reality and tried to *justify* it as a solution to the problems of romantic dualism and alienation. "For true transcendence [Wagnerian redemption] substitutes the mirage of the enduring upwards-soaring individual who vanishes into thin air at the moment of his annihilation.... In the innermost core of Wagner's idea of redemption dwells nothingness, it too is empty."[11] For Adorno, transposing Shaw into Marx, this doctrine of redemptive annihilation can be seen clearly in *The Ring* as Wotan expresses the death wish of capitalistically alienated society, a society built on the manipulation of others and the denial of individuality. Wotan's will to power denies the freedom of others as surely as Alberich's enslavement of the proletarian Nibelungs. For both Adorno and Nietzsche, Wagner advocated a Schopenhauerian religion of resignation from the phenomenal world. For Adorno, it was a religion of pure sociopathic alienation, epitomized in *Parsifal*.

In his understanding of *The Ring,* Adorno, like Nietzsche, emphasizes the pessimistic antithesis to optimistic readings such as Dahlhaus'. The end of *The Ring* glorifies self-destructive transcendence through death rather than the victory of love over power because it portrays the "bourgeois revolution" of industrialized Europe as an idealized escape from capitalism through romanticized subjectivity. Where for Dahlhaus the end of *The Ring* heralds the advent of a liberating utopia of compassion and justice along Feuerbachian lines, Adorno sees the self-destructive, Schopenhauerian denial of freedom and the rejection of Feuerbach's socialism. But we should ask whether Adorno, and Nietzsche in his similar attack, confuses Wagner's *representation* of love or resignation as these have sometimes operated in our society with an *ideological commitment* about what they *ought* to be. If his works accurately portray the mythologies of romantic love, of domination through social power and the hope for redemption as these have formed our civilization, do they really try *to get us to believe* that sex and death are the only means of redemption from industrialized inhumanity—that we should take Tristan and Isolde, or Wotan and Brünnhilde as role models?

The Ring does indeed tell the story of a society that objectifies value and idealizes power, a society that "reifies production" and seeks domination by transferring value and power into capital, alienating labor and destroying love and freedom (to give the Marxian analysis Adorno rather mechanically employs). But Adorno begs the question: I contend that Wagner does not *advocate* resignation and self-destructiveness. He is not a "nihilist," a "lackey of imperialism," a champion of decadence (pp. 154 f.). If he sees that love can be destructive as well as redemptive, or that redemption can be destructive, why is that not exactly right? In my view, understanding our participation in the construction of our society depends on comprehending the interdependence of creation and destruction, the interdependence of power and love as I have tried to describe it. Wagner's point is really quite simple: sex cannot be an escape from politics if it expresses the fundamental connection between humans and the world that makes society possible. But we can surely distort sexuality by believing that it transcends society, portending something more important for us than the phenomenal world. I contend that Wagner rejects *that* view as decisively as Adorno and he does it by exploring the social implications of transcendent love.

In what follows, I will avoid the temptation to dwell on Adorno's no-holds-barred polemic against political intentions in Wagner's music. There are hundreds of miniature *ad hominum* attacks in his book resting on the belief that Wagner's music clearly and uniformly expresses social nihilism and subjectivist self-destructiveness. By way of attacking that assumption, I will first discuss his general argument that Wagner uses music to thwart our rationality, to get us to deny the phenomenal world and to transcend it for Schopenhauer's metaphysics—decadence and sociopathic subjectivism over healthy social responsibility (to use Thomas Mann's favorite dichotomy). Secondly, I will try to show how Adorno's own view of the critical role of art in society in fact resembles Wagner's in important ways.

6. Music as Drug

Adorno claims that Wagner used music as a technological system of sub-rational psychological stimulation for creating images and feelings with the intention of *controlling* the minds of his audience: one of the first attempts at mass psychological, social control (what we, of course, think of as advertising). He claimed that Wagner's music-dramas do not challenge our intellects, that his music contains "no development" and lacks structural integrity, that it simply substitutes repetition for movement (see pp. 119 f.). The leitmotifs are merely "gestures" possessing no true musical content (I discuss Adorno's metaphor in more detail in Section 7).

Turning first to the leitmotifs, critics as different in their understanding of *The Ring* as Cooke and Dahlhaus, or Newman and Donington, have convincingly demonstrated that there are major differences, for example, between motifs such as the Sword, the Spear, Alberich's Curse, and the Ring, which hardly change at all, and the complex, associative families of thematic material that undergo continual and constant variation. The motifs of Erda and Nature provide key examples of the latter kind (as I outlined them in Chapter 1, Section 8). The Freia motif, the love themes linked to Love's Redemption (not so isolated as was once thought, as I pointed out in Section 2), the harmonic changes in the Rhinegold motif from its earliest occurrences to the dissonant form associated with Hagen are also examples. The music associated with Brünnhilde's compassion, Brünnhilde's Holy Love, the Volsung music, Siegfried's Destiny, and the Power of the Ring are further key examples of transformation by variation. I will mention others shortly. The Valhalla motif falls into both groups. Very often the harmonization and orchestration of that motif remains constant; but, especially in *Götterdämmerung*, it also undergoes extensive variation, sometimes used as suggestive fragments juxtaposed with other motifs as well as appearing in different orchestral and rhythmical guises. Fate also falls into the latter group. Sometimes hardly recognizable, it often forms a harmonic basis for entire scenes. This can be seen in *Die Walküre* IIIiii with Brünnhilde's Reproach and its inversion of the Spear motif. In this scene Wotan's Frustration motif usually ends in Fate. These motifs, woven together with great complexity, lead to the closing of Brünnhilde's eyes and her magic sleep, her quest for understanding temporarily interrupted. The motif of Brünnhilde's Sleep undergoes a good deal of modification in the final scene with its first appearance just after Brünnhilde's "Soll fesselnder Schlaf/fest mich binden":"If fetters of sleep/ come to bind me," urgently underscored in the violins and cellos in dramatic contrast to its later, more pacific appearances.

In my discussion of the last scene between Wotan and Brünnhilde in Chapter 2, we saw that *Die Walküre* ends with an augmented version of the Fate motif, and this eventually connects their moving farewell to the world of *Realpolitik* in *Götterdämmerung* through the Dawn music of *Siegfried* IIIiii. When Brünnhilde mentions Siegmund in her final scene with Wotan ("Siegmund I beheld./I said/you had marked him for death":"Siegmund musst' ich sehn./Tod kündend/trat ich vor ihn"), the motif of the Annunciation of Death reappears. She refers to Siegmund's death but, along with the Fate motif, this moment also characterizes Wotan's farewell to Brünnhilde. That wonderfully affecting moment also marks them for death. In this scene the Annunciation motif takes on a vastly expanded scope as it applies to its later meaning in Wotan and Brünnhilde's last scene. When Wagner uses the more rigid, shorter motifs such as the Sword and the Ring, he usually does so through the gradual evolution of their meaning in the course of the work. They cannot be the kind of Pavlovian stimuli Adorno claims them to be because they are part of an unfolding story requiring our fullest attention (and rational ability). We do not simply react to these motifs if we hear connections between them, and because of these associations, they do not always mean the same thing.

Although Wagner claimed that he wanted his music to effect us directly through emotion, we cannot understand very much of it without intelligent listening. It is one thing to experience music analytically, breaking it up into its various sections, understanding tonal relations, thematic development, and so on, but without experiencing the flow of the work. It is quite another to listen to its changing web of sound actively, recognizing variations, recurring motifs, orchestral modifications, participating in the work as a dramatic event. In both cases we listen actively, not passively. The second kind of listening, however, while not focusing on musical structure, still requires a level of attentiveness not possible in the kind of pure receptiveness Adorno thinks of as the passivity of the "Wagnerian experience." But *those* listeners are predisposed subjectivists—they *want* to be passive, to wallow in sound. It is hard to see how Wagner could have been writing for them (or them alone) given the complexity of his music. If he sometimes goes for 'effects', he always has a reason that ties into the dramatic structure.

For Adorno, as we have seen, Wagner deliberately used music to induce a state of mystical *Einfühlung,* or collective subjectivity, resulting in a denial of rationality—"feeling is everything" universalized—enabling the "dictator conductor," through an inflexible beat, to deny the "rupture between subject and object," (the rational autonomy of the subject). Wagner's "denial of freedom" finds its roots in the almost subliminal stimuli of his manipulative technology, the mechanism of totalitarian mind control. Just as Siegfried becomes an "accomplice" of Wotan's will to self-destruction (p. 131), so too are all of Wagner's dramas directed at creating the ideology of transcendent individuality (really the *loss* of individuality) freed from the oppression of society through the power of sound. His characters are completely determined manifestations of the Will in Schopenhauer's sense, society thus amounting to the enemy of true individuality. In the transcendence of the phenomenal, social self, there can be no further distinction between subject and object ("no more Tristan; no more Isolde," to quote from *Tristan* II) and Wagner therefore follows Schopenhauer in glorifying death as a form of ecstasy (p. 147). Finally, Adorno claims that redemption in Wagner always comes from some transcendent agency, never from inside, never from the characters themselves. The Will subsumes individuality as universality.

The end of *The Ring*—like the end of *Tristan*—is certainly concerned with the nature of individuality but not with praise of its transcendence through death. Adorno assumes that Wagner was straightforwardly Schopenhauerian in his rejection of individualism for universalized subjectivism. For Adorno, Schopenhauer expressed philosophically the deepest desires of a passive bourgeoisie, separated from production through dependence on the labor of others. I contend, however, that Wagner does not reject the importance of individuality even though he continually directed our attention at the larger processes that make it possible. This can be seen in the starkness of the Prelude to Act III of *Tristan*, with its bleak anticipation of transcendence in death. The harsh reality of this music, the cold light of day shed on the metaphysical-sexual night-world fantasy of the lovers, stands as one of Wagner's greatest musical-dramatic achievements. Adorno accurately describes this music as "black, abrupt, jagged" but says that it *unintentionally* subverts the dream of transcendence through death. Why "unintentional"? How *could* that be? Adorno might say that the contrast between it and the Prelude of *Tristan* itself increases *our* desire for transcendence, but just try listening to it with that escapist assumption—it fails because the end of *Tristan,* Isolde's *Liebestod,* remains the *unfulfilled* dream the Prelude tells us to expect as the outcome of the work itself. But understanding the Act III Prelude, and indeed to the Prelude to the work itself in this way, is possible only at the *end* of *Tristan.*

We have also seen a similar contrast used effectively in *The Ring.* The dream-shattering Prelude to *Die Walküre* II also contrasts with the love of Siegmund and Sieglinde by looking at it's delusory self-sufficiency from the larger perspective of Wotan's struggle for control. Their love will be destroyed because of his need for power. For Adorno, the contrast between love and power proves that Wagner was, again, the "diligent lackey of imperialism and late-bourgeois terrorism" because he epitomized the "neurotic's ability to contemplate his own decadence and to transcend it in an image that can withstand the all-consuming gaze [of the Will]" (p. 154), and we do indeed see something of this in Wotan as he wanders about in *Siegfried* waiting for his hero to reject his authority. He possesses full realization, but remains numbly detached uninvolved and disengaged—for Adorno, the epitomization of bourgeois decadence. The painfulness of the confrontation between myth and reality expressed in the preludes to *Die Walküre* II and *Tristan* III, or in the Prolog to *Götterdämmerung,* becomes yet another "commodity" for bourgeois society to savor in its self-destructiveness. For Adorno, however, Wagner does not take the next step. In his denial of the social reality of the self, he perpetuates the primacy of subjectivity that has allowed capitalism to retain its control, to treat *us* as pure consumers. The contrasts between love and power, and between individuality and society in the three examples I have just cited therefore, for

Adorno, encourage *us* to seek love as a subjective withdrawal from social responsibility, as an antidote to politics.

In the Appendix (Section 4), I try to show how *Tristan* (in the interpretations of Peckham and Tanner) revitalizes and transforms our interest in the role of love in society by showing the power of love over our beliefs about ourselves as social beings. Why was Wagner not aware of the social and philosophical implications of that self-image, as well as its effect on our ideas of society and individual autonomy? Why does not the starkness of the Prelude to Act III of *Tristan*, in its vivid contrast with the pure subjective yearning of opening Prelude and the sensual dream-world of Act II, give us the pivotal contrast between illusion and reality that makes up the core of the work? Does the love between Siegfried and Brünnhilde not involve them socially despite their attempts at remaining outside of Wotan's society? Siegmund and Sieglinde are also unintentionally politically involved, as we see in the Prelude to *Die Walküre* II. In these examples, how could Wagner not have been aware of the ambiguity of romantic love and its vision of the transcendence of self and society? Why are not Tristan's protest, his curse on love as he sacrifices himself to the Will in Isolde's arms, or Siegmund's refusal of Valhalla's pleasures, or Siegfried and Brünnhilde's "laughing death" to the world of politics, perfectly understood in their self-destructiveness *when seen in the light of the contrast between these preludes*? Wagner in effect asks: Where does the greater reality lie—in the subjective world of love, or in the social world?

It seems to me that Wagner does not answer that question directly and therefore was not a Schopenhauerian in holding the Will to be the ultimate reality (our only access to it being through our own willing). My general point is that, for Wagner, we can never escape the grip of our illusions. To prioritize the social in human identity does not secure a foundational source of value for him, since our relation either to the Will or to society must always be as individuals: we cannot transcend our world except by changing ourselves *within* society, by substituting one role for another, or creating new ones, as do Wotan and Brünnhilde. I agree with Peckham and Tanner that Wagner's later works reject any source of redemption lying outside of human life.[12]

Failure to see Wagner's refusal to transcend has been a pervasive fault in Marxist criticism. Like Adorno, composer-critic Hans Eisler utterly misses this point:

> The content of [Wagner's] works is always the sufferer's redemption through divine grace, through compassion or love, but always redemption from without, from on high, never redemption through the suffering individual himself. The redeemer and redemption play such a significant role that, in

Parsifal, Wagner is able to write, "Redemption to the redeemer."[13]

In *Parsifal,* however, redemption *does not* come from outside. The mystical, transcendent power of Christianity does not save anyone, indeed waiting for God to work a miracle, to save the Brotherhood of the Grail, is the source of everyone's problems in the work! These difficulties Parsifal himself overcomes through his internal transformation from aimless detachment to socially responsible agent of change (in part centered on his encounter with the dehumanized Kundry in Act II, Wagner's most powerful picture of the failure of the hope of transcendent salvation). In *Parsifal,* as in *Die Meistersinger,* we see the connection between the personal and the social represented through the effects of illusions on people. That these *are* illusions seems to me to be Wagner's point.

In his search for a connection between musical analysis and cultural criticism, Adorno unequivocally saw the sonata form as the paradigm of development and Beethoven as its greatest practitioner. For him, it paralleled musically the dialectic of Thesis/Antithesis/Synthesis, with progress towards the recapitulation as an *Aufhebung* of the exposition and development, whereas Wagner's "commodity-like" motifs were strung together like "discrete objects" with no fundamental musical (or analogously social) relationships to each other (p. 48).

I will turn to Wagner's conception of musical form in the next section and devote the remainder of this one to other aspects of musical development in *The Ring,* describing some of the evidence against Adorno's charges. I begin with some further examples of Wagner's use of his leitmotifs that show him in a more innovative light. In "Wagner's Musical Language" (p. 234), Cooke discusses the close connection between the Volsung and Siegfried motifs. After pointing out how they are both based on the Fate motif, he describes how alterations of tempo radically change the significance of their occurrence. For example, Siegfried's up-tempo motif usually expresses heroic vitality—until it appears as Siegfried's funeral music in *Götterdämmerung* where (as Cooke suggests) its effect recalls the Funeral March of Beethoven's *Eroica* Symphony, heroism defeated (even though Beethoven tries to reverse defeat in the final two (unconvincing) movements). I have mentioned several times the almost unnoticeable drumroll on the timpani heard in *Das Rheingold* when Fricka in Scene 2 begins to notice the deleterious effect of Freia's removal from their midst by Fasolt and Fafner, and again when Fafner kills Fasolt in Scene 4. This motif becomes the rhythmical basis for the Funeral Music and we then see the point towards which it has been heading.

Variations in tempo sometimes disguise a motif. For example, the Magic Sleep music changes greatly from its first occurrence in *Die Walküre* IIIiii to its later uses in that same scene; also, the usually slow music of the Volsung Race reappears greatly accelerated in *Die Walküre* I when Siegmund pulls the sword from the tree, a reference connecting him directly to Wotan's plan and underscoring the significance of Siegmund's identity.[14] The Sword motif here emerges out of the Volsung motif thus connecting Wotan's fate with the hope of heroic redemption. More often, however, slower versions of the Volsung motif are connected with the increasingly complex role played by Siegfried and Brünnhilde in the clash between power and love. Siegmund too finds himself caught in that opposition, for he is intended to use the sword to defend his love for Sieglinde and eventually Wotan's love for his society. Hence the fateful, minor tonality of the motif. The fate of the Volsungs becomes fully apparent in Act IIiv when Brünnhilde reveals to Siegmund that he must die. The motif of the Annunciation of Death in that scene derives from the Volsung music (as both derive from Erda's motif) and ties the original optimistic connection between Siegmund and the sword to his death. I pointed out earlier how the Annunciation motif, along with Fate, form the basis for this entire scene. Wagner's technique of using a single motif or a related group of motifs to characterize an entire scene becomes increasingly prominent from the middle of *Die Walküre* to the end of the cycle.[15] The musical relations between the motifs show the significance not only of events in the lives of the characters but also of their beliefs. Even when a motif does not change very much, because of the context of those beliefs, it can sometimes act as a semistable signpost in a complex developmental process made up of variations in the motifs that *do* change.[16]

In his study of Wagner's music-dramas, Jack Stein points out that the motif of the Sword occurs forty-nine times and that of Love (in various forms) fifty times in *Die Walküre*.[17] Does it have the same sense each time? Does it evoke the same idea or emotional response? Do we react in a purely mechanical way at the end of *Die Walküre*? As the events of the drama unfold, each occurrence of a basic motif takes on a different significance as it refers forward and backward in time. Our response to this can vary tremendously as we come to realize the existence of these variations and they cannot all possibly be heard the first time, or even perhaps the first dozen times. Indeed, in *Götterdämmerung* many of the variations occur in layers of conjoining motifs, often in such degrees of density that one cannot hear them except through repeated listening with the score.

One example of this complexity involves the Servitude or Bondage motif, a special application of the motif of the Power of the Ring. I pointed out in Chapter 1, Section 8, that the latter is closely related to the motif of the Rhinegold, for example, as sung by the Rhinemaidens when they lament the loss of their gold. As Servitude, this simple two-chord motif comes to symbolize the destructive power of the ring. It appears in this connection along with the Fafner or Dragon motif in the Prelude to *Siegfried* II. An example of this transformation occurs when, in *Siegfried* IIIii, we can hear it in the accelerated woodwinds as the Wanderer claims that Siegfried's wood bird flew away to save its life rather than to stay with Siegfried ("Es floh dir zu seinem Heil!") and that a terrible fate follows its flight. The accelerated motif symbolizes the flight of the bird but also reasserts the power of the ring that has lain dormant until Siegfried recovered it from Fafner. It too now takes wing and reasserts its power when the fairy tale heroism of Siegfried's *Bildung* encounters Wotan's symbol of power. The power of the ring will soon destroy Wotan's spear, the last vestige of his control over society. Siegfried's helpful bird flies away, however, at the outset of his emergence into the real world and his knowledge of nature does him no good at all from that point on. After this moment he has no one to tell him about the significance of what happens as the power of the ring takes him under its control. If we recognize this little motif, we will see Siegfried's heroism in the very different light of its destructive potential.

At the end of his last scene with Erda in *Siegfried* IIIi, when Wotan desires his own end so that a redeemer free of Alberich's curse can free his world from it, we have a further example of motival development in *The Ring* and how they are brought together to convey the underlying significance of events. When he says: "Then your wisdom's/child [i.e., Brünnhilde] will achieve/that deed that will free our world":"wachend wirkt/dein wissendes Kind/erlösende Weltentat" we hear an unresolved chord. The deed may free the world, but in what sense? When Wotan says: "Whatever may happen,/the god will gladly/yield his rule to the young!":"Was jene auch wirken,/dem ewig Jungen/weicht in Wonne der Gott" the motif of Siegfried's love for Brünnhilde appears in the violins; but when Wotan tells Erda to return to her depths we hear a distorted version of Freia II in the trombones and tuba rather than its characteristic orchestration in the strings, and then finally the Fate motif. Why are *these* instruments used for the Freia motif (usually heard in the violins)? Here Freia II recalls the need for compassionate love (the true need of the gods), but that love will destroy Wotan, as we realize when that motif appears in the instrumentation usually associated with Alberich's curse.[18]

One of the most striking instances of Wagner's layering technique occurs in the Prelude to Act III of *Siegfried*, written after the long hiatus that included the composition of *Tristan* and *Die Meistersinger*. Here Wagner uses the Wanderer motif to indicate the immanent meeting between Wotan and Siegfried. This motif, now urgent and troubled, as Cooke points out, is based on Loge's motif as it was modified in the Magic Sleep music at the end of *Die Walküre*.[19] In the Prelude, the Wanderer motif appears against the Twilight of the Gods and the Power of the Ring, together indicating the several threads of the drama about to be woven together. The terrific vitality of this Prelude also indicates the increasing complexity of the relation between power and love. But, once again, these motifs are brought together in such density that we cannot possibly grasp the significance of this Prelude without attending to its details.

An example of how Wagner uses a related family of motifs to unify an entire scene occurs in *Die Walküre* IIIiii: the music associated with Brünnhilde's "Was it so shameful,/what I have done":"War es so schmählich,/was ich verbrach." In Chapter 2 Section 5, I noted Cooke's association between this music and Wotan's Spear motif as it symbolizes Brünnhilde independence from Wotan's control. She is no longer the extension of his will that she described herself to be in Act IIii. Cooke also points out that "War es so schmählich" derives from the last segment of the music associated with Wotan's denunciation of Brünnhilde earlier in Act III. But, significantly, the music of the reversed or inverted Spear motif becomes that of the compassionate, "You, who this love/in my heart inspired":"Der diese Liebe/mir in's Herz gehaucht."[20] Brünnhilde's reversed spear motif in "War es so schmählich" recalls the motif of Renunciation: indeed, *she* embodies and will personify the renunciation of Wotan's power. In this scene one can clearly see Wagner's economical use of counterpoint (although far richer in *Tristan, Die Meistersinger* and, above all, *Parsifal*), but he also achieves an overall intricacy of development through the juxtaposing and layering of other motifs (Fate, Frustration, Renunciation), in ways reminiscent of Beethoven. Because the motifs used in this scene are closely interrelated musically, Wagner, like Beethoven and Brahms (both of whom also used short, motif-like fragments), can move easily between them within the framework of tonal possibilities they outline (see Cooke, "Wagner's Musical Language," pp. 235 f. and Dahlhaus, *New Grove Wagner,* p. 99).

Adorno's claim that this music contains no structural integrity, or that it evolves only by a superficial mimicry of variation forms, fails to take account either of Wagner's use of classical forms or his modifications of them—modifications that laid the foundation for twentieth-century music. Wagner's use of "endless melody," a particular annoyance for Adorno, the bad part of nineteenth-century music, in fact almost always consists of long series of variations, cross references, and reminiscences rather than unstructured, amorphous meandering. In his brief discussion of Wagner's music, Peckham points out (p. 267) that Wagner's frequent use of canon and fugue forms was different because he introduced other musical material after he had begun what initially appear to be a rather formal exposition—and the most dramatic precedent for this technique was (Adorno's hero) Beethoven.[21]

Turning to harmonic development, one of the most complex systems of motifs of *The Ring* centers on the interval of the fifth. Siegfried's Horn-Call motif serves as a key example of a motif involving this interval, its rising motion conveying the energy and optimism of the young hero. However, the music of Gutrune in *Götterdämmerung* also involves this interval, although inverted in her falling, deceptively submissive motif that symbolizes the seduction of Siegfried. That same falling motif also characterizes Hagen in the form of a diminished fifth—a defeated fifth—thus linking the innocent Gutrune to

Siegfried as part of Hagen's plot to destroy him. Hagen's single-bar motif almost directly transcribes the music associated in *Das Rheingold* (Scene iv) with the Purpose of the Sword when Wotan sings: "So I greet the hall,/safe from all fear and dread": "So grüss ich die Burg,/sicher vor Bang und Grau'n." That safety proved to be entirely delusory. Similarly, Siegmund also sings the music of the Purpose of the Sword in *Die Walküre* Iiii when he pulls Notung from the tree ("in hour of need,/now it is found":"In höchster Not/fänd ich es einst"). This occurs immediately after the Volsung and Sword motifs, underscored in the cellos and basses by Wotan's descending Spear motif while the Sword sounds in the trumpet (one more example of the dense concatenation of motifs at significant moments in *The Ring*). Wotan's vision of the power of the sword proves to be illusory.

The music of Gutrune also resembles the horn call of the Gibichungs as they assemble in *Götterdämmerung* II. This horn motif, anticipating Siegfried's doom, is an inversion of Siegfried's harmonically major horn call, heard to its full effect in Siegfried's Rhine Journey at the end of the Prolog of *Götterdämmerung*. Indeed, as a subversion of his heroism, this motif occurs at the point when Hagen's plan begins to get its grip on Siegfried and Brünnhilde. Siegfried's "blood-brotherhood" oath of friendship with Gunter and its falling fifth (as I pointed out in Chapter 2, Section 6) actually derives from Hagen's descending motif, showing his control over others. Gutrune's music, deceptively submissive in its reliance on parallel thirds, also disguises Siegfried's fate since his arificially induced 'love' for Gutrune relies again on Hagen's deviousness. In Hagen's plot to deceive Siegfried, Gutrune's deceptively innocuous music disguises Hagen's influence, shown by the fact that her motif is also based on his falling diminished fifth.

The friendship between Siegfried and Gunther, also associated with a falling fifth, parallels Gutrune's motif in suggesting the manipulative control of Hagen over Siegfried through Gutrune and Gunther. Significantly, the control of Siegfried through Gutrune and Gunther, symbolized by these motifs, all derive from Hagen's motif (and are developed in the scene known as Hagen's Watch at the end of Act Iii). But Hagen's motif, as we saw in the last chapter, derives directly from the falling fifth at the end of Siegfried's horn call, as can be seen in *Götterdämmerung* Ii when Hagen and Gunther see the approaching Siegfried on the Rhine—just before Gunther says "On the Rhine I can hear a horn":"Vom Rhein her tönt das Horn."[22] This motif becomes the developmental core of the next scene when Siegfried and Gutrune meet and Siegfried's fate comes under the control of Hagen—all symbolized by the connection between the end of Siegfried's horn call, Gutrune's motif, and Hagen's basic motif portending the rapid change from Siegfried's optimism to Hagen's demonic intent. As Cooke says, "during the great scene in Act II[v] of *Götterdämmerung,* in which

Siegfried and Brünnhilde both swear on Hagen's spear, there is a tremendous conflict between the upward and downward-leaping fifths."[23]

Hagen's control eventually extends over Brünnhilde as well as Siegfried. The motif of Siegfried's Death that closes Act II follows from Hagen's falling motif—with which the act begins. Here an entire act—depicting the rise of Hagen—gains its unity through his motif and those developed from it. Both rising and falling intervals of the fifth are contained in the oath sworn by Brünnhilde and Siegfried in *Götterdämmerung* IIiv ("Shining steel!/Holiest weapon!/Help me defend my honor!":"Helle Wehr!/Heilige Waffe!/Hilf meinem ewigen Eide!"). The clash between Siegfried's redemptive role and his inability to save anything at all important reaches its climax in Brünnhilde's vengeance for having been deceived by her lover, even if unwittingly. The more solid interval of the rising fifth is reduced to unstable fourths and diminished falling fifths; Siegfried's good intentions, his friendship with Gunther, all fall into Hagen's hands—one further example of how a family of musical interconnections dramatically unifies *The Ring*.[24]

One final example of development: in *Siegfried* Ii, Siegfried and Mime discuss Siegfried's parents (Mime trying to claim that he is both). This scene rests on two basic motifs: the first associated with Siegfried's youthful exuberance, which goes through several variations, and the second known as Siegfried's Yearning for Love, a slow, rising and continually varying melodic texture in the lower strings. The relation between these two thematic groups, the first fast and the second slow, suggests the introduction of a sonata. Furthermore, as the scene progresses, the music of the second part of Freia's motif, the basic love music identified by Cooke, appears along with theVolsung motif—all of which then undergo variations connected with Yearning for Love (see Siegfried's "Es sangen die Vöglein/so selig im Lenz"). The overall design of this scene resembles that of a sonata exposition and development: the rise of Siegfried and the beginning of his 'symphony'. Indeed, as one begins to notice features like this, *The Ring* possesses much more musical sophistication than may appear superficially. However pragmatic Wagner's use of musical forms, he clearly employed them imaginatively in ways Adorno simply refuses to recognize, or attributed to his Composer-Dictator theory. Indeed it is Adorno who looks backward rather than forward in his surprisingly conservative conception of development. In the next section I turn more directly to these issues of musical form.

7. Adorno's Enlightenment Sonata Ideal

In the late eighteenth and early nineteenth centuries, the sonata form was taken by some, then and now, to be an expression of utopian mythology—a musical counterpart to the inner-workings of history.[25] This suggestively

Hegelian approach, linking the sonata to parallel forms of conceptual evolution, holds true for Adorno as well. Under this view, the developmental structure of the sonata contains the implication of historical evolution towards an implicit goal, a structure paralleling the development of human consciousness itself. Politics, art, and philosophy are, of course, also seen developmentally in a way Adorno wanted to borrow from Hegel without becoming too 'idealistic' in Marx's sense (that is, not directly concerned with the 'material' story of historical existence at the economic level). But, like other members of the Frankfurt School, he also wanted to avoid the extremism of contemporaries such as Georg Lukács who for a time had an unfortunate tendency to apologize for the 'social necessity' of Stalin's all too materialistic atrocities. As postwar Eastern Europeans, Adorno and his colleagues were understandably sensitive about such things. Adorno especially tried to reconcile 'spirtuality' with individualism.

For Adorno, the sonata along with its essential dependence on Major/Minor tonality, remained the paradigm of musical structure until Schoenberg who, through a suitably internal and dialectical criticism of the principles of tonality in Western music, created a new theory of music.[26] Ironically, however, it was due to Schoenberg, among others including Mahler and Berg, that a more sophisticated understanding of Wagner's music has emerged. What appears to be an absence of form to Adorno in fact heralds the beginning of a reconception of the very idea of musical development that eventually led to Schoenberg's revolution. The point is not that Wagner tried but failed to use classical forms to impose a merely superficial order in order to manipulate feeling, but rather that through original modifications of those forms in the service of music-drama he helped to create a different conception of musical development and expression.

Adorno's model for musical form and development derives from what he sees as the high point of Western music until Schoenberg—that beginning with Bach and ending with Beethoven. Adorno shares the nostalgia of his colleagues for the art if not the philoisophy of the Enlightenment. Arnold Hauser, for example, writes:

> The men of the eighteenth century strive to extract a clearly definable doctrine and world-view from everything, even from their emotionalism and irrationalism; they are systematists, philosophers, reformers, they make up their minds...they follow principles and are guided by a plan for the improvement of life and the world.

While those of the nineteenth century, on the other hand:

> lost their faith in systems and programs and see the meaning
> and purpose of art in a passive surrender to life, in seizing
> hold of the rhythm of life itself, in preserving the atmosphere
> and mood of it; their faith consists in an irrational, instinctive
> affirmation of life, their morality in a resigned acceptance of
> morality.[27]

In the nineteenth-century, the middle class lost touch with its Enlightenment roots, with its belief in the controllability of society, and contented itself with irrelevant ideological debate rather than finding practical solutions to its problems.

> Under the influence of this opiate, the German intelligentsia
> lost its feeling for positive and rational knowledge and replaced it by intuition and metaphysical vision. Irrationalism
> was certainly a universal European phenomenon, but it was
> expressed everywhere essentially as a form of emotionalism,
> and first received its special quality of idealism and spiritualism in Germany; it was only here that it developed into a
> philosophy of contempt for empirical reality, based on the
> timeless and the infinite, on the eternal and the absolute. (p. 105)

For Hauser, the subjectivism of Schubert and Schumann exposes a socially pessimistic view of humanity, a metaphysical seriousness in contrast to the "playful exuberance" of Mozart, "the purest ethos transfiguring the whole of life." Beginning with Beethoven, however, music became gloomy, metaphysical and "spiritual." "It is [Hauser writes] sufficient to compare the serene, clear and calm humanity of Mozart, its freedom from all mysticism and turbid emotionalism, with the violence of Romantic music, to realize what had been lost with the eighteenth century" (p. 212). Later on the social pessimism of romanticism was "entirely dependent on music," reaching its climax (or collapse) in Schopenhauer and Wagner (p. 213). Adorno clearly shares Hauser's sense of loss in trying to reconcile the two sides of Hegel: the one looking back to the Enlightenment (from which he took his ideas about reason and science, (radically transforming both)), the other into the "abyss" of subjectivity (for which Hegel tried to find a philosophic transformation in the union of subject and object as the "life of the whole").

In an article not (as of 1994) translated into English, Dahlhaus points out that Adorno relies heavily on Alfred Lorenz's, *Das Geheimnis der Form bei Richard Wagner* (Berlin, 1924).[28] The first part of this huge work deals with *The Ring*, the second with *Tristan*, the third with *Die Meistersinger,* and the fourth with *Parsifal*. Lorenz tried to show that Wagner used traditional compositional techniques. But, in rightly finding that account distorted and deficient, Adorno concludes there to be no developmental or compositional integrity of any kind in Wagner, a conclusion undoubtedly reinforced by his own predilection to see the late eighteenth- and early nineteenth-century sonata as the paradigmatic historical manifestation of dialectic in music. He sees the failure of this tradition in Wagner as the basis for his "gestural" approach to music. Since there supposedly exists no real development beyond the arbitrary association of finite, unchanging motifs, no real principle of musical development, the stimulation of emotion of emotion remains the only role for music. Such fragmented and episodic musical 'stimuli' cannot constitute an intellectual experience, nor can it be the kind of emotional experience I have been claiming for it.[29]

As Dahlhaus points out, Adorno's criticism should be directed at Lorenz and not Wagner, who in fact was well on the way towards a conception of musical development that cannot be fully understood by the analytical methodology of classical musical architecture employed by Lorenz.[30] Wagner's views on musical development, as Dahlhaus argues, paralleled those of Brahms. Both were able to create large musical structures out of small musical units (usually one to four measures long). Schoenberg, for one, conceived his idea of continuous development specifically through Wagner's analogy of a web of developmental variations held together by purely internal rhythmical, harmonic, and melodic means depending on the repetition and regrouping of small cells into larger and more complex wholes.[31] The change of metaphor from the 'architectural' conception of the sonata to the 'organic', evolutionary complex or web envisaged by Wagner at the end of *The Music of the Future* indicated major changes in his conception of musical form. For example, instead of the Tonic/Dominant, Major/Minor opposition between the first and second themes of the classical sonata, harmonically reconciled through development, dramatic movement in Wagner resembles that of a Schubert *Lied*, simple and indivisible. This is not to say, however, that Wagner's (or Schubert's) developmental techniques avoid contrast, but that it occurs between thematic groups, each of which also has its own developmental complexity rather than the relationally dependent tonality of the classical sonata where, for example, seemingly independent tonic and dominant themes are brought together in the development. This movement towards unity often does not occur in a Schubert *Lied*. We can see this in the example of the quasi-sonata form of *Siegfried* Ii, to which I referred at the end of the last section. As with many Schubert *Lieder*, Wagnerian development occurs internally within distinct thematic contexts, heightening contrasts between them, but without leading to a resolution.[32] We are usually left with a sense of suspended contrast rather than finality.

Such changes in the idea of musical form stand as one reason why Wagner, when he returned to *The Ring* after *Tristan* and *Die Meistersinger,* saw it through a new perspective reinforced by Schopenhauer—as a "symphony" out of which the events on the stage emerged as expressions of deeper, underlying processes that could only be conceived and experienced musically. Music became the most important part of music-drama in this later conception. As with *Tristan,* but not as extremely, the visible events on the stage became one more voice in this symphony (although what is said (or sung) remains important—as it often does not in *Tristan*). The music of *The Ring* thus took on an importance it previously lacked (clearly evident in whole of *Siegfried* III, beginning with its Prelude). In this shift from its earlier conception, music-drama was supposed to be the culmination of the concept of musical development begun by Beethoven who, by taking sometimes considerable liberties with the sonata, transformed the symphony from its classical ideal in Haydn and Mozart into a new means of emotional and even philosophical expression.

Wagner's conception of tonality also differed significantly from that of the early nineteenth century. For one thing, as Charles Rosen points out, later nineteenth-century composers began to weaken the polarity between tonic and dominant essential to the classical sonata's internal contrasts.[33] We can see this in *Tristan* and *Parsifal,* especially with the chromaticism of the former and the extensive use of counterpoint and harmonic suspension in the latter; but it exists in *The Ring* too despite its simpler diatonic framework. Long sections—such as the scene of Brünnhilde's Reproach and her reconciliation with Wotan—rest on implied Tonic/Dominant contrasts, often avoiding a clear arrival at either.

Another example involves the relationship between the motifs of Alberich's Curse and the Tarnhelm in *Götterdämmerung* I: Bailey points out (p. 60) that, at the end of Brünnhilde's monologue after her scene with Waltraute, Alberich's (firmly diatonic) Curse avoids its usual tonic triad ending because the tarnhelm is about to work its magic on Siegfried in Hagen's capture of Brünnhilde. The harmonically unambiguous Curse motif here connects with the tonal ambiguity of the Tarnhelm motif. Consequently, in this scene, we avoid any sense of a resolution of conflict in the way one achieves it in the classical transition from dominant to tonic. In *The Ring,* there are many such instances where an apparently approaching resolution slips through our grasp. Because of the harmonic ambiguity of the Fate motif within the repeated tonic modulation of the Fire music and Brünnhilde's Magic Sleep, the end of *Die Walküre,* for example, constitutes a pause rather than a resolution.

Dramatically, many questions are indeed left unanswered and the musical tensions contained in the final moments of *Die Walküre* help to create the knot of problems confronting the Norns at the beginning of *Götterdämmerung*. Even with the final appearance of Love's Redemption, Wagner does not shift back to anything we can identify as a tonic or dominant harmonic center, except in relation to the dream of redemption—but that has become the most ambiguous idea in the entire work, set as it is against the flames of Valhalla and all those associated with it. We have reached this point by evolutionary means having nothing to do with the final triumph of a basic idea either musical or moral. No such basic idea exists in *The Ring* as a point of return. The mood at the end of *Götterdämmerung*, once the waters of the Rhine have quenched the fires of Valhalla, conveys the ambiguous potential of nature, as it was in the beginning. The tonal resolution of the final chord following Redemption Through Love cannot have its traditional effect because of the psychological and philosophical ambiguity leading up to it. The 'resolution' contains the potential for more of the same.

Dahlhaus argues that Wagner's use of consonance and dissonance is not, as Adorno claims, directed towards a "false resolution"—a transformation of redemption into sensual transcendence through death (see *In Search of Wagner*, pp. 118 f., p. 142). As Dahlhaus points out in the *New Grove Wagner* (p. 139), we actually experience very little resolution in *The Ring*, indeed as it progresses the balance usually tips in favor of dissonance. Often, in reaching a point of apparent resolution, the immediately succeeding events pull the rug from beneath that illusory stability. When it does occur, musical resolution contrasts with social or moral conflict: the ending of *Das Rheingold* contrasts the reality of Wotan's moral compromises with the illusion of his dream-world. The ending of *Siegfried*, with its transcendence of love, contrasts with the social world typfied by power. I showed in the previous chapter that the ending of *Siegfried* only seems to be an ending; that world of isolated love—depicted in music suggesting ideally harmonious resolution—rests on an illusion—indeed a delusion—immediately evident in the opening measures of *Götterdämmerung*. (The same fundamental Wagnerian contrast between the Preludes to Act III of *Tristan* and Act II of *Die Walküre* and what preceded and follows them.)

Like Redemption Through Love, Brünnhilde's awakening music in *Siegfried* contains the Fate motif—and recall its 'questioning' role at the end of *Die Walküre*. The awakening scene in *Siegfried* III 'answers' that question. I have tried to show how that distinction between illusion and reality emerges as one of the dominant themes of *The Ring*. These are indeed false resolutions, as Adorno says; but he sees in this a retreat from humanity while I have described how it fits in with a general interest of the nineteenth century concerning the contingency of value and identity. Though without the chromaticism and harmonic ambiguity of *Tristan* or *Parsifal*, *The Ring* also avoids traditional climactic resolutions, as I have suggested, through dramatic irony and through the musical technique of building one set of variations onto another, of taking the action of the stage to be part of a continual musical development.

I have summarized how Adorno understood Wagner's music as a decline from the purity and cultural integrity of the classical sonata. But, like it or not, Wagner changed the idea of form in ways that escaped Lorenz. Surprisingly, Adorno's own view of Schoenberg as the contemporary cultural hero who redeemed twentieth-century music from the reactionary Stravinsky should have led him to see Wagner's innovativeness (although he grudgingly admits the musical importance of *Tristan*). Wagner did not impose an arbitrary external scheme by organizing his musical 'gestures' for ulterior political purposes. The structure of his music has proven to have internal coherence even in its 'external' references to physical objects, people, or what they symbolize. His politics was really a complex social individualism, not the totalitarianism seen by Adorno and other, more doctrinaire Leftists. Far from there being "nothing to analyze in his music" (*In Search of Wagner*, p. 41), virtually every measure consists of a variation of previous ones—a distant motif, a recapitulated phrase or texture. But appreciating this requires a different conception of development than Adorno was willing to consider. *Tristan* and *Parsifal* are far more harmonically advanced than the *intentionally* old-fashioned *Ring*, but all these works share a true complexity of structure that changed the concept of form by introducing fluidity and cell-based development.

A more constructive view might be that Wagner was not trying to emancipate us from form altogether. For the reasons I have suggested he wanted to change our idea of musical experience just as Beethoven had done with the sonata form he inherited from Haydn and Mozart, and just as they had done in their perfection of that form from its haphazard baroque origins.[34] I have tried to show how Wagner's use of form should be seen in the light of its evolutionary connection to Beethoven, Mozart, Haydn, and Bach—just as we should see Schopenhauer, Nietzsche, and Wagner in relation to Hegel, and Hegel in relation to the entire history of Western philosophy (as he wanted to be seen). These two lines of development in music and philosophy come together in the nineteenth century, its confluence essential to our understanding of Wagner today.

Adorno's epitomization of the sonata as the deepest principle of musical development expresses a curious antihistoricism for someone who wanted to define a clear sense of cultural evolution. On the one hand, he sees musical style resting on historical, social change (and, even as influencing it), but he also clearly believes that there is a *normative* judgment to be made between Beethoven and Wagner: Beethoven was right and Wagner wrong because there is something *right*, something true about the sonata as a representation of the social, dialectically oriented essence of human identity. Adorno prefers the sonata as a paradigm of development because it looks like a musical anticipation of Hegel and Marx. But the sonata was transformed; not only was it *never* a single, monolithic form, but the role it played within the history of music also underwent considerable and rapid change. For example, in the final paragraph of *The Classical Style*, Rosen argues that:

> [a] style, when it is no longer the natural mode of expression, gains a new life—a shadowy life-in-death—as a prolongation of the past. We imagine ourselves able to revive the past through its art, to perpetuate it by continuing to work within its conventions. For this illusion of reliving history, the style must be prevented from becoming truly alive once again. The conventions must remain conventional, the forms lose their original significance in order to take on their new responsibility of evoking the past. This process of ossification is a guarantee of respectability.... The sense of the irrecoverable past...is omnipresent in the music of Brahms, resignedly eclectic, ambiguous without irony. The depth of his feeling of loss gave an intensity to Brahms's work that no other imitator of the classical tradition ever reached: he may be said to have made music out of his openly expressed regret that he was born too late. For the rest, the classical tradition could be used with originality only through irony—the irony of Mahler, for example, who employed sonata-forms with the same mock respect that he gave to his shopworn scraps of dance-tunes. The true inheritors of the classical style were not those who maintained its traditions, but those, from Chopin to Debussy, who preserved its freedom as they gradually altered and finally destroyed the musical language which had made the creation of the style possible.

It seems to me that Wagner also belongs on Rosen's list, between Chopin and Debussy. Perhaps more than anyone else in the nineteenth century, it was he who turned away from the classical style in the way Rosen describes in his last sentence and opened the door into the twentieth century.

8. Art and Morality

Concerning *The Ring* itself, to summarize, Adorno describes the destruction of the world as a "happy ending" because it adjusts all the events of the cycle to the "scheme of death and transfiguration which reveals its commodity character." It does this by stripping redemption of any prior theological content, transforming it not into Feurbachian naturalism but the pure sensuality of the asocial self. In the self-destructive world of *The Ring,* power alienates through "an interlocking system in which the more ruthlessly the individual tries to prevail, the less he succeeds" (*In Search of Wagner,* p. 117). Adorno continues:

> If in *The Ring* mythic violence and legal contract are confounded, this not only confirms an intuition about the origins of legality, it also articulates the experience of the lawlessness of a society dominated in the name of law by contract and property. [In such a society, one which] has been socialized through and through, [it is not possible for an individual to alter anything].... The opacity and omnipotence of the social process is then celebrated as a metaphysical mystery by the individual who becomes conscious of it and yet ranges himself on the side of its dominant forces. Wagner has devised the ritual of permanent catastrophe. His unbridled individualism utters the death sentence on the individual and its order. (p. 119)

It would seem clear that true redemption must be social for Adorno and that Wagner denies this possibility in favor of confused Schopenhauerian romantic subjectivity, symbolized by the unifying transcendence of the Will. The "happy ending" of *The Ring* destroys both society and most of its members through the desire for transcendence—isolated individual and Will are finally united through the destruction of the phenomenal and social world. These characters "deserve death" in the sense of its requirement in the process of "self-actualization" (alienated subjectivism leading in desperation to the myth of the self transcending society). The mystery of the self has been explained: the true goal of the quest for truth lies in unity with the Will, to be accomplished only through the denial of the priority of social value and the assertion of self-destructive individuality. *The Ring* portrays, therefore, a "homecoming without a home, eternal rest without Eternity, the mirage of peace without the underlying reality of a human being to enjoy it" (p. 149). The totality of Wagner's fatalism eliminates freedom and individuality by transcending the deterministic power struggle in society through the illusory comfort that one is but a part of a larger (but equally determined) whole. In short, Wagner possessed no irony. If his depiction of Wotan's society cannot be social criticism, it must be a revelation of his anti-individualistic politics.

Here is Adorno's most succinct description of *The Ring*:

> If we were to summarize the "idea" of *The Ring* in simple words we would say that man emancipates himself from the blind identity with nature from which he springs; he then acquires power over nature only to succumb to her in the long run. The allegory of *The Ring* asserts that dominion over nature and subjugation by nature are one and the same. The division of the world into nature and individuation is parallel

> to the split between authority and rebels.... But to emerge the winner is also to succumb to the power of the ring. The music leaves us in no doubt about this. Accompanying the Wanderer's last words, "forward then! I cannot stop you," we hear the motif of the Twilight of the Gods. The parable of the man who dominates nature only to relapse into a state of natural bondage gains an historical dimension in the action of *The Ring*: with the victory of the bourgeoisie, the idea that society is like a natural process, something "fated," is reaffirmed, despite the conquest of particular aspects of nature. (p. 137)

Except for the last two lines, this is an accurate and insightful account of *The Ring,* much like the one for which I have been arguing. Why is it not also a description of exactly what Wagner himself set out to achieve? Adorno's insights describe precisely what *The Ring* conveys: a denial of the Enlightenment conception of autonomous individuality as the primary social force, rationally independent and capable of utopian control, ironically contrasted through Wagner's appreciation of the tragic conception of winning one thing but losing another. Adorno's criticism appears in his last sentence: in *The Ring* society becomes "like a natural process," deterministic in its denial of freedom and its ritual of "permanent catastrophe." The "totality [of *The Ring*] is the bad eternity [infinitely repetitive, no progress] of rebellion as anarchy and unrelenting self-destruction" (p. 132). For Adorno, this leads to the socially detached subjectivity of the nineteenth-century bourgeoisie and its denial of public moral value.

Adorno admits that Wagner strips redemption of its theological meaning, but the conclusion he draws implies that Wagner therefore believed individuals to be part of a monstrous *naturalistic* machine that trivializes the power of protest and the values of creativity and freedom—all the elements making socially responsible individualism possible. Adorno's almost mechanical connection between the desire for transcendence and desire for death in *The Ring,* in his view, reflects the nihilism and self-destructiveness implicit in the romantic escapism of bourgeois society. In such a world, transcendence without God is a "homecoming without a home" because nothing human survives; no justification for human value can be found in the nature of things because, deep down, nature has nothing to do with the self or with social value (thus, in the destruction of Valhalla, the conclusion of *The Ring* rejects the unity of Spirit and Nature visualized in the ending of *Faust*). We continue to hold onto the myth of transcendently endowed value in the belief that we are united with the universe through the Will.

Adorno's Schopenhauerian, deterministic interpretation of *The Ring,* however, does not accurately describe what happens in the final version because Wagner rejected the transcendent spiritualism and universalized subjectivism implicit in Schopenhauer's conception of the Will. Just because we discover human life and value to be contingent, changeable, fraught with threats to the hard-won stability of our values, does not mean we should then want to escape society. If we recognize that Mankind and Nature are interdependent (not the same as reductively describing society as a natural process, explained by laws of nature), the 'fate' of this contingency *galvanizes* us for Wagner. Recognition makes us *responsible* for those values and for the conception of personhood connected with them. Increased comprehension of that responsibility, rather than resignation to inevitable failure and the denial of freedom, comes with our recognition of the contingency of our social values and the implicit conflict between them and our personal desires.

Wagner's "indifference towards the inner-life of the individual" (p. 117), not by disregarding individuality but by portraying it as pathetically ineffective, was the result of his Hegelianism, for Adorno: his belief that parts are determined by the whole. But we have seen several examples of how this description does not fit *The Ring* and that it consistently escapes the absolutism of Hegel *and* Schopenhauer. True, the characters are often under the illusion (or delusion) that they are free when they are actually projecting hopes and fears reflected by their circumstances in the world, but to call this "determinism" confuses conceptual constraint with causal necessity. We are always 'constrained' by our beliefs and values, by our social institutions; but changing them surely involves the creation of *other* constraints. To say that my alternatives are restricted to either A or B *constrains* my choice, it does not *determine* it (in the sense that it would be determined if A and B were *logically* possible but B was the only *causally* possible alternative[35]). Why is not *The Ring* instead a story about *constraints* effecting the inner-life rather than *determinants* trivializing it? And if there is a general, inevitable result ("all things that are pass away"), is it not very important for us to realize that there can be no utopia, that the human self-image undergoes constant change, as do our values and our conception of reality, and that these changes are sometimes destructive? I have been trying to show that the result of our realization of the ultimate constraints on human striving need not be pessimism or escapism, it can be renewed *social* energy in the creation of new constraints—*Die Meistersinger* in reality as well as in art.

Speaking generally about the doctrines of *Opera and Drama*, many commentators have noted that Wagner's characters, and his music-dramas, possess certain generic characteristics. As Brian Magee summarizes it:

> ...there is something passive about [music-drama]—and also something solipsistic, the two being related. By filleting drama of motive and presenting it almost entirely in terms of emotional response Wagner shows things acting on people

> but not people acting on things. Their feelings in relation to situations and each other are poured out in unparalleled fullness, but this very fact means that the situation itself, or the relationship, is somehow "given." We see the characters almost entirely from the inside—very little as active in the world, motivating events, assuming control of situations and changing them.... [Wagner's] characters are subjects only of feeling: of action they are always the objects. One can go even farther and say that his main characters are victims[36].... Solipsism is suggested by that fact that reality for Wagner is always to be found in the psyche, not in the external world. Inner emotion is so overwhelmingly experienced that everything else, including other people, has only a shadowy existence on its periphery.... It has been said of *The Ring* that in the deepest sense there is only one character, the different "characters" being aspects of a single personality, so that the work is a portrait of the psyche as well as a depiction of the world. (Brian Magee, *Aspects of Wagner,* pp. 33–34)

These are not so much criticisms, I think, as they are *characterizations*. Peckham, for example, whose view reflects more of Schopenhauer than does mine, believes that the Will, expressed through the orchestra, stands as the *only* character in *The Ring*. But one can find counterexamples to everything Magee says: there *are* many moments of dramatic interaction between characters in *The Ring* and, if those characters have richly portrayed inner-lives, and if a sense of isolation and victimization ultimately intrudes, why should this be taken as a criticism rather than as Wagner's all-too accurate description of the gulf between modern psychological and social reality? Not much later, for example, the 'monodramas' of Schoenberg (*Ewartung* and *Pierot Lunnaire*) and even the later works of Mahler, develop this sense of isolation as an aesthetic category. Much earlier, in 1827, Schubert's *Die Winterreise* clearly established this very sense of psychological isolation as an aesthetic category. Even so, as Magee quotes Edward Dent:

> Wagner, through his writings and through his own personal influence, has converted the musical world, or a good part of it, to something like a new outlook on music in general. It may be that he was mistaken in supposing that the modern world could ever recover the attitude of ancient Greece to the religious aspect of musical drama, but he certainly induced it to take music, and especially opera, far more seriously than it had ever done before. (*Aspects of Wagner,* p. 35)

Turning lastly to the politics of freedom, to which he continually appeals, Adorno's conception seems best symbolized by *Fidelio,* with its pathos of the unjustly imprisoned arising from their dungeons, a metaphor of resurrection, shaking off the chains of oppression in a chorus of solidarity filled with the Enlightenment's symbolism of light. Adorno's image of freedom clearly reflects this romantic ideal. Beethoven's political point in *Fidelio,* for Adorno, was to protest the terrible fate of those who stand by their beliefs and conscience, and who thereby uphold the value of the individual, symbolized by Leonora's love for Florestan as it stands against social oppression. Adorno finds no such protest in Wagner because the characters of his dramas are not individuals, they do not, for him, have social consciences but only desires for escape. But surely Siegmund and Sieglinde are Wagner's protest against totalitarianism, as is Brünnhilde through her compassion, and the death of Siegfried carries with it the pathos of hope defeated at the hands of expediency and the distortions of erotic idealism. Is the effect of Siegfried's Funeral March on us really the *acceptance* of determinism and the glory of escaping social constraint? Does it symbolize *our* resignation, our status as 'victims' of the world-process?

Siegfried's death cannot, I contend, simply depict the injustice of the world against the purity of love (given Brünnhilde's role in his murder). The complexity of our response to this moment depends on what has come before (I will have more to say about the Funeral March in my Conclusion). Cooke points out that the decisive moment of the whole cycle rests on Siegmund's refusal to go to Valhalla:

> In the long struggle between power and love, begun in *Das Rheingold,* love has always—despite its apparent triumph in [*Die Walküre* I]—been totally on the losing side; but now that it has its back to the wall, and seems certain to be extinguished, it makes a tremendous come-back, through Siegmund's love-motivated act of rebellion against the highest manifestation of power. (*I Saw the World End,* pp. 336–7)

From that moment on, love and power are explicitly involved in a desperate struggle. But that conflict was implicit in *Das Rheingold* when Freia, in her role as the sustaining force of Valhalla (its source of continual youth), was objectified, made into a commodity—she had what would be called by Adorno and the Marxists "exchange value" for Wotan in his attempt to gain the ring. By treating her as goods to be bargained away, Wotan transformed Freia into a "fetish" (most obviously seen in the giants' reaction to the possibility of possessing her). I noted in Chapter 1, Section 8 how the motif of Freia's life-sustaining golden apples clashed with that of the gold in Scene 2 of *Das Rheingold,* and how this was, in a single stroke, the story of *The Ring.* Remember too the contrast between Nibelheim and its slave-labor, its deafening anvils, and Valhalla's rich brass lullaby and its relation to the motif of the Power of The Ring: the contrast between heaven and hell, with heaven itself compromised and set against the Rhinemaiden's lament. In these instances, Wagner makes Adorno's point for him and, I have been saying, it is really *Wagner's* point. I have also noted how Freia's music becomes the basis for the Love music of *Die Walküre* in its association with Siegmund and Sieglinde, and later with Brünnhilde. The idea of love, derived from Freia II and from Wotan's treatment of Freia, and its impact on Brünnhilde through Siegmund's refusal to go quietly that causes Valhalla's collapse.

But if love transforms the Old Wotan, the Wotan who manipulated the giants and Alberich, who gave away Freia, who created Siegmund and Sieglinde as a reflection of his own *eros* and for his own redemption, love also makes it easy for the New Wotan to renew his desire for control since he uses Brünnhilde's compassion in his search for a redeeming hero. Even as they try to establish their autonomy from power and oppression, they cannot escape the constraints of power entirely. Is this not true of the prisoners of *Fidelio* as well? If the characters of *The Ring* protest power and fate, what do they do about it? Even Brünnhilde's love becomes a will to power for her. I contend that this makes up the understanding of the relation between individuality, humanity, and society contained in *The Ring*. There is no such thing as unconstrained freedom, complete autonomy, but we continually change those concepts in practice. Freedom has no absolute definition. As a result, even in defeat, Wotan and Brünnhilde change the system. Wagner tells us a story *about* the problems of freedom in society including the transcendence of society through love. But what are the effects of that belief on those who hold it?

In his major philosophic work, Adorno summarizes his general view of aesthetic-philosophical understanding as follows:

> The only philosophy which can be responsibly practiced in the face of despair is the attempt to contemplate all things as they would present themselves from the standpoint of redemption.... Perspectives must be fashioned that displace and estrange the world, reveal it to be, with its rifts and crevices, as indigent and distorted as it will appear one day in the messianic light. To gain such perspectives...is the simplest of things,...but it is also the utterly impossible thing.... Even its own impossibility it must at last comprehend for the sake of the possible. But beside the demand thus placed on thought, the question of the reality or unreality of redemption itself hardly matters.[37]

Again, this seems to me to fit the conclusion of *The Ring* pretty well: hope certainly matters—even if the kind of redemption dreamt of by Wotan (or Brünnhilde) never occurs, hope guides their actions. And it may be, as Nietzsche suggests, that the actual structure of the world cannot be fully grasped because it is inherently indeterminate. But we must try to gain understanding of it in relation to our own interests even against that realization, for only through the attempt at creating order can we establish anything valuable. Surely the achievement of any such orientative drive would itself be redemptive because it shows humans at work at what they do best. Striving for understanding, even in defeat, has usually been the source of the social freedom and stability we have been able to achieve. The drive for orientation and value, for understanding, the will to power, has always kept humanity going. But, I have maintained, Wagner refuses to transcend, to give a final picture of humanity beyond *Die Meistersinger,* beyond society. Like others in the nineteenth century, he denies that understanding has its ultimate stopping point in absolute truth, and thus we exist forever within 'illusions'. If we can never escape the process of managing our illusions, we can never get a completely outside view, a God's eye view, of our inventions (including our self-images).

Like his colleagues at Frankfurt, Adorno rejected the materialism and economic determinism of the later Marx. He took the nineteenth century seriously in his interest in consciousness and spirituality; he did not simply dismiss them, or dismiss social value and individualism as mere 'products of economic forces'. He did believe in freedom. But he sometimes shared with the earlier Hegel the idea of what he called a "synoptic imperative," an "imageless," non-deterministic, general comprehension of the intersection between humanity, society, and nature reconciling individuality and freedom with social responsibility. In his desire for 'synopsis', he remained Hegelian in a way Wagner did not. The point of *The Ring* might be that this urge for totality requires exactly the mythology of freedom and inventiveness necessary in periods of conceptual and social revolution. Of course, as Kant was the first to argue, we cannot ever *know* whether we are 'free' in that sense, because the whole point of these global revolutions in self-understanding rests on the rejection of previous synoptic imperatives even if they envisage a new one.

Adorno's artistic conservatism led him to emphasize the development of the sonata form in the late eighteenth and early nineteenth centuries as an aesthetic idealization of the synoptic imperative. Indeed, he believed it to be a more coherent historical period than more recent commentators have shown it to be (Rosen, for example, and Dahlhaus). But if we see that fertile period more dynamically, the way Hegel might have seen it, then Beethoven shows one side of that myth, while the political paintings of Goya and Géricault show the other. We do not end with the creation of an ideal form of expression because the thoughts expressed in this period are as destructive as they are creative—and they are both at the same time. *The Ring* in effect recasts the image of cultural revolution: *Fidelio* and *The Raft of the Medusa*; the *Ninth Symphony* and *Götterdämmerung*.

9. Nietzsche's Wagner

For both Nietzsche and Adorno, Wagner not only denies the existence of absolutes, of which they both more or less approve, but in so doing, they say, he reduces values to subjective states, and then implies that anyone who can manipulate the experiences of others can create values in accordance with *their* subjective states. This has become a familiar argument: since there are no absolutes, no transcendental standards of comparison, no values can be valid for all. Values are mere sentiments. *Therefore* the only foundation for value lies in the interests of whatever establishment controls the subjective mechanism of value creation—capitalism for Adorno, Christianity and its descendants (including Wagner) for Nietzsche. These *virtual* absolutes will do just as well. But while the values implicit in a work of art like *The Ring* may well express the interests of its creator, it does not follow that it advocates or serves those interests or values, that works of art inculcate, engender a world view. My point has been that *The Ring* does not *advocate* subjectivity or self-destructiveness but that it sees these as part of a larger context of change and contingency. Like Adorno, Nietzsche's Wagner-critique also has a tendency to reproduce this fallacious inference.

Turning to the character of Siegfried, Nietzsche captures the irony of his character perfectly in that important #4 of *The Case of Wagner*: Siegfried wages war against the laws and contracts of Wotan's compromised society and overcomes its decadence through purely natural impulses. As Nietzsche describes him,

> [Siegfried] starts early, very early: his very genesis is a declaration of war against morality—he comes into this world through adultery, through incest.—It is not the [ancient Norse] saga but Wagner who invented this radical trait; at this point he revised the saga. …Siegfried continues as he has begun: he merely follows his first impulse, he overthrows everything traditional, all reverence, all *fear*. Whatever displeases he stabs to death. Without the least respect, he tackles old deities. But his main enterprise aims *to emancipate woman*—"to redeem Brünnhilde"—Siegfried and Brünnhilde; the sacrament of free love; the rise of the golden age; the twi-

light of the gods for the old morality—*all ill has been abolished.*[38]

Nietzsche refuses to see Wagner's irony here, or to see that Siegfried can be understood ironically: he intended his description as a criticism, as a parody of what he claims to be Wagner's absurd conception of redemptive hope. But with the character of Siegfried, Wagner shows the impossibility of the kind of heroic redemption Wotan desired, the kind Nietzsche saw at the end of the first versions of *The Ring*. As Nietzsche describes it, when he returned to *The Ring* after a hiatus of ten years or so, Wagner "translated it into Schopenhauerian terms." Instead of the original optimistic ending with its triumphant emergence of a humanist utopia, we get resignation, withdrawal and decadence. "He flatters every nihilistic (Buddhist) instinct and disguises it in music" (*Nietzsche contra Wagner*, Postscript). Why was Wagner not perfectly aware of all of Siegfried's absurd ineffectiveness just as Nietzsche described them? The contrast between his natural origins and the seemingly unnatural problems of Wotan's society could hardly be more clearly drawn. But the defeat of Siegfried's natural purity does not launch us into Schopenhauerian pessimism and resignation about the human prospect. As Peckham points out, the action on the stage

> can be thoroughly pessimistic, yet value remains in the world of human experience. It is the self, embodied in the music, that endures even though society and the hero have both been destroyed, even through the divine world has been eliminated, even though the problem of society is seen as absolutely unsolvable.... *The Ring* strips the self of...divine authority and asserts that...heroic effort [for transcendent justification] is futile and must necessarily be frustrated. The self is now absolutely—and terribly—free, neither supported nor justified. For the first time it is really stripped bare, its value entirely self-generated. (p. 269)

The destruction of the ("theological") myth of transcendence leads to a clearer view of our illusions: 'the self', whatever its natural instincts, cannot fill the gap left by the death of God because it has no absolute nature. I agree with Peckham (and Adorno) that Wagner "strips the self of divine authority" and that, because it has no implicit authority of its own, heroic redemption can now be seen to be at least problematic. But his last sentence implies too much existential autonomy for the final version of *The Ring* (and probably too much for Nietzsche too). In this I think Nietzsche's characterization of Wagner as an unreconstructed Schopenhauerian, and still looking for an absolute, also fails to capture an important aspect of the work—nothing remains of Wotan and Brünnhilde at the end of *Götterdämmerung* because their *society* has been destroyed, every other person who means anything to them has been destroyed. Just as there could be no freedom for Tristan and Isolde once they have transcended their society, including their physical identities, it is unclear at the end of *The Ring* what it would mean for value to be completely self-generated by a being (or by a force such as the Will) with the awful autonomy Brünnhilde achieves under that view. At that point, society is the least of her interests. Value in relation to what? While this question may be perfectly appropriate to Sartre, Wagner has an answer: value lies in the relation of individual to individual in the creation of shared goals, interests, and affections.

The self does not, therefore, possess isolated, universalized identity for Wagner; nor can it generate values in isolation. Subjectivity has no essence either. He seems to be telling us the same thing as Adorno: that too much autonomy leads to the loss of identity because no self can be purely self-constructed. We are shaped by factors such as community, tradition, and history but these should not be thought of as *external* factors, as something added to an identity the self already possesses. They too are part of ones identity (the point of *Die Meistersinger*). One exists as a member of a community, one exists at a certain point in the history of that community and moral authority rests on the interdependence of self and society—not absolutely but as an ongoing invention, both precarious and hopeful. Certainly Wagner took society and community to be part of the constraints on selfhood in all of his works and it seems to me that, in his view of constructive and destructive identity, he avoids both the romantic, metaphysically autonomous self and the Hegelian conceptually determined identity of the self in his refusal to transcend. However much I may be able to hold myself autonomous from these factors, I cannot transcend society for something more basic to selfhood, something more valuable, because they are interdependent and connected with who 'I' am.

Furthermore, it is a very misleading view of *The Ring* to think of the self as a substitute for the Will (or the Will as an abstract self), as Peckham suggests, and its endurance in some absolute sense after all the major characters have been annihilated. When Peckham speaks about the self "embodied in music," the orchestra indeed expresses and extends the beliefs and desires of the characters, but it does not become a (symbolically) transcendent being—the orchestra as pure spirit, as God, or what was left of God in the late nineteenth century, the absolute self. Although this view has some appeal, I have tried to show how this music expresses in a general way the fateful potential for conflict in the universe as it unfolds in *The Ring*. The danger of seeing the orchestra as a generalized self—or of overextending the metaphor that it becomes a character in the work—simply makes Wagner *too* Schopenhauerian—Nietzsche's mistake in thinking that Wagner denies individuality. The orchestra shows us the beliefs and emotions of the characters on the stage, it shows us the connection between the microcosm and the macrocosm, and sometimes it comments on the actions of the characters with irony, recollection, and projection. But neither Schopenhauer's determinism nor his pessimism comes through in anything like their full power in the diminishment of the individual. The orchestra-as-Will shows us the conflict-orientation of the world through its own musical development, but it does not transcend as ultimate reality beyond the phenomenal world. It characterizes *that* world from the point of view of conflict between its members but our focus remains on the characters—on ourselves—even in the orchestra's final generalization.

Perhaps Nietzsche would have been sympathetic to this kind of an account had he seen that by the time he reached the final version of *The Ring,* Wagner's Schopenhauerianism was as selective as his own. But he also felt overpowered by Wagner's domineering personality, and there is no doubt that he felt his own creativity threatened by the subordination demanded of him. To psychoanalyze for one brief moment: How much of Nietzsche's opposition to Wagner was the result of trying to pull himself out from under this undeniably powerful, ruthless influence, to establish his own creativity? To think of *Parsifal,* for example, as a work *expressing* the beliefs of Christianity (undoubtedly in a particularly perverse way), rather than a work *about* the mythology of transcendent redemption, is a mistake others besides Nietzsche have made (as Tanner points out); but Nietzsche associates that work with Wagner's own personal need to play the savior in his egocentric spiritualization of humanism. For Nietzsche, *Parsifal* became a "religious" work, and a fantasy of autobiography. Of all of Wagner's works, *Parsifal* was most explicitly about *himself.* This clearly precludes any understanding of the quite nonreligious, humanistic conclusion of the work and its clear rejection of transcendent mythology as the source of redemption. I explore these more positive views in the Appendix, Section 6.

It should also be noted, in conclusion, that there seems to be a big difference between Nietzsche's public view of Wagner in his later work and his private view. For example, Newman quotes from late letters (1887) in which Nietzsche compares *Parsifal* to Dante: "Has any painter ever depicted so sorrowful a look of love as Wagner has done in the final accents of his Prelude?" And to his sister he describes himself as "violently shaken" and "deeply moved" by the work. He writes:

> It is as if someone were speaking to me again after many years about the problems that disturb me—naturally not supplying the answer *I* would give, but the Christian answer, which, after all, has been the answer of stronger souls than the last two centuries of our era have produced. When listening to this music one lays Protestantism aside as a misunderstanding—moreover, I will not deny it, *other really good music,* which I

have at other times heard and loved, seems, as against this, a misunderstanding.[39]

Nietzsche's best public discussion about his ambivalence towards Wagner occurs, much earlier, in *Daybreak* (#255) in his "Conversation about Music." There he draws two distinctions, between 'good' and 'bad' music, and between 'innocent' and 'guilty' music. The latter distinction cuts across the former: there can be good or bad music of either kind. Innocent music "thinks wholly and solely of itself, believes in itself and has forgotten the world in contemplation of itself," while guilty music strives for effects and has designs on the moral autonomy of its listeners. 'Good' innocent music may well sweep us into its sound world, but in so doing it need not change us into less creative, less critical, less responsible human beings.[40] Good, innocent music encourages us, enhances our humanity—as Nietzsche himself argues Wagner's music does.

Notes

1 An important study of early audiences and performances of *Tristan,* for example, can be found in Elliot Zuckermann, *The First Hundred Years of Tristan*, (New York: Columbia University Press, 1964).

2 Carl Dahlhaus, *Richard Wagner's Music-Dramas*, trans. Mary Whittall (New York: Cambridge University Press, 1979), pp. 92–104 for a discussion of the various endings of *The Ring.* See also Carl Dahlhaus, "Über den Schluss der *Götterdämmerung,*" in Carl Dahlhaus (ed.) *Richard Wagner: Werk und Wirkung* (Regensburg, 1971). As I indicated in the previous chapter, Dahlhaus also wrote the entry on Wagner in the *New Grove Dictionary of Music and Musicians,* published as the separate volume cited above.

3 Ronald Gray, "The German Intellectual Background," in Burbidge and Sutton, *The Wagner Companion*, p. 47.

4 See Roger Hollinrake, "Carl Dahlhaus and *The Ring,*" in Steward Spencer (ed.), *Wagner 1976: A Celebration of the Bayreuth Festival* (London: Wagner Society, 1976), pp. 68–82.

5   Although I occasionally employ their terminology, I do not discuss the psychoanalytic interpretations of *The Ring* such as Robert Donington's Jungian *Wagner's Ring and its Symbolism* (London: Faber and Faber, 1963). See Cooke's discussion of both Shaw and Donington in *I Saw the World End*. Of Donington he writes that "the central weakness of Jungian interpretation [is that] [a]nything and everything is enclosed within the narcissistic magic circle of the individual psyche, into which no image of irrevocable external catastrophe can enter without being gelded of its manifest meaning, so that black becomes white, and all is always for the best" (p. 29). No one should deny the importance of Donington's interpretation, however, and I certainly include psychological symbolism as one level of *The Ring* but, along with Cooke (and Tanner), I see it as *one* of its levels, not its deepest. See also Robert L. Jacobs, "A Freudian View of *The Ring*," *The Music Review*, XXVI, 3, 1965, pp. 201–219. Reprinted in J.L. DiGaetani (ed.), *Penetrating Wagner's Ring* (Tcancck: Fairleigh Dickinson University Press, 1978).

6   See Cooke's discussion of the theory of leitmotif, *I Saw the World End*, pp. 37 f., and Dahlhaus, *New Grove Wagner*, Chapters 4 and 5. I refer to some of their points in what follows.

7   Dahlhaus, *Richard Wagner's Music-Dramas*, pp. 102–104.

8   The *Leviathan* was published in 1651; Charles I was executed in 1649 and Cromwell became Protector in 1653. During this period the *Leviathan* was widely discussed as a characterization of political sovereignty. See Cooke's discussion of Old/New Wotan, *I Saw the World End*, pp. 324 f.

9   Thomas Hobbes, *Leviathan,* C.B. Macpherson (ed.) (London: Penguin, 1968), Part I, Chapter 11, p. 161.

10 George Windell, "Hegel, Feuerbach, and Wagner's *Ring*," p. 45. See Cooke, *I Saw the World End,* p. 159 for an important comparison of parallels between Alberich and Wotan as Wotan becomes aware of his ambiguous identity.

11 Theodor Adorno, *In Search of Wagner*, trans. Rodney Livingstone (Manchester: NLB/Schocken, 1981), p. 149. First published as *Versuch Über Wagner* in 1952. It was, however, written in 1937–8, in the last years before the outbreak of World War II: Hitler invaded Poland on September 1, 1939.

12 In particular see Tanner, *Wagner,* pp. 180 f. and Peckham, *Beyond the Tragic Vision,* Chapter 15.

13 See David Cormack, "Thomas Mann, Hanns Eisler and the 'New Bayreuth'," *Wagner*, II, 2, pp. 44–63, esp. pp. 58 f.

14 In Chapter 1, Section 8 I noted another important instance of this technique in Wagner's use of the second part of Freia's motif in the music for Loge and Wotan's descent into Nibelheim in the Interlude between Scenes 2 and 3 of *Das Rheingold.*

15 Bailey discusses the Annunciation scene at some length in "The Structure of *The Ring* and its Evolution," pp. 55 f. His analysis shows the musical complexity of the scene as it is connected to the dramatic structure. He also usefully discusses the beginning of *Götterdämmerung* in corresponding detail. See also Grey's discussion in *Wagner's Musical Prose*, pp. 233 f.

16 In *The Case of Wagner*, #7, Nietzsche describes Wagner as "our greatest miniaturist." "His wealth of colors, of half shadows, of the secrecies of dying light spoils one to such an extent that afterward almost all other musicians seem to robust." This entire section contains many valuable insights, although Nietzsche meant them as a rejection of Wagner's "decadence."

17 Jack M. Stein, *Richard Wagner and the Synthesis of the Arts* (Westport, Connecticut: Greenwood Press, 1960), p. 110.

18 The richness of the instrumental texture in *The Ring* results in part from Wagner's use of at least four instruments within almost all choirs—thus there are four flutes, four oboes, four trumpets, and so on. Many orchestras also double some of these lines. This allows not only for tremendous volume (which should be carefully controlled) but also for genuine four-part harmony from each instrument. A study of the orchestral score clearly shows this complexity. Motifs are also associated with specific instrumental groups: the Sword with the trumpets, Love with the strings, and so on. Alberich's Curse, for example, begins as a single line for the trombones, but ends in three- and sometimes four-part brass cadences. The Love music often divides up the strings into complex groupings (see Act I of *Die Walküre,* or *Siegfried* Ii); the Rhinegold and Servitude motifs usually occur in the woodwinds, Death on the drum, and so on. But they will also occur

along with other motifs so that their instrumental associations are essential to their identity.

19 See Cooke, *Introduction to Wagner's Ring*, p. 29.

20 See Cooke, "Wagner's Musical Language," pp. 250–252, and his *Introduction to Wagner's Ring,* p. 19.

21 It might be observed that some of Beethoven's contemporary critics claimed that he could not write a decent fugue. Taking Bach as the model, Beethoven's fugues are certainly 'deficient'. But this misses the point that Beethoven—even if he *could* write a decent fugue in the baroque sense—nevertheless transformed it into a much freer form so it could play a role within the development section of the sonata where he used it to great effect. Without taking up this complex point here, Wagner initially intended that melody, in music-drama, should be motivated by the text and become like speech. See Grey's discussion of melody as form in *Wagner's Musical Prose,* p. 270 f. and his discussion of Dahlhaus on endless melody, p. 252 f. In part, Wagner wanted to eliminate the recitative, which he regarded as completely unmotivated musically—ironically, the same criticism Adorno made about Wagner's monologues. See Martin Jay's discussion of Adorno's "diametrical opposition" between Beethoven and Wagner: Martin Jay, *Adorno* (Cambridge, Massachusetts: Harvard University Press, 1984), pp. 144–149. Unlike his criticisms of Enlightenment philosophy, which he described as alienating Mankind and Nature through scientific instrumentalism, for Adorno, Beethoven unified them through his "nonconceptual" approach to music. Wagner's later view of music-drama shares this point.

22 Donnington also points out the connection between Hagen's motif and the first bar of Valhalla. Hagen's bass line also resembles the opening of Erda's motif and the rising dotted-eighth motif of the Twilight of the Gods (see *Wagner's Ring and its Symbols,* p. 296).

23 See also Cooke, *Introduction to Wagner's Ring*, p. 26.

24 In *Götterdämmerung* Wagner also used some components of grand opera (an anachronism he had ruled out in *Opera and Drama*) such as ensemble singing (in the trio at the end of Act II) and even a chorus, first in the ironic Hagenesque celebration of the marriages and then in the wonderfully confused betrayal of Act IIiv.

25 For a discussion of this point see Maynard Solomon, "Beethoven, Sonata, and Utopia," *Telos*, VI, Fall 1971. See also Solomon's *Beethoven* (New York: Shirmer-Macmillan, 1977). For criticism see Robert Solomon (no relation), "Beethoven and the Sonata Form," *Telos*, VII, Winter 1972. M. Solomon replies to this in "Beethoven and the Enlightenment," *Ibid*. See also R. Solomon's introduction to nineteenth-century intellectual history, *History and Human Nature* (New York: Harcourt Brace Jovanovich, 1979), Chapter 12, for another discussion of Beethoven and summary of this debate.

26 Adorno argues for this in *Philosophy of Modern Music*, trans. Anne G. Mitchell and Wesley V. Blomster (New York: NLB, 1973). In it, the "revolutionary" Schoenberg opposes the "reactionary" Stravinsky who, as a neoclassicist, merely imposed old forms on equally old music and made no new theoretical advances. Unlike Stravinsky, for Adorno Schoenberg accomplished a genuine *Aufhebung* of classical form through the transformation of the language of tonality.

27 Arnold Hauser, *The Social History of Art*, Volume III (London: Routledge and Kegan Paul, 1951), p. 206.

28 Carl Dahlhaus, "Soziologishe Dechiffrierung von Music: Zu Theodor W. Adornos Wagnerkritik," *International Review of Music, Aesthetics, and Sociology*, I, 2, 1970, p. 141. See also Bailey's discussion of Lorenz, p. 54, endnotes 10 and 12.

29 Adorno devotes an entire chapter of *In Search of Wagner* (Chapter 2) to this point. For him, Wagner's music enacts "no historical process" (p. 35) because the motifs are in principle musically isolated from each other. There is no development for them because they "detach themselves from the temporal continuum that they seemingly created" (p. 37). Wagner's motifs are "gestures" because they merely imitate some natural object; they have no conceptual depth and exist only to refer, not to mean anything. Wagner did indeed conceive of his motifs 'mimetically' but only a very few of them actually retain that kind of ostensive simplicity. See Cooke, *I Saw the World End*, pp. 37 f. for the discussion to which I implicitly appeal throughout this section. Nietzsche also argued, in *The Case of Wagner*, that Wagner merely tried to simulate meaning through theatrical gesture rather than rational thought. See Grey, *Wagner's Musical Prose*, pp. 258–259.

30 *Loc. cit.* See also *The New Grove Wagner*, pp. 98–106. Dahlhaus discusses form more generally, and Adorno in particular, on pp. 124–126. See also Grey's extensive discussion of Dahlhaus in *Wagner's Musical Prose,* see: Index: Dahlhaus.

31 See Arnold Schoenberg, "Brahms the Progressive" in his *Style and Idea* for the origin of this view.

32 Schubert's *Impromptus*, for example *every one,* consists of sonata expositions followed by sometimes very complex variations, but with nothing like a sonata development. *Always* the thematic groups consists of developmental variations, often brought together as a *coda* in a series of contrasting developmental stages. The listener is left with the sense of contrast without resolution.

33 See Charles Rosen, *The Classical Style: Haydn, Mozart, Beethoven* (New York: Norton, 1972), Epilogue, for a discussion of the contrast between the sonata and other forms in Schubert and Chopin.

34 It should be noted that Adorno's idealization of the sonata proves all the more ironic since, as Rosen puts it, "Haydn was almost completely ignored, Mozart admired but misunderstood, and the reverence for Beethoven can be accounted only a pernicious influence for at least a generation after his death, producing with few exceptions only the most lifeless and academic imitations of forms no longer either comprehensible or acceptable," *Loc. cit.*

35 For example, it may be logically possible for me, a philosophy professor, to have been the Prime Minister of Canada instead. But given the actual history associated with John Tietz, only the former has come about. This does not, by itself, imply that causal histories are deterministic.

36 See Sandra Corse, *Wagner and the New Consciousness: Love and Language in The Ring* (London and Toronto: Associated University Presses, 1990). Corse believes that only Wagner's female characters are victims, totally overlooking Siegfried or Siegmund (for example). Nevertheless, there is much that I agree with in Corse's book.

37 Theodor Adorno, *Minima Moralia: Reflections from Damaged Life*, trans. E.F.N. Jephcott (London: NLB, 1974), Section 153. See a discussion of this passage in J. Hillis Miller, "Some Implications of Nietzsche's

Thought for Marxism," *Telos,* XXXVII, 1978, p. 38. See also Chapter 4 of Martin Jay's *Adorno*. I thank my colleague Samuel Black for suggesions about my discussion of Adorno.

38 Nietzsche also compares Brünnhilde with Emma Bovary (Flaubert's novel, *Madame Bovary*, was published in 1856, three years before *Tristan*): "transposed into hugeness, Wagner does not seem to have been interested in any problems except those which now preoccupy the little decadents of Paris. Always five steps from the hospital" (*The Case of Wagner* #9). See Peckham's discussion of *Madame Bovary*, pp. 276 f. Briefly, the difference is that Brünnhilde has serious problems understanding the moral dimension of her universe while Emma Bovary simply avoids morality altogether in her pursuit of sensuality. My point is that Brünnhilde's death involves a level of conceptual understanding, however incomplete, impossible for Emma. Emma's sensuality became destructive because she could not see its effects; but Brünnhilde's love cannot be (just) a form of sensuality because of its moral dimension, its concern with Wotan's world (look at the conceptual sophistication expressed in Brünnhilde's awakening scene) and with Siegfried's apparent betrayal of that love.

39 Quoted in Newman, *The Wagner Operas*, Vol. II., pp. 672–3. Newman's discussion of this passage should be read as well. See also Lucy Beckett's discussion of this letter in "Wagner and His Critics," in Burbidge and Sutton, *The Wagner Companion*.

40 See Tanner's discussion of this passage in his Introduction to R.J. Hollingdale's translation of *Daybreak: Thoughts on the Prejudices of Morality* (New York: Cambridge University Press, 1982).

Conclusion

What Does *The Ring* Mean?

I have tried to show how *The Ring* aesthetically exemplifies the great changes in our conceptions of meaning and value that began to take place in the nineteenth century. By way of conclusion, and at the risk of some repetition, I will first summarize the main points about *The Ring* that I have tried to make in the course of my examination. Section 1 will be devoted to this review. In Sections 2 and 3 I return to the ending of *The Ring* to contemplate its meaning in a more general way (I also make a few more specifically philosophical remarks at the end of the Appendix).

1. Redemptive Fire

With its great length, *The Ring* generates such tremendous momentum that it takes quite a while to conclude. There are in fact two long stretches of music in the final version of *The Ring,* but it could not plausibly have ended with Siegfried's funeral, except anticlimactically. For then Siegfried's death would be, as Mann suggests, a merely sentimental remembrance of heroism destroyed with little connection to the larger dramatic and philosophical context that emerges during the drama.

After her extraordinary adventures, Brünnhilde at last says that she understands what has happened to her in the long journey from her subservient role in her father's kingdom to the side of her lover, a lover she helped to destroy during her long journey towards self-consciousness. What does she comprehend? What *we* understand emerges in the music at the point of her cryptic realization: "Alles, alles/alles weiss ich." Has she "studied Schopenhauer," as Nietzsche says in *The Case of Wagner* (#4)? She knows, conceivably, what her mother Erda knows—that all things change and that, in particular, power and love cannot be pulled apart. I contend that this sentiment applies in a general way to self and society too, that they are inherently unstable, in constant change, undergoing continual reinvention. This ending, Wagner said, retained by implication the sense of the earlier ending containing the phrase "I saw the world end." Wotan's denial of his will to power opened the way for radical changes in his society, but those changes did not lead to its replacement by a better one based on love and somehow forestalling the forces of change. Along with Brünnhilde's last words, we also hear the motif of the Power of the Ring followed by Alberich's Curse. The music indicates, I suggest, what Brünnhilde understands through this last constellation of motifs: Alberich's Curse leads into the Rhinemaidens' "Rhinegold" motif (absolved of its Hagenesque distortion), becoming Valhalla at "Ruhe, ruhe du Gott" (but we should also remember that the Rhinegold motif forms the basis for the Power of the Ring and Servitude motifs—recall the transition from the Renunciation, Gold, and Ring motifs to Valhalla between Scenes 1 and 2 of *Das Rheingold*). *Das Rheingold* is thereby connected to *Götterdämmerung* establishing the historical link Wagner intended in his account of the creation of society out of self-consciousness. We then hear the Erda-derived Rise and Fall of the Gods and the Need of the Gods (has this need been satisfied—is it unsatisfiable?). The significance of these references will be completely lost without having seen and heard how they have been built up throughout the rest of the cycle, and the choric function of the orchestra, its 'comment' on the general meaning of the drama, is essential to this ending.

Although Brünnhilde has been the focus of the final events of the visible drama, I agree with Tanner ("The Total Work of Art," p. 172) that neither she nor Siegfried have become the real center of the work. The music increasingly alludes to the larger context of the Will as the opposition of power and love at all levels, the metaphysical, the personal, and the social. As we proceed to the end of *Götterdämmerung,* we encounter more and more references to the events of the past, reminding us—if not through conscious recollection then indirectly—of the many variations of conflict that have brought the characters to this point. Furthermore, the ending of *The Ring* in its final version takes us beyond the hope of utopian redemption, in its Feuerbachian sense of social mission of humanity, because the Will, as Wagner came to understand it musically, simply represents the tension between power and love in the self and society. By the middle of *Götterdämmerung,* Brünnhilde has become a symbol of that tension but not its resolution. Her own, internal discord between love and rage was to be resolved in the death of Siegfried and in the symbolic destruction of Valhalla and Wotan, both by now completely superfluous. I have maintained that the dynamic nature of the Will as Wagner sees it in *The Ring* engenders both creation and destruction. In this metaphysical environment of continually evolving conflict, there can be no ultimate triumph of love in the form of compassionate humanity over power and evil for there are no universal truths established to underwrite such a victory, to eliminate the possibility of conflict. In this I agree with Adorno. However, the final moments of *Götterdämmerung* do not envisage a transcendence of conflict and change but a vision of their centrality to civilization.

It should also be observed that placing two powerful and relatively long stretches of music so closely together not only allowed Wagner to highlight the various conceptual elements of the drama but also to bring the orchestral interweaving of these elements to center stage. Again, the role of the orchestra as chorus becomes increasingly prominent as the music-drama becomes symphonic. The significance of *The Ring,* once again, lies in its music. The Funeral March and the end of Valhalla are in effect two large recapitulations. Siegfried's funeral music brings together the many elements associated with heroism, hope, the sword, the destiny of the Volsungs, Brünnhilde's love, the second part of Freia's motif, the Dawn music, Alberich's Curse and death. Brünnhilde's last scene brings together the motifs associated with Valhalla, with love, the Curse, Fate, the Power of the Ring, and Love's Redemption.

Returning to the characters of Siegfried and Brünnhilde, by the middle of *Götterdämmerung,* Siegfried has become a mere symbol for the hopes and dreams of both Wotan and Brünnhilde. But he also symbolizes heroic potential, otherwise his funeral music would be grotesquely out of place since—as Tanner asks—after Siegfried leaves his fairy-tale world and climbs Brünnhilde's mountain into the real world of his sexuality and then, in *Götterdämmerung,* the world of politics, what does he accomplish? What has he done to *deserve* his funeral music? He sails off to set the world aright at the beginning of *Götterdämmerung,* but immediately encounters Hagen. With his arrival at the House of Gibichung, Siegfried already has a 'reputation' as a great hero, his great life work being to make the world safe for love. Love, however, destroys him.

Let us look specifically at the motif that unifies the Funeral March: the drumbeats symbolizing death. We have seen that this motif has been associated specifically with death since *Das Rheingold* and brings together the entire cycle in the Funeral March. It accompanies Alberich's renunciation and curse in *Das Rheingold,* usually appearing whenever twists of fate portending death occur. It points to the motif of Alberich's Curse its role in Wotan's monologue during *Die Walküre* IIii, foretelling the deaths of Siegmund and Siegfried. Along with the Fate music, the drumbeats accompany Brünnhilde's revelation to Siegmund of his impending doom. The motif thus ultimately establishes a symbolic interconnection between Brünnhilde's destiny and redemption. As the forces of power and love are brought together in Siegfried's funeral music, we see the result of Wotan's dream of heroic redemption. What began as a barely noticeable drumroll in *Das Rheingold* becomes the basis for the music of Siegfried's death in *Götterdämmerung,* and for the great Funeral March that follows, where it appears in tremendous and harsh brass chords along with the timpani motif. This music portrays the failure of Wotan's hope; the recurrence of the Volsung motif and the Sword point up the symbolic significance of Siegfried in the drama as the focus of that hope. Its *Eroica*-like outburst of nobility and sadness brings together all of the events in Siegfried's life, interweaving the many motifs accompanying his progress from individual to symbol. The reference to the love music of his parents, Siegmund and Sieglinde, express the hope for Siegfried while the joys and triumphs of his youth are enshrouded in the mists of death, in the Nothingness opening before Wotan's world at the failure of his redemptive ideal.

In the final sequence of *The Ring* (also discussed in Chapter 2, Section 3) we hear the deceptively hopeful motifs of Valhalla (deceptive because of its close resemblance to that of the Ring and hence with the desire for power), Death, and Alberich's Curse, the Twilight of the Gods, and finally Love's Redemption. Immediately following the moment of Brünnhilde's "Alles, Alles,/Alles weiss ich,/Alles ward mir non frei!" we again hear the solo timpani and its death motif followed shortly by Alberich's Curse, cut off as Hagen and the ring are submerged. We then hear the Rhinegold motif, Valhalla, the Rise and Fall of the Gods, and then the motif of sleep originally associated with Brünnhilde at "Ruhe, ruhe, du Gott!" Finally, just before Brünnhilde calls on Loge to light the fire, the Ring motif along with the Curse and a reference to Renunciation reappear, followed by Wotan's Spear motif—the outcome of his authority in the conflagration initiated long before by his daughter. The motif of the Rise and Fall of the Gods (reminiscent of the rising and falling piano theme in the second movement of Beethoven's "Kreutzer" violin sonata (op. 47)) provides the backdrop for much of the final scene. This motif combines a version of the rising Nature motif with the falling motif of the Twilight of the Gods.

In the end, the ruins of Valhalla remain to be contemplated by the survivors of the House of Gibichung who have witnessed these catastrophic events. What do these events symbolize? I have argued that from Wagner's point of view, the essence of the world manifests conflict through the Power/Love dichotomy. Society and selfhood are essentially impermanent because they are changing, as we have seen in the characters of Brünnhilde and Siegfried. Yet persons can, through their creations, control the forces of power and love at least to the extent that we can see the dialectics of opposition and resolution as the root of our impermanence, and through that understanding perhaps we can establish some relative stability within such a world. The self does not achieve independence from politics at the end of *Götterdämmerung* by at last establishing utopia. Nor, contrary to Peckham (Appendix, Section 4; Chapter 3, Section 9), should we think of the Will as an "absolute self," as transcendent individuality (for Wagner, this must be an oxymoron). At the end, the dynamic forces of the universe remain, but they contain no absolutes except change through conflict. The power of both love and politics lies in their ability to effect change. The concluding moments of the cycle, I have argued, do not portray the triumph of love but the interdependence of power and love. Valhalla was deceptive in its illusion of permanence, its motif indeed the "lullaby of the bourgeoisie" (as Adorno described it). Furthermore, we have seen the deceptiveness of love in its transcendent power through its connection with fate.[1]

I suggest that these two extended recapitulations show, firstly, the connection between hope, redemption, and change. Society and the self in nineteenth-century German philosophy and art are not only conceived as fundamentally changing but, when understood as the underlying source of the desire for permanence and stability, change and contingency has the character of irony. What happens through our hope for permanence will not always be what we expect, and sometimes it will be the opposite. For example, Wotan's search for social stability only ensures its change and Brünnhilde's desire to live for love as the only real value has direct political and social consequences. Secondly, the last recapitulation joins together power and love as two sides to the same force of change forming the images of self and society in *The Ring*—and for us as well. In the last moments of *Götterdämmerung*, Redemption Through Love does not, I have argued, signal the victory of love over power; it shows the power of change in our conceptions of self and society. When the Dawn music occurs for the final time at the moment of Siegfried's death, it portends the dawn of the gods' final day but it also constitutes a moment of comprehension. Brünnhilde begins to see the interconnectedness of power and love, the essential orientation of life: she has become like her mother, Erda.[2] The two great orchestral montages immediately following this final occurrence of the Dawn music at Siegfried's death take us to this more general level of understanding. What, exactly, is the *victory* of love in this context?

By bringing together the contrary symbols of nature and society—the World Ash Tree and Valhalla—and then unifying them in the fire that consumes both, Wagner retains something of Schopenhauer's scepticism about the ideals of the Enlightenment and romanticism. Nature and spirit cannot be brought to unity in human civilization, or through art or emotion, or transcendent selfhood, because they embody principles of change inconsistent with the illusions of permanence that have sustained Western civilization, at least until the nineteenth century. When we see and hear the collapse of Valhalla at the end of *Götterdämmerung,* we witness the destruction of our own symbols of permanence. To use Nietzsche's terminology, love and redemption are reduced to the primal force of the will to power (exemplified in *both* Brünnhilde and Wotan), their illusoriness, the desire for permanence, thus made evident to us. If the essence of self and society lies in change rather than permanence, how can we achieve order and value if the hope for redemption rests on the will to power rather than permanent values and truths? Is this not, after all, exactly Adorno's complaint about "permanent catastrophe"?

I have tried to show that understanding the self as an illusion does not necessarily lead to the abandonment of the concept of morally active, creative personhood. Just because the self is a kind of action does not mean that we should eliminate the concept and speak only of economic forces, social institutions, atoms in the void, or whatever we might think of as the originating conditions of selfhood. Understanding the forces that constitute our Western images of selfhood does not necessarily make them superfluous. Kant was the first to say that the constituted nature of the self does not eliminate the concept of Responsibility from our self-image. Similarly, for Nietzsche, if self-images *are* results rather than discovered essences (however much they may so appear), the question of the importance or value of the self cannot be settled by realizing it to be a construct rather than an irreducible substance. Either way, life goes on.

Turning to the motif of Redemption Through Love, we should again ask not only what Siegfried redeemed but what Brünnhilde accomplished at the end of *Götterdämmerung*. (I noted in Chapter 3, Section 2 that Wagner did not associate the defeat of power with redemptive love.) I also pointed out that this motif, although added to *Die Walküre* later by Wagner, should not be considered in isolation from others in *The Ring* because of the late date of its actual composition since it and the several forms of love music share elements derived from Freia I and II. *It also contains the Fate motif* in its first measure. Redemption Through Love does not symbolize the overcoming of power and the victorious assertion of love over, but the destructiveness of love itself, its power as a force of change. Love, as much as hate, initiates the great conflicts in *The Ring*. Wotan's world is destroyed as much by love as by the machinations of Alberich and Hagen.

Renunciation stands with redemption as the other main theme of *The Ring*. Neither the renunciation of love nor the renunciation of power accomplishes what it is supposed to. Siegfried's loss of identity in *Götterdämmerung* Iii exposes the delusory romantic ideal of *das Ewigweibliche* (the Goethean ideal of eternal passive feminine as the goal of masculine active striving), as Peckham suggests (see Chapter 2, Section 4). It shows that love as the pure desire to control its object destroys its freedom. Indeed as a response to Siegfried's 'deception', Brünnhilde becomes the active agent. But Siegfried's anonymous sexuality also destroys the autonomous existence he and Brünnhilde thought they had achieved. In one of Wagner's many anticipations of Freud, Siegfried not only opposes (his grandfather) Wotan's world but, subconsciously, the exclusive bond between two individuals as well. Siegfried's sexuality is easily manipulated by Hagen, Gutrune easily substituted for Brünnhilde (as Peckham says of Siegfried, sexually any woman will do), and Siegfried can even dominate Brünnhilde through the persona of Gunther.[3] Not until he regains his memory, just before his death, does his identity through his relation to Brünnhilde return.[4]

In the Appendix, Section 4 I point out the similarities and differences between the hope of transcendent love in *The Ring* and *Tristan*. Although I do not know how degrees could be measured very finely here, *The Ring* ended up less Schopenhauerian than *Tristan* because the lovers in *The Ring* do not believe they will achieve the union of their identities in death. Their love, they believe, will take them beyond the world of Wotan's struggle for control; but while they are deceived in believing that they are no longer involved in that struggle, that they have transcended it, they perish as direct a result of their renunciation of that world. Alberich's renunciation of love destroys him, Wotan's renunciation of power, as well as Brünnhilde's and Siegfried's "laughing death" in the face of Wotan's world, proves only, in *Götterdämmerung* II, that renouncing politics for love leads only to more politics.

At the end of *Götterdämmerung* the violins play the motif of Love's Redemption and the personal, human level of compassionate love becomes the impersonal Will. As Tanner describes it, the instrument nearest to the human voice shows us how the personal is also the universal, how "unconscious Nature rolls peacefully forward, and human creativity, wonderful but containing the seeds of dissolution (how Lawrentian Wagner was!) is celebrated without irony even as it is incinerated, and the misnamed Redemption theme promises that there will be new conscious life" ("The Total Work of Art," p. 173). Is that "promise of new conscious life" utopian—Feuerbachian—as Dahlhaus argues? Does *The Ring* tell a story about how we leave behind earlier stages of conflict for unity and resolution, or does it tell a Schopenhauerian, anti-utopian story about how new life will repeat the same cycle of destruction? My point has been that *The Ring* does not advance our capacity for *transcending* conflict except in our understanding of its formative power. But this *is* an advance: we are not caught up in Schopenhauer's bad infinity of the Wheel of Ixion (explained in the Appendix, Section 3) and the denial of human significance. Redemption simply amounts to the *management* of our tendencies towards conflict rather than their *elimination* (the point of *Die Meistersinger*). It comes down to the realization that we cannot get beyond change, that we can only manage its forces in accordance with the values we have established for our survival and for the survival of what we hold dear. To understand ourselves in this way, to have reached the stage of *aufheben* that allows us to see ourselves as both constituted and constituting, amounts to no more than our grasp of the role of conflict and change in our self-imagery.

In its final appearance, the motif of Redemption Through Love should include *an experience of loss*. Brünnhilde's reunion with Siegfried would not have the powerful effect it does without the *defeat* of that hope in her actual death. Her *Aufhebung,* her understanding, takes place in life as constituted by conflict. Heard in this light, her final moments are not an anticipation of utopia but a reminiscence of the hope that drove her (and others) to terrible depths as well as to great heights. With Tanner I suggest that any promise of new life contained in the final moments of *The Ring* also holds out the essence of the world as change—life as Becoming rather than Being, process rather than stasis. But, reminiscent of Greek tragedy, it also tell us that everything can come to an end because of our lack of understanding, as it did in Wotan's case and, of course, we never understand *everything*. It may well be that, like Wotan and Brünnhilde, we simply bring about our own destruction through our best intentions, and in the twentieth century we have certainly been able to envisage that possibility. In an image I used earlier (Chapter 3, Section 2), the campfire of our civilization may be the only light of any value in the entire universe, but it may be a light that eventually burns out. Our only hope lies in maintaining that fire, not in transcending it for something better; we must have faith in our own redemptive powers.

Tanner also, appropriately, quotes from Yeats's *Sailing to Byzantium*.[5] To this one should add, from *Second Coming,* the now often-quoted lines:

> Things fall apart; the center cannot hold;
> Mere anarchy is loosed upon the world,
> The blood-dimmed tide is loosed, and everywhere
> The ceremony of innocence is drowned;
> The best lack all conviction, while the worst
> Are full of passionate intensity.

Yeats invokes a mood reminiscent of the end of *Götterdämmerung*, the somberness of its visage, and even its circumspectiveness about redemption. We should also remember the passage from Conrad I quote at the end of the Appendix: only by understanding the destructive *and* creative elements of life enables us to understand it—a sentiment Nietzsche wholeheartedly supported in the passage about the joys of creation and destruction from *Twilight of the Idols,* also quoted in the Appendix. If we are beings who become, who *establish* values and truths rather than *discover* them, we must see ourselves as *both* creative *and* destructive.

I have tried to show how every major character in *The Ring* embodies an illusion that has both positive (creative) and negative (destructive) potential. In Chapter 2 I showed how the two pairs of endings to the four parts of *The Ring* bring together two principle groups of illusions. The first pair: *Das Rheingold* ends with the myth of social redemption and Enlightenment order established by Wotan having taken up the sword (in his imagination), thereby embarking on the path of intervention that eventually destroys his hope as he presciently envisages the very thing that will shatter the spear, the symbol of his power. *Siegfried* ends in the mythology of romantic love. The second pair: *Die Walküre* and *Götterdämmerung* end in the destructive fire of truth, the Heraclitean symbol of change. The implicit power of change contained in love (in the form of the sleeping Brünnhilde) ironically arising out of the clash between love and power at the end of *Die Walküre*. The interdependence of power and love, as the mechanism of that change, connects directly to the image of Brünnhilde's achievement of self-understanding implicit in the illusion sustaining her as she escapes from Wotan's world to create another with Siegfried. She does not escape the destructiveness of her illusion of redemption, however, and lives it to its conclusion. In understanding that change and illusion are the fabric of life, she nevertheless does not abandon all myth. That would be to abandon her identity altogether and this she does not do. She encounters death as "Siegfried's bride," united with him in death and the destruction of her illusion by the very powers she believed she had transcended. We soon hear the music of Brünnhilde's Magic Sleep from *Die Walküre*—when it occurred there, it's falling movement paralleled the motif of the Twilight or Decline of the Gods thereby symbolizing Brünnhilde's destructive potential.

In discussing the theme of understanding in *The Ring,* I pointed out the symbolic phototropism implicit in its dramatic and musical movement. We continually move towards or away from understanding, towards light or towards darkness (in this Wagner retained a fundamental Hegelian metaphor that derives from the Enlightenment); but sometimes the light proves to be a false dawn—for example, the endings of *Das Rheingold* and *Siegfried.* What appears to be the light of day or the triumph of noble intentions—the dream of redemptive resolution—takes us instead further into the larger drama of conflict. As we see at the beginning of *Götterdämmerung,* the Dawn music of *Siegfried* III, the music of Brünnhilde's awakening, reappears but in a disheartening reversal of that earlier hope and optimism in its transposition from dawn to dusk. The fire at the end of *Die Walküre* and *Götterdämmerung,* through its power of transformation, takes us closer to an overview of the elements of conflict in the work as a whole. But we nevertheless can experience the hope of redemptive transcendence in Siegfried's arrival at Brünnhilde's mountain fortress: his ascent into the sky, his movement upwards towards Brünnhilde's light in the sky so marvelously depicted by the orchestra in the Prelude to *Siegfried* IIIiii, again based on Freia's motif. Cooke points out that Siegfried's search for Brünnhilde dwells on the first part of that motif, the part associated with sexuality (*I Saw the World End,* p. 49). Here, to take the psychological approach, Siegfried's assent symbolizes his libidinal search for love. We hear musical references to Wotan and Brünnhilde's reconciliation at the end of *Die Walküre,* but finally the opening of Brünnhilde's eyes—her "Heil dir Sonne" referring ambiguously to the sun and to Siegfried—directly quotes the motif of Fate. Our understanding through this reference to light is that we see the reactivating of Erda's prophecy. The Renunciation music also reappears when Siegfried sings: "Since you have bound me in powerful fetters, give me my freedom again!":"in mächtigen Banden,/birg meinen Muth mir nicht mehr!" The sentiment could also be Wotan's: at that moment showing how this love—seemingly so completely removed from Wotan's world—mirrors his struggle. Brünnhilde's passion determines the future for Siegfried in ways he will never know.

When the Dawn music occurs for the third and last time (at Siegfried's death), we have seen its evolution through degrees of realization and comprehension that make up the epistemological subplot of the entire work. Just before the beginning of the Funeral March, Siegfried relives the scene of Brünnhilde's awakening. This music also portrayed her awakening to her human identity and to the love that became its basis. Just before Siegfried dies he remembers her eyes: "Ah! See those eyes,/open forever!/Ah! Feel her breathing,/loving and tender!/Joyful surrender!/Sweet are these terrors!/Brünnhilde waits for me here!":"Ach, dieses Auge/ewig non offen!/Ach, dieses Atems/wonniges Wehen!/ Süsses Vergehen,/seliges Grauen—/Brünnhild bietet mir—Gruss!" In his remembrance of that first moment, Siegfried also points ahead to Brünnhilde's moment of understanding at the end of *Götterdämmerung*. His reference to her eyes, "open forever," retains its Buddhist connotation of the all-seeing eye of the enlightened, but (I have argued) we do not get the existentialist metaphysics of absolute selfhood that Peckham finds so tempting.

The imagery of vision should include the *closing* of Brünnhilde's eyes at the end of *Die Walküre*. There, love first opened her eyes and gave her wisdom, but through an extremely destructive route. It may be possible here to see 'understanding' in its Hegelian form, as the placing the microcosm within the macrocosm. As power was transformed into love at the end of *Die Walküre* associated with Brünnhilde's potential as her eyes close, so love is transformed into power in *Götterdämmerung,* partly because of Hagen's passionate intensity, but ultimately through Brünnhilde's illusion of transcending her society. So important was the idea of love for Brünnhilde that (what she saw as) betrayal by her lover was the deepest possible threat to her human identity, newly created and entirely defined by her relation to Siegfried. This *idea* of love became a motive for Brünnhilde's exercise of power and it's resulting annihilation of the object of her love, Siegfried the *individual*. Ironically, Brünnhilde denies his importance to her as an individual because of the *symbolic* role he came to play in her emotions. When she earlier refuses to return the ring to the Rhinemaidens she has, in effect, adopted its power for her own idealization of love.

For Peckham, Wagner's goal was "to free people from...illusions" such as the asocial value of romantic love, the belief in transcendent and permanent values, and in a conclusive representation of the nature of the self as Will (*Beyond the Tragic Vision,* p. 260). This is, I contend, overstated: *The Ring* certainly shows us how the illusion of redemptive love works and how it forms the specific images of self and society that make us what we are. But can we ever be completely freed from all illusions, from *all* myth, from *all* perspective? As long as change is part of our nature, as *The Ring* suggests, I do not think so. I have taken this Wagnerian-Nietzschean theme of the constitutive power of illusion to show how there can be no perception without selection, without potentially destructive (as well as potentially constructive) interpretation. The essence of human life centers on the activity of *Bildung* for Wagner, the creation of understanding and character, and while its goal should be, as Nietzsche suggests in the epigraph at the beginning of Chapter 1, to understand itself as an illusion, in the sense of a creation, it should also be to understand itself as self-creative and responsible. How this view of personhood could work obviously takes us beyond the scope of this book, but it has been one of the central questions in twentieth-century philosophy, one that has its origins in the nineteenth century.

2. The Metaphysics of *The Ring*: Optimism or Pessimism?

The early, Feuerbachian ending of *The Ring*, discussed in Chapter 2, saw the dawn of a new age of humanity in the clear, objective light of day, *eros* evolving into socially responsible compassion. Dahlhaus' reading of the ending to the cycle, which I have used as my primary example of this optimistic reading, was that Wagner returned to this original ending in the final version, thus contradicting some of his own statements about the radical changes *The Ring* had undergone. I have argued that this view does not hold up in the face of internal evidence. In my interpretation of the final version of *The Ring*, we do not see the historical transition from a world in the grips of divine, autocratic power to a new order of freedom and renewed social value (anticipated in Brünnhilde and Siegfried's love). We see the very essence of the world as change resting on conflict represented by the music. In *The Ring*, I have suggested, Wagner conceives of the Will as eternal conflict (that Schopenhauerian principle remains strong in all versions); I have suggested that the ending of *Götterdämmerung* tells us that creation and destruction are counterparts with no ultimate supremacy of freedom or love. Freedom and love are achievements that have to be reinvented virtually every day because they do not remain static, they cannot be taken for granted.

Through its emphasis on conflict, *The Ring* retains some elements of Hegel's theory of self-consciousness, insofar as Wagner understood it. Hegel would claim that the interdependencies of selfhood, society, and reality consist of change, that change driven by conflict has a structure that can eventually be explicated in the historical comprehension of higher levels of civilization, although he also believed that, for individuals, history is a "slaughter bench." What appears in the short run to be irrational or destructive, however, will in the long run be seen to fit into a rational scheme of development—this he called "the cunning of reason." Wagner clearly rejected the rationalism and determinism implicit in that view, the unity of reason with civilization in spirit. What we understand and feel at the end of *The Ring* does not resemble the higher *rational* order of the universe contained in Hegel's concept of Spirit, one civilization succeeding another through the process of growth and decay leading inexorably to higher forms of culture. In *The Ring* we encounter the possibility of destruction instead of progress, no new values established, no final vision put into practice. The point that stuck with Wagner after Schopenhauer was that while humanity can never eliminate conflict and change from its constitutive processes, it can never achieve the kind of rational/emotional integration envisaged by Hegel.

By placing his earlier, optimistic Feuerbachian (and Hegelian) conception of *The Ring,* with its emphasis on progress and development, within a larger *anti*-Hegelian context denying a final resolution of conflict, an 'ultimate' last word, Wagner nevertheless accepted only *part* of Schopenhauer's thesis of the destructiveness of the Will. If he did not see his characters as expressions of a rational Hegelian Spirit, neither did Wagner disparage the world of phenomenal individuals when he moved to the subrational level of Will (Adorno's characterization of the sensual transcendence of reason). Schopenhauer appealed to the contrast between the reality of the Will and the illusions of selfhood as a justification for his cynicism about the value of civilization. Where is this dualism in *The Ring*? Wagner allows the spectators of the fall of the gods to occupy the center of the visible drama. The phenomenal world remains at the center of our understanding at the end of *Götterdämmerung* when the orchestral Will, summarizing the essence of both politics and love as creation and destruction. 'World as Will' just *is* that world described as the dialectic of conflict. The illusions that make up selfhood and value simply reflect the relative stability of historical moments—including the belief in an absolute foundation for truth and value. Although Schopenhauer believed there *were* absolutes here, which he characterized as the Platonic forms, they performed the role of abstract standards by which to measure changes in phenomena (see Appendix, Section 3), I have suggested that both Nietzsche and Wagner reacted to Schopenhauer by thinking of the Will naturalistically rather than transcendently (for Schopenhauer, nature was a representation of the Will). They also see the desire to transcend the impermanent as a *natural* rather than a supernatural desire. Real effects on real people (however grandly conceived).

I have also maintained that love does not defeat power in the resolution of conflict because they are both features of the 'essence of the world' in *The Ring.* Consequently, we see how love itself can be a form of power, a source of change as well as stability. The ambiguity of love lies in its hope of transcendence and redemption on the one hand, and its controlling domination of the self on the other. For Schopenhauer, love destroys individuals in the conflict between the desires for unity and for self-assertion, but its universal potential rests on the perpetuation of the species, of willing in general, rather than on individual identity. Wagner's "slight modification" of Schopenhauer's Will, ironically, was to completely interpret it as sexuality, and specifically the sexuality of individuals rather than sex as the secret of metaphysical unity. Even at our most spiritual, as searchers of unity, we are still sexual individuals. This seems to be one of the lasting influences of Feuerbach on Wagner and one of the reasons neither he nor Nietzsche could follow Schopenhauer in *his* irony about *apparent* individuality. One way or another, sex is everything for us, not merely a symbol for the Will, for something abstract and general. Wagner also modified Schopenhauer's view of the denial of the Will to show how resignation fits into the illusion of transcendence—as we see in Wotan's case and, I have argued, in Brünnhilde's as well. He *inverts* Schopenhauer's claim that our highest goal in life is the *denial* of the Will in ourselves, that is, that we should somehow escape the illusory principle of individuation in life. If personhood depends on myths, it is also real in the sense that myth can only be replaced by myth: we can give up one conception of selfhood only by inventing another and the real choice lies between myths that are creative and myths that are self-destructive (and, again, which is which is not something that can be known *a priori*). In so doing, by concentrating on individuals and their illusions, Wagner thus put love and conflict together in a way that the optimistic interpretations of *The Ring* simply cannot explain.

As we saw in Chapter 3, for example, Dahlhaus argued that Siegfried and Brünnhilde's love was destroyed by "an outside agency and falls victim to a world in opposition to it" (*Wagner's Music-Dramas*, p. 104). They *were* deceived, and their love *was* a promise of redemption at the end of *Siegfried*. But is that promise fulfilled? Is not Brünnhilde herself responsible for her own refusal to return the ring even before her deception by Hagen and Siegfried/Gunther? Is not her love destroyed from *within* because of its transcendent mythology, its self-deceptive dream of romantic detachment from Wotan's world in her idealization of Siegfried? That world may be in opposition to Brünnhilde, but *she* also opposes *it* by her refusal to help Wotan or even to try to understand why Siegfried acts so strangely. The world has become alien to her. Later, in *Götterdämmerung* II and III, she has become so dominated by her image of love that she denies the importance of Siegfried, the mere *object* of that love because of its apparent inadequacy. Her own actions then help to unleash the destructive power of Hagen's revenge for Wotan's original injustice to Alberich. But *renunciation* as much as *deception* catalyzes the action of *The Ring*: Brünnhilde and Wotan renounce power, Alberich renounces love, and Hagen renounces the good. They are destroyed by what they desire in their renunciation: Alberich by the power he desires, Brünnhilde and Wotan by the love they hope will redeem them from the horrors of uncontrolled power.

I have occasionally used Nietzsche to help me understand the nature of illusion as a constitutive force in human life, and then to apply it in my view of *The Ring*. But in what I take to be their common refusal to transcend by seeing contingency rather than permanence in the concepts of Truth and Value, have Nietzsche and Wagner eliminated the whole point of civilized existence and morality, namely the importance of social stability that stems from a shared understanding of our self-imagery and its world? Perhaps Adorno was right after all. Indeed, in showing us that power and love are interconnected, that destructiveness cannot be eliminated from our images of humanity, no matter how strongly we desire peace and harmony, are not pessimistic resignation, or sensualistic escapism, the only courses open to us? Why take them seriously if our most important values are simply illusions, if whatever we accomplish will pass away? If we have moved beyond good and evil, how can there be any purpose to life? My reply has been that if Wagner and Nietzsche are ironic they are not cynical. But, even so, do not Wagner and Nietzsche give us only a theory of disillusionment? If irony leads to inaction, why bother? Where is their positive contribution? These are indeed questions raised by and in their works and they have not been fully answered even though we have been trying hard to do so for over a century. These two still have much to say to us, with Wagner emphasizing the problematic relation between personhood and society, and Nietzsche the problematic nature of creation and value as constitutive of personal identity.

Nietzsche's view of creative individuality rests on his point that creativity does not just come down to the invention of something new but of something different *relative to what we have got*, what we are bored with, what restricts or constrains or offends us. 'Creativity' comes down to the invention of something valuable in relation to negative values, something that helps us see differently, act differently, and feel differently, something that enhances life by extending our comprehension of its processes. Creativity thus usually rests on responses to perceived needs in one's environment or society, or in oneself. But, if we are lucky enough or smart enough, something quite new sometimes occurs, something that changes our perspective. For Nietzsche, creativity turns its culture in a new, unpredictable direction by giving it new myths and therefore new energy. But every myth will find its demythologizing nemesis, laying open the way for new ones. We can never transcend myth and so, Nietzsche argues, let us learn to control it as best we can where "control" means to create myths that enhance our understanding of contingency—and that encourage us to create more myths, new ways of seeing ourselves and the world.

In one of his letters to Röckel, Wagner wrote: "to be at one with truth is to give oneself up as a sentient human being wholly and entirely to reality—to encounter birth, growth, bloom, blight and decay frankly, with joy and with sorrow, and to live to the full this life made up of happiness and suffering—so to live and so to die." Later in the same paragraph he reiterates his view that "love in its most perfect reality is only possible between the sexes; only as *man* and *woman* can we human beings can truly love. Every other love is merely derived from this."[6] But in this context love cannot be the transcendence of life; and here, clearly, the world should be *not* left to Alberich (as he said to Liszt): we should live to the fullest the life we have because that is all that we have. *How* to live it depends on exactly the kind encounters between individuals that Nietzsche depicts in his account of truth and morality and Wagner in his cautionary and inspiring tales.

3. The Survivors

Deryck Cooke suggests that "the story told in *The Ring*, undeniably, is the history of a whole world, from its origins to its dissolution, since nothing is imagined as having happened before its first event, or as capable of happening after its last event."[7] Well, perhaps not quite: at the end of *The Ring*, the House of Gibichung silently remains. In the Chereau Bayreuth production of 1976, the survivors, a mute, questioning, proletarian chorus, turn to face the audience indicating that we too are among the survivors symbolically present at the ending of the world and the creation of a new one.[8] Our understanding has been increased; we too have moved towards the light. So *The Ring* cannot be the bad infinity Adorno claimed it to be. The cycle of creativity and destruction will continue— *that* is the nature of both Spirit and the Will—but we might better control it through our experience of works like *The Ring*. We cannot halt the process of change and conflict, but we can try to establish and protect what we cherish through our responses to its inevitability. We have recognized something about the character of our world and of ourselves: in essence, the new world will be like the old one. The universe has not been returned to a state of nature in the sense of an ideal condition of pacified purity, the ultimate Goethean fantasy (and one he knew could never be achieved so long as human redemption lies in its striving, in its *quest* for truth, in journey rather than arrival). Nature, for Wagner, has no intrinsic value beyond its portentous symbolism of potential conflict, as frightening as it is attractive, existing simply as the raw material of change.

Wagner's view seems to be that individual autonomy has significance only *within* social contexts, only through the interaction between individuals and the moral forces that envelop them. The tension between individual autonomy and social cohesiveness defines the structures of his music-dramas. *The Ring* focuses on death but celebrates life as the process of renewal *and* decay, of our own individual selfhood *and* civilization. The music of *The Ring* goes beyond its physical referents (such as the sword, the gold, the ring and so on) to portray the dynamic flow and collision of forces underlying the conceptual level of action and belief in the visible drama. The objective referents of the music are taken into a larger developmental, philosophical realm of increasing complexity. In my appeals to musical examples, I tried to show how the leitmotifs are totally misconstrued when thought of as isolated Pavlovian cues to recall specific images. The specific referents of motifs such as the Sword, Valhalla, the Gold, and so on, are swept along in constantly varying contexts which change their meaning and significance. Contrast, for example, the first occurrences of the Valhalla theme in *Das Rheingold* with its distorted corruption in *Götterdämmerung*, and its final, nostalgic reminiscence at the end. Is this not foretold in that brief and condensed interlude in *Das Rheingold* (between Scenes 1 and 2) where the Ring/Power motif changes into Valhalla? What has happened to the idea of Wotan's noble society in the course of *The Ring*? What has happened to Wotan's nobility, to Siegfried's heroism, to Brünnhilde's love? As Cooke says, Wagner intended the music behind these events "to express the profound emotional and psychological realities behind the concepts."[9]

By connecting motifs to events, and to the hopes, fears of the characters, the orchestra shows us how the characters hope that they can overcome their limitations and the contradictions implicit in their moral values. If fear, hope, aggression and the death wish are let loose in *The Ring* (along with the desires for pleasure and sex, to finish Cooke's list[10]), our comprehension proceeds through the musical connection of their world to the desire for understanding on the part of the characters. Both Wotan and Brünnhilde are driven by the need to understand and, although Siegfried's motivation remains primarily sexual, he too achieves a larger, if still only partial, perspective on his life. Brünnhilde's love was destructively transformed by her participation in Siegfried's death. Her realization of what happened to her love released the compassion and desire for reconciliation that ends both Valhalla and her own life. Just before Siegfried's death—after the last recurrence of the Dawn music and directly parallel to the awakening scene in *Siegfried* III where Siegfried awakens Brünnhilde from her renunciation-induced sleep—he again exhorts Brünnhilde to open her eyes and to see him for what he is. When he asks: "Who has forced you/back to your sleep?":"Wer verschloss dich/wieder in Schlaf?" he refers to the moment when he found her (and indirectly to Wotan who put her to sleep the first time), but the refererence attaches to her delusion about his betrayal of her love. At that moment we hear the Fate motif in the violins followed by a reference to the second part of Freia's motif in the basses and cellos—the problematic role of love in a world of change and power.

Brünnhilde's problematic vision—distorted by a love that expresses her own fears and desires—comes to its musical climax just after Hagen runs Siegfried through with his spear. When the vassals ask: "Hagen, what have you done?":"Hagen, was tatest du?" we hear twice in the horns the Sleep music from the last scene in *Die Walküre*. Brünnhilde's potential destructiveness has been actualized by her love, Siegfried's death the result of awakening Brünnhilde. When Siegfried woke the sleeping Brünnhilde, he reactivated that potential. Her own desire for revenge also became a kind of sleep and her lack of understanding the cause of Siegfried's death. Immediately after, we hear the demonically slithering motif in the basses and cellos associated with Siegfried's death (and reminding us of Alberich's original motif in *Das Rheingold*), the first part of which includes the death motif from the timpani that becomes the ostinato of the funeral music to follow. This early motif in *Das Rheingold* leads to Siegfried's death as the outcome of Alberich's renunciation. The Dawn music of *Siegfried* IIIiii then appears for the third and final time as a preface to Siegfried's final moments and the return of his identity. The Magic Sleep music clearly refers to the last act of *Die Walküre* when Wotan and Brünnhilde experience reconciliation. But that reconciliation will not be possible for Siegfried and Brünnhilde.

Brünnhilde's ultimate state of comprehension would not have been possible had her love not been transformed into her desire for domination and revenge. Her reconciliation with Wotan required transgression; but her understanding now seems possible only through the kind of development we have witnessed. So the wonderful cello theme in their final scene together, recapitulating Wotan's "Der Augen leuchtendes Paar," takes on an even deeper significance when we realize the symbolic role that Brünnhilde's sight plays in the larger drama. The closing of her eyes in *Die Walküre* should be understood in connection with their reopening at the end of *Götterdämmerung*. That higher state of comprehension was possible only through the loss of what was dearest to her. Is the same not also true of Wotan and his desire for redemption through Brünnhilde at the end of *Die Walküre*? This moment means so much more when one looks back on it from that later vantage point.

The ending of the world *is* the subject of *The Ring*. The world of Wotan and Alberich ends. Power and love destroy each other but they also sustain each other. God is dead; there are no absolute foundations for our values or our particular perspectives of understanding and knowledge—no 'perspectiveless' perspective beyond the pervasiveness of change. The survivors on stage have witnessed the end of a life, the end of a civilization, the end of a world. We contemplate the Heraclitean fire of change, with its potential for success and for failure, standing as the great truth at the end of *Die Walküre* and *Götterdämmerung*. The Rhinemaidens survive and there are human witnesses to the end of Wotan and Brünnhilde's world. But for these survivors (including ourselves, symbolized by those left on stage) the question should be whether we are about to embark on a repetition of the cycle we have just witnessed, for no absolute values, no universal social principles, have been established to prevent it—beyond love, which we have seen to be a cause of change. Wagner's answer seems to me to be: 'Yes, this will happen to you too because life is change, so be careful how you manage it'. As Boulez puts it: "without going so far as Joyce's literal solution in *Finnegan's Wake*, the impression remains at the end of *The Ring* that Wagner has set the scene for a future beginning; without wishing to implicate Nietzsche in the matter, one cannot help thinking of the *ewige Wiederkehr* [Nietzsche's "eternal return"]."[11] Still, because we have been witnesses to this cycle, it should be (contrary to Adorno) a repetition *with understanding*—what Nietzsche himself hoped to achieve in his fantasy of the eternal return—nature always contains the potential for conflict. In Wagner's world, the universe cannot redeem us, as it did Faust. What disturbed Adorno about this view of truth was that it seemed to imply no socially redemptive value for love, nothing we can count on. But *something* has to hold society together. I have argued that Wagner agrees: if anything stands as the essence of society it is, as Feuerbach suggested, love. However, love is also a power, also potentially destructive. Adorno's non-materialist socialism cannot easily accept that view because it remains millennial in its conception of human nature. We did not know *that* before. Wagner envisaged humanity without that kind of hope but still capable of generating others in response. I think that Nietzsche's view of truth as an illusion helps us to understand Wagner's imagery better.

In my appeal to the ancient Greek metaphors of fire and water, one other allusion suggests itself: Heraclitus' pun that life is a bow (*bíos, biós*). In *The Will to Power* (#967) Nietzsche refers to this very metaphor: "the greatest human beings perhaps also possess great virtues, but in that case also their opposites. I believe that it is precisely in the presence of opposites and the feelings that they occasion that the great person, the bow with the great tension, develops."[12] The string that keeps the bow tense is our understanding of the world. The bow itself comprises our life, our civilization. It seems at rest but contains forces of great power. If the string loses tension, the bow will not work. Pericles, the greatest of the Greek soldier-rulers, held that everything declines (like Yeats, "Things fall apart," like Erda, "All things perish"); the bowstring will loosen, every society will lose its creative edge even if their heroes accomplish their goals.

In their rejection of the metaphysics of tragedy, Plato and Aristotle took the ancient distinction between *physis* and *nomos*, between the impersonal workings of nature and the gods on the one hand and human convention and society on the other, and brought them together in their antitragic view that human reason is the crown of nature, thereby establishing one of the major dreams of Western civilization. For Plato, nature itself provides us with standards and, if we understand them, we can flourish. Understanding the natural order, rather than on faith in tradition or luck, thus became central to virtue; knowledge unifies the virtues and reason closes the gap between our desires and the Good. This antitragic metaphysics became the basis for Christianity and for the rise of science in the Enlightenment. For Christians, humans cannot fully understand because they are imperfect. But perfection must exist, even though it "passeth the understanding." Divine perfection exists as a principle fundamentally opposed to the possibility of tragedy. Damnation is not tragic if salvation, however unlikely, remains *possible*. Removing theological blinders in the form of the limits of human reason, as the Enlightenment did, simply enabled human beings to understand what before only God could comprehend.

Since the nineteenth century, we have seen many challenges to this optimistic relation between mankind and nature in the criticism of the tradition of metaphysical realism that has held Western civilization together from Thales to Kant. *The Ring* shows us how profound this challenge has become. It also shows us that the *inventiveness* of human practices, the core of Plato and Aristotle's view of virtue, has been the real source of value even if it does not reflect a redemptive relationship between truth, nature, and the Good. Plato, at least the younger Plato, held that we cannot be good without knowing what is true. Aristotle's conception of virtue was designed to work without an *absolute* value, but not without a conception of happiness as an objective biological feature of human nature. But if, as I have suggested, our social inventions are *contingent,* not based on universal truths, it remains for us to show that liberal democracy can sustain a conception of value rich enough to preserve its resilient and continued reinvention.[13] Heraclitus' bow depends on tension, on the conflict implicit in human practices and, again, The Ring shows us how powerful that tension remains. The pessimism that often arises out of contingency, however, can also drive us back into life, as it did for Hans Sachs and for Parsifal, by showing us the real conditions of creativity—an insight that must be optimistic, even against the recognition that all things change. Tanner describes this attitude as "moral vitalism"[14] and I suggest that Nietzsche exemplifies it in his later works. His view about creativity in *The Genealogy of Morals* is that value arises as a responsiveness to threats. For Wagner, Siegmund's sword becomes valuable to him as a symbol of his love for Sieglinde. She satisfies in him a deep need—hence the name of the sword: "Notung" (expressing also Wotan's need for a redeemer). But creation must have a goal, for Nietzsche, an end, and this points to the problem with love—love can also destroy.

Our experience at the end of *Götterdämmerung* thus centers not on victory but on downfall—the downfall of our noblest ideals of redemption, love, freedom, law, and heroism. These are *all* symbolized by the sword, indeed, all of those ideals, so important to our civilization, were created in our attempts to minimize the flux of life and the world, to eliminate tragedy, the condition of their creation. In *The Ring,* Wagner emphasizes process through the motion of the music: we have experienced the upward movement of Wotan's optimism (positive needs), the rising motion of the Nature motif and of its permutations in Siegfried's sexuality and Brünnhilde's love set against the downward plunge of Wotan's spear, Hagen's downward-moving destructiveness, disguised in the falling motif of Gutrune's innocence, and the permutation of this at the end of *Götterdämmerung* IIv when Brünnhilde's revenge is combined with the Renunciation and the Power of the Ring motifs—the denial of the will to life. But these are needs too—negative needs possible only as destructive reactions to other hopes. This is Wagner's bow.

For the most part, so far at least, the defeat of these hopes has also been part of the movement towards the light, towards new hopes, and in this way *The Ring* preserves an element of Greek tragedy. Tragedy finds its expression in the final scene through the metaphysical dimension not present at the end of Siegfried's Funeral Music: despite the pyrotechnics of Valhalla's destruction, the climax suggests an open-ended, forever incomplete understanding of ourselves and the universe. The Funeral Music, the Death motif of the timpani (connecting with such poignancy the lives of Siegfried and his father Siegmund, and *his* father Wotan, all touched by Brünnhilde's love), the memories of the love music in the final concatenation: the upward movement of heroism, hope and love contrasting with the downward motion of the decline of the world, the twilight of the gods and their dream of permanence, Brünnhilde's final encounter with the fire of truth told to us in the music. In that complex image, we are still caught within the brooding presence of its vision.

Notes

1 In "Richard Wagner and *The Ring*," Mann describes Siegfried's Funeral Music as an "overwhelming celebration of memory and mind" because it brings together the motifs of hope and heroism that have appeared throughout the drama: "all these splendid, reminiscent phrases, weighted with fate and feeling, should pass by amid earth-shakings and thunderings, with the body borne high on its bier—and that was only one instance of all the significant solemnity and mythical exaltation promised by this drama turned scenic epic. Back to the beginning, the beginning of all things, and its music! For the Rhine depths with the glittering hoard, round which the Rhine daughters sported and played—all that was the innocent, primitive state, still untouched by greed and curse; and one with it was *the beginning of music*." When Siegfried ascends Brünnhilde's rock in the Prelude to *Siegfried* IIIiii, every musical event implies something about Siegfried. We hear the Sleep music from *Die Walküre*, indicating Brünnhilde and her potential for love, Siegfried's Horn Call, the Bird motif, symbolizing the quest for knowledge in preparation for his discovery of Brünnhilde, and the Bondage or Servitude motif indicating not only the problems of Wotan's world but the power that the ring will have over Siegfried too.

The Prelude to *Siegfried* III comprises one of three encapsulations of Siegfried's significance for the drama. Two others occur in *Götterdämmerung*: first, the Rhine Journey interlude at the end of the Prolog, which (despite its projection of heroism) takes Siegfried directly into the clutches of Hagen, and second, Siegfried's funeral music. These three interludes sum up Siegfried's search for love, his heroic potential, and the failure of heroic redemption and Wotan's hope. (Interestingly and significantly, the introduction to the Rhine Journey begins with Brünnhilde waving good-bye to Siegfried—

the motif of that waving motion is based on the augmented Freia II motif and becomes the basis for the Rhine river as Siegfried sails off to his doom.) Once again, it is impossible to make *all* of these associations as one hears this music for the first time (or even several times). This is just one of many such instances where Wagner abandons the doctrines of *Opera and Drama*. The music does not *support* the drama here, it *becomes* the drama. By the time Siegfried's Destiny occurs in the final kaleidoscopic moments of *The Ring*, it has returned to its original status as a pure ideal. But we have seen what has happened to that hope in the course of the attempt to achieve it in a world constituted by the process of conflict.

2   After Erda's warning in *Das Rheingold,* Wotan followed her to the underworld and fathered Brünnhilde. She therefore has a direct connection to Wotan's desire for domination.

3   For the psychological interpreter, it is irrelevant that all of this is done by magic potions and trickery: these are merely symbols of a deeper libidinal motivation. His initial fear of Brünnhilde (quite justified) matches Brünnhilde's fear of her sexual power over Siegfried. For psychological interpreters, their "death to the world" symbolizes the libidinal power of sex.

4   The relation between conscious knowledge and unconscious instinct in the character of Siegfried requires more attention than I can give it here. S.K. Land, in "The Rise of Intellect in Wagner's *Ring*," *Comparative Drama*, V, 1, Spring, 1971, for example, identifies three stages of Siegfried's learning: first, the biological facts of life (symbolized by the bear in Siegfried's first entrance); second, learning language (Fafner's blood and the woodbird); and third, love (with his discovery of Brünnhilde) (pp. 38–9). But equally important to Siegfried's character are the cases of personality transformation, forgetting, and then the regaining of his identity in *Götterdämmerung*. Land's point that the movement of intellect in *The Ring* points toward reflective consciousness, if taken in the way suggested by Land, seems clearly not to fit the understanding of either Siegfried and Brünnhilde at the point of their deaths. We have not reached the point of "conscious intellectual processes." They do not conceptualize their understanding; the music conveys a significance only dimly grasped by Siegfried, and Brünnhilde's "Alles, alles weis ich" must be conveyed by music; prose will not do at this point. Furthermore, his claim about Siegfried's "impregnable strength" resting on the sensible and the emotional nature of his being (and its Feuerbachian naturalness) (p. 39) clearly stands at odds with the events of *Götterdäm-*

merung depicting Siegfried's vulnerability. Like many other commentators, Land fails to see the irony of Siegfried's characterization.

5   See *The Total Work of Art*, p. 173: "so, in *The Ring*, Wagner has sung of 'what is past and passing, [or] to come', and he came very close to answering to Yeats's more detailed specifications:

> ...The young
> In one another's arms, birds in the trees
> —Those dying generations—at their song,
> The salmon-falls, the mackerel-crowded seas,
> Fish, Flesh, or Fowl, commend all summer long
> Whatever is begotten, born, and dies.
> Caught in that sensual music all neglect
> Monuments of unageing intellect."

6   See Cooke, *I Saw the World End*, pp. 17-18. Wagner also says: "I had (unfortunately!) never really sorted out in my own mind what I meant by this 'love' which, in the course of the myth, we saw as something utterly and completely destructive," quoted in Tanner, *Wagner*, p. 177.

7   *I Saw the World End*, p. 248. Also quoted in Darcy, "The Pessimism of *The Ring*," p. 41.

8   See Tanner's discussion of the Boulez/Chereau productions in Chapter 4 of *Wagner*.

9   "Wagner's Musical Language," p. 227.

10   *Ibid.*, p. 243.

11   "Time Re-Explored," p. 30.

12   See also *Twilight of the Idols*, #38. This passage is quoted and discussed by Nehamas, p. 221 (see Appendix, Section 6).

13   The work of Richard Rorty stands as one of the most important contemporary discussions of this point and an exemplar of what I have referred to as moral vitalism. I include references in the Bibliography. Although I will not to discuss this connection here, I look forward to an opportunity to do so elsewhere. Two provocative quotations must suffice for now. Rorty, like

Nietzsche, holds to the contingency of selfhood and, in his demythologization of romantic metaphysics, says: "To say that we become different people, that we "remake" ourselves as we read more, talk more, and write more, is simply a dramatic way of saying that the sentences which become true of us by virtue of such activities are often more important to us than the sentences which become true of us when we drink more, earn more, and so on," *Philosophy and the Mirror of Nature* (Princeton: Princeton University Press, 1979), p. 359. Concerning the ideology of conclusive philosophical refutation (bearing MacIntyre in mind (see the Appendix, Section 6)): "any attempt to drive one's opponent up against a wall...fails when the wall against which he is driven comes to be seen as one more vocabulary, one more way of describing things. The wall then turns out to be a painted backdrop, one more work of man, one more bit of cultural stage setting. A poeticized culture would be one which would not insist we find the real wall behind the painted ones, the real touchstones of truth as opposed to touchstones which are merely cultural artifacts. It would be a culture which, precisely by appreciating that *all* touchstones are such artifacts, would take as its goal the creation of ever more various and multicolored artifacts" (*Contingency, Irony, and Solidarity,* pp. 53–54).

14 I discuss this concept in the Appendix, Section 6. See Tanner's "The Total Work of Art," p. 175.

Appendix

Philosophical Contexts and Applications

This appendix contains some philosophical background relevant to my discussion of *The Ring* that may be helpful for some readers. The first two sections discuss Kant, Hume, Goethe, and Hegel. Therein I summarize Hegel's Master/Slave parable, which Wagner seems to have used in his characterization of Wotan's conflicted life. Sections 3 and 4 discuss the Schopenhauerian aspects of *Tristan und Isolde,* drawing some comparisons and contrasts with *The Ring.* Section 5 includes a brief account of *Die Meistersinger* and his use of the concept of Illusion. Section 6 introduces Nietzsche's "perspectivism" in comparison with Wagner's conception of illusion as I have attributed it to him, again with some connections to *The Ring*. Section 7 summarizes an explicitly positive Nietzschean interpretation of *The Ring.*

1. Kant and Hume: the Nineteenth Century Begins

Although Immanuel Kant stands at beginning of a new era, he saw himself as the defender of Enlightenment principles—its faith in science, in social and political rationalism, its vigorous antimysticism and passionate belief in the transformation of religion into humanism (thus reaffirming the ideals of the French Revolution). Just prior to Kant, Hume had raised serious questions about the nature of scientific universality and, consequently, the extent and nature of human knowledge. Hume's scepticism about the foundations of knowledge threatened the entire intellectual and social project of the Enlightenment. Where earlier rationalists, such as Leibniz and Descartes, tended not to distinguish between logical and natural necessity, thereby yielding a very powerful conception of science, placing heavy nonempirical demxands on the concept of Knowledge, Hume was one of the first to draw a distinction between mathematical or logical necessity, on the one hand, and "natural" necessity on the other.

The laws of science, Hume argued, are not based on logical necessity, like the universal truths of mathematics (which, for Hume, are only "relations between ideas" and have nothing to do with the real world). Natural laws rest on psychological expectations built up through continual experiential repetition. To deny any truth of mathematics or logic asserts a contradiction, but to deny the truth of the law of gravity does not. We are not, therefore, absolutely justified in saying that the future will be like that past or that the sun will rise tomorrow by appealing to the laws of nature. For Hume, these laws contain nothing but factual summaries of past observation plus our expectation, our hope, that the world will continue to behave that way. We have no reason to believe that it will other than our faith in continuity. (Ironically, Hume thought he was *defending* science by grounding it in human psychology and common sense rather than in the fancies of speculative metaphysics, which of course included theology.) Because there seemed to be no necessity in nature akin to that of a mathematical proof, and hence no *experience* of necessity, there seemed to Hume to be no apparent metaphysical glue, no *logos,* holding the world together. (Hume's philosophic views, not surprisingly, threatened the complacency of many: he was twice turned down for academic posts at the universities of Edinburgh and Glasgow on grounds of religious radicalism.)

As Kant described his intellectual history, he was awoken from his dogmatic slumbers (his rationalist faith in metaphysical absolutes) by Hume's suggestive arguments, which implied that the emperor had no clothes, that the universe itself might not be a reasonable place after all. Kant claimed in *The Critique of Pure Reason* (published in 1781, eight years before the fall of the Bastille) that we indeed cannot find any necessity in particular experiences of natural events, nor can we justify the universality of science if we simply measure things. Science does not consist of catalogues of data and summaries of experience. What justifies the trivial but absolutely necessary assumptions that measurements of objects are uniform between different corners of a room, between different corners of the world, the solar system, and the galaxy? Why is "F=ma" true *everywhere*? If the laws of science are not as certain as "2 + 2 = 4," are they *more* certain than empirical generalizations? What justifies our reliance on the principle of induction, upon which we base our belief that the future will be like the past? Necessity and universality, Kant agreed with Hume, are not properties of things or events; if they exist "in nature," must therefore have another foundation if we are to be scientific *at all.*

The search for natural necessity, Kant argued, required a rethinking of the nature of cognition tantamount to a new "Copernican Revolution": instead of looking to nature for necessity, look instead at the mind that perceives and judges. For Kant, the mind must be so constructed that it understands nature through universal laws by ascribing necessary connections between events and uniform properties to objects. Our minds *impose* regularity on the universe rather than *discover* it. How could we be sure that what we experience actually meshes with the *actual* structure of that reality? Because, due to the mind's structure, we *must experience* the world in a certain way. We do not have the option between organized and disorganized experience. Experience, by its very nature must be organized. To paraphrase Kant, perceptions without concepts (ordering principles) are blind; but purely rational concepts without experience are empty. This summarizes the whole point of the vast, bewildering *Critique of Pure Reason*. He described himself as an "honest broker," bringing together the good parts of rationalism and empiricism. For Kant, the necessity and universality of scientific law owes its foundation *not* to psychology, as Hume said, but to the principles of "logic," as he broadly characterized it, implicit in the mechanisms of experience and and the way we objectively understand the world. Kant's great revolutionary proposal was that our cognitive machinery must be programmed to operate in certain definite ways by universal principles that define its output, objective experience. The universe, insofar as we experience it, he argued, is rational only if we can experience it rationally.

Kant thought he had filled in the missing part of Hume's view of natural necessity by supplying the conceptual structure that accounted for the uniformity built not only into the scientific image of nature but also the recognition of oneself as the regularizing observer of nature. We *must* view the world—and ourselves—through the concepts of Substance, Causality, Quantity, Quality, Modality (possibility/necessity), and so on (there are in all twelve categories roughly corresponding to Aristotle's, thus establishing an historical link to the early days of science, as Kant saw it).[1] Objective experience requires that we attribute separate existence to the objects that we experience, and this separate existence assumes a space-time continuum that conforms to the laws of science. Can we know that the sun will rise tomorrow, that the future will be like the past, that the table on which I am typing will be the same table after I blink my eyes? Yes, said Kant, because it is not a rational option to believe otherwise— we can only explain *why* changes occur *in accordance* with the laws of science (since experience must be organized, worlds *must be* coherent to be worlds at all).

In this view of natural necessity, Kant saw himself answering Hume. Almost all of our experiences ascribe order to the world, an order imposed by the structure of the mind, Kant claimed. We do not experience causes, we experience the world causally; the world consists of *uniformly* related events. The world thus constituted, made up in accordance with the concepts of the understanding as the source of organization and rational order, becomes the world science tells us about: an independently existing, rational continuum of spatiotemporal objects. So Hume was partly right: necessity *is* a matter of psychology, but what explains the tendency to form such expectations? What supplies regularity to psychology? The mind must be *predisposed* to experience in certain ways and not others, but what explains that disposition? Here Descartes and Leibniz were right: the regularity of nature requires universal principles of rationality built into the mind. There are, then, universal truths about rational minds similar to those about coherent worlds. But the earlier rationalists could not justify that inference (Descartes argued we had to trust in God's benevolence on such matters). For Kant, rationality and experiential coherence both rest on the same logical processes: again, he was only concerned about how we *experienced* the world. We can know for sure, he thought, achieving scientific certainty if we *limit* ourselves to describing possible experience and, because of his logical principles, the universe *as we represent it* must be rational. The order of the world rests on *a priori* logical principles that are not derived from experience, and hence they are general and universal, giving it its form. This is the world *as it is experienced.* The actual nature of the world *in-itself,* apart from our experiences, is another matter. What justified *these* principles and assured their universality? He attempted to prove that only with them can experience have the order we experience it to have. We *do* experience it that way, so the principles that constitute such order *must* be implicit in all cognition.

Hume also raised a problem about the self. A century and a half earlier, Descartes said he experienced himself as a "thinking being." In his own attempt at introspective discovery, however, Hume could find only this experience or that experience of the world but never an experience of the self that *had* them. This was also a confusion that Kant brilliantly exposed: do not confuse the unity of experience with the experience of unity (as Peter Strawson puts it in his commentary on the *Critique of Pure Reason*). Self-identity results from the unifying operations of the various faculties of the mind. There is no unity *per se*, no Cartesian thinking subject, no 'I' that thinks, perceives, doubts, etc. Unity results from the way in which our diverse psychological faculties operate and the phenomenal self, for Kant, was simply the biological organism with a brain possessing a level of conceptual complexity great enough to produce the illusion of a self. But what produced this illusion? What is the principle that underlies organized experience? Here Kant introduced his troublesome conception of the "transcendental ego," which we do not experience and which is nobody in particular, nevertheless standing as the origin of whatever unity we do experience. The transcendental ego has no personality, no selfhood; it is simply the implicit logical of psychological processes "summarized" in personal identity. Kant's principle was that experience is always 'owned', experience is always someone's. But the spatio-temporal location of my physical body is only a necessary condition of experience: What *unifies* experience, what makes it "mine" if "I" am not myself a "unity"? Kant argued that we must grant the origin of this unity "transcendental" status because unifying activity itself must exist beyond the level of experience while still being necessary for it. We never experience the unification of experience: experience is already organized. He used the word "transcendental" in this context to specify those necessary inferences that we must draw concerning the *conditions* of all experience. Accordingly, for Kant, we must infer the existence of some logically-based process whereby our experience of the world becomes the experience of a self, of our experience.

The main point of Kant's theory was that, instead of drawing a line between *objective* reality and *subjective* experience, we should draw it between subjective *experience* and objective *experience*. Experience is the product or result of a process, of many processes. To maintain this Kant also introduced a new distinction between "phenomena (the organized world according to our subjective and objective experience: reality, including ourselves, as we know it) and "noumena" (whatever lay *beyond* possible phenomenal experience). Kant called himself a "transcendental idealist" in the sense that he did not think *all* reality to be a product of mental activity, just the part of reality we experience. He claimed, modestly and judiciously (he thought), that objective reality (the sum total of all possible objective experiences and the universality they project) was a function of mental activity responding to its noumenal source. We only *know* about phenomenal reality, however, reality as constituted by the conceptual structure of experience. "Representations," conceptually ordered experiences, were experiences of the *phenomenal* world, not the *noumenal* world transcending possible experience. The experiencing subject, for Kant, is thus a point of view on a world conceived spatio-temporally. All rational minds have the conceptual structure to so conceive and experience the world. The 'objective world', then comes down to the projections implicit in the representing abilities of the minds that encounter it. Representations of the world are simply the perspectives of the world as experienced, as these perspectives are determined by the conceptual framework underlying all representational activities. Beyond lies the noumenon.

The unobservable noumenal realm made ethics and religion possible for Kant. Since the phenomenal world was rigidly deterministic and contained no freedom, the noumenon could not be described scientifically since it was defined as that part of reality lying beyond our cognitive capacities (the functioning of which were predetermined in accordance with the laws of science). Kant was quite clear that in order to think of ourselves as moral agents we had to *assume* that we were freely choosing beings. We cannot *prove* that we are actually free because freedom is not an objectively discoverable fact about human beings—no empirical investigation of them as biological organisms will find it (indeed, quite the contrary). Nevertheless, we literally create ourselves as moral beings through the assumption of freedom and through the description of human beings as ends in themselves. Because morality requires freedom, moral beings must never be treated as means but only out of respect for their freedom: this principle is fundamental to morality. Kant described himself as "criticizing reason to make room for faith" by showing how the laws of science were limited to a certain kind of experience: objective experience. He wanted to find a place for morality and religion in the rampant materialism and scientism of his age without denying the power of science to explain the phenomenal world. Beyond objective experience, we could believe in moral value and even in God as aspects of noumenal reality. Here Reason, unhindered by appearances, has a role to play. We could understand ourselves to be free, morally responsible beings as well as the rational machines envisaged by La Mettrie and Hobbes. But reason in morality had to depend on different principles since values are not objects. Reason tells us that in order for us to describe ourselves in moral categories, for example, we must "posit" a free ("autonomous") self—not the self that appears to us (our "empirical ego") or even the structuring self (the "transcendental ego"), but a being listening only to the commands of Reason. What were those commands?

Kant believed he had defended universality and necessity in science by limiting its scope to objects of actual and possible experience, objects that could be measured, predicted, and categorized. These are the activities of the Understanding. Ethics, religion, and art were not about the material world analyzed by science because they were not about objects. Therefore, they engaged the world beyond objective experience. In providing a justification for scientific method that avoided Hume's scepticism, Kant also showed just what the problem was for the Enlightenment. If *science* defines rationality in relation to objectivity, how can we achieve it in ethics, politics, and religion? The French Revolution, for example, began optimistically in the effort to rebuild society on rational foundations (just as Descartes had envisaged over a century earlier), but how could that goal be accomplished if reason was limited and if selfhood escapes scientific analysis? What then was to be the source of value in that society? For Kant, values had to meet the test of his 'universalization principle': we must will that any moral command worthy of the title must become a universal law for all humanity. That could be the only rational test for moral responsibility—if we cannot universalize, we remain forever mired in parochial, local interests, preoccupied with means rather than ends, utility rather than goodness. He concluded that moral imperatives must be *categorical*, universal for all. In this way Kant was able to show how reason applied to the noumenal realm as well as the phenomenal. The principles of morality could be generalized only by the test of universalization—the ideal test of Enlightenment respectability. This appeal to universalizable moral principles underlay the Declaration of the Rights of Man at the beginning of the French Revolution and the American Bill of Rights.

2. Goethe and Hegel: Beyond Enlightenment

The problem with Kant's distinction between phenomena and noumena was this: he seemed to apply his concept of Causality, or *some* relational concept, beyond possible experience—*between* phenomena and noumena—in order to get his theory of knowledge to work. Something had to provide the raw data for the mind to organize and something had to power the organization itself. Kant argued that this was a *necessary* inference and was therefore not subject to his re-

Philosophical Contexts and Applications 171

strictions on metaphysical speculation (which, he argued, was never restricted to *one* explanation about anything). But such a problematic differentiation hardly resolved the difficulty of the source of experiential unity. It is one thing to infer that unity must have a source but quite another to explain what that source must be like (must *it* be a 'unity', or rational?). Kant thought that the noumenon must be rational in some larger sense than that defining objective experience and it needed to be for his view of morality to be grounded on reasons. But for Kant's successors, the question was: What was this larger sense of rationality?

It was on this question that Fichte, Schelling, and Hegel attacked Kant's fundamental distinction between phenomena and noumena. If there could be such a grand metaphysical distinction, it must be rationally understandable (the very idea of a *connection* is itself implies a rational explanation), but the Understanding was restricted to phenomenal reality and became merely speculative (without rational restraints) when it moved beyond the limits of objectivity. Kant's successors, however, saw the faculty of Understanding simply as reason restricted to space and time. Rather than two separate faculties with two sets of rules (that Kant never satisfactorily disentangled), there is one faculty with two applications: pure and applied. But what controlled pure reason? For Kant it was the possibility of practical reason based on noumenal assumptions (such as freedom). He assigned reason a "regulative" use in the attempt to project subjective organization on the noumenon, to organize it relative to our speculative interests. The result was the absolute idealism of the early nineteenth century. Because reason must be universal, the individual mind, or even the scientific mind, does not create reality, reality is the result of 'thought in general', reason universalized unifying phenomena and noumena. Hegel's early work, *The Phenomenology of Spirit* (1807), presented a vast summary of anti-Kantian arguments, some shamelessly stolen from Fichte and Schelling. Instead of Kant's thesis that all we can know are the actual and possible phenomena of experience, Hegel saw history as the development of "Mind" or "Spirit," in a sense that included Kant's phenomenal experience, but which also studies itself. The comprehensive history of Mind was in fact self-knowledge of the noumenon.

Hegel wrote eloquently of 'Spirit' (*Geist*). It included the history of all thought, all experience, all of our social and political institutions, all art, all religion, of civilization itself. The noumenal essence of *Geist*, for Hegel, was that reality itself—including the persons contemplating it—changed from one historical period to another. The concept of *Bildung* that I introduced in Chapter 1, Section 1 applied not just to persons but to their cultures as their conceptions of the universe matured through history. The Enlightenment had held that reality was permanent and unchanging, a principle of metaphysical realism that has its origin in Plato. Even for Kant, the ordering activities of the mind were not affected by history. As it was for Plato, mathematics was the model of such truths: "$2 + 2 = 4$" cannot be true today and false tomorrow *and so* the ultimate nature of reality *must also* be unchanging. But Hegel raised serious doubts about that inference.

What is Reason? What is its scope and limit? By the late eighteenth century, the traditional distinction between reason and passion became blurred. Hume had even gone so far as to call reason a "slave" of the passions. Where the Enlightenment saw the relation as the problem of *controlling* passion, even at the outset of the Revolution, early nineteenth-century idealism and romanticism saw reason itself as a passion (as Hegel himself brilliantly argued in the *Phenomenology of Spirit*). The rejection of the Enlightenment, or rather, ironically, the fulfillment of its dream of unity, was at hand in morality and art as well as philosophy. Goethe's *Faust* stands out as one of the most dramatic exemplifications of the ambiguity between reason and passion (Goethe completed *Faust* in 1832, just a few months before he died, but it was a life-long project going back as early as 1772). During the French Revolution, Goethe was quick to see, people realized that life could be stranger than any art up to that time; but, reflecting this tumultuous period, art quickly became overtly political. Politics, morality, even philosophy became subjects of aesthetic discourse. The work of artists such as David for example, contained messages cleverly expressed in his painting of the death of Marat (as a revolutionary who used sex for political purposes, or perhaps *vice versa*) as well as with his ancient Roman scenes of republican virtue, conveyed contemporary messages for the French Revolution. Here was a convergence of art and concept, sensibility and thought. Mozart's portrayal of invigorating evil in *Don Giovanni*, rebellious spirituality in *The Marriage of Figaro*, and love transcending social repression in *The Magic Flute* brought drama, music, and politics dangerously close together. Then, early in the nineteenth century, Beethoven and Goethe took the very concept of Reality itself into their works, combining art and metaphysics.

At the beginning of the second part of *Faust*, for example, Faust turns his back on the sun, the Enlightenment symbol of truth, the natural light of reason. Here Goethe rejected the new world order of rationalism and materialism, laboriously and triumphantly established during the two centuries connecting Galileo to Newton and Descartes to Kant, simply turning his back on its inhumanity and its repudiation of emotion. "By God," Faust says of his desire for Margaret, "I have no name for it! Feeling is everything!" And, using imagery Hegel would also employ, "Gray…is every theory,/And green alone life's golden tree."[2] What was the point of rationality in such a world? It was too limited to tell the truth.

The story of Faust goes back to the Middle Ages; in the sixteenth century Christopher Marlow had given it the quality of a morality play, about retribution for the rejection of morality. Marlow's Faust wanted pleasure and knowledge, selling his soul to the devil, in return briefly getting both pleasure and knowledge, but was deservedly punished for harming others and offending God.

Goethe's *Faust*, however, more complex and ambiguous, ends not with the punishment of evil (for Faust's abandonment of civilized restraints) but in transformation and redemption. In this version of his pact with Mephistopheles, Faust does not even want knowledge, explicitly rejecting an earlier offer. He wants the thrill of pursuit. Indeed, because of his striving, his *immer streben*, for an unattainable ideal characterized as the eternal feminine—every object of desire is sexual, but desire is also a transcendent force—Faust actually achieves salvation. Even God expresses no commitment to "the Law," as opposed to interest in Faust's potential in adversity. The Enlightenment dichotomy of Good/Evil is replaced by another: Activity/Passivity (as T.J. Reed summarizes it).

This was a far cry from the passionless objectivity of Enlightenment scientism, although Descartes and Kant could be quite passionate about being passion free. Now the spiritual essence of humanity lay in emotion, not reason: indeed, reason defeats our humanity, our concern for the particular individual, the unreplicatable situation. In Part II of *Faust*, Goethe substitutes the image of the waterfall for the symbol of reality (Part II, Act I). Kant also used similar imagery in his *Critique of Judgment* (1790) Part I, Book II. He appealed to nature as a metaphor of the sublime; but for Kant, sublimity was an experience of the ultimate rationality of nature, the unity of nature and reason, whereas Goethe, taking this imagery further, used his waterfall as an expression of the dynamic force of life itself—the ultimate source of reason but not itself comprehensible through it. The rainbow thrown off by the waterfall seems to be real, yet even as an illusion it still, Faust says, "mirrors human love and strife" rather than Reason. The colors of the rainbow are the result of the interaction between the (unseen) sun, water droplets, and the observer—all three necessary for the rainbow, for phenomenal reality. Human life—and reality generally—are similarly results rather than givens, process rather than stasis.

Ultimately, Goethe brought the sea into the concluding scene of *Faust*, a culminating metaphor of unity. Nature, the world now no longer a machine but a dynamic organic process "over-flowing, ever gleaming,/Watering worlds with endless flow." Against covert, but (at least today) unmistakably erotic visions of Christ coupled with sexual metaphors in nature and culminating in a unifying process of salvation through which the universe itself redeems him, Faust's quest for the "eternal feminine"—the responsive, receptive but elusive essence of nature, the counterpart to male striving. 'Striving' is thereby revealed as the primary (and purely masculine) motivation in the quest for truth. Nature and Spirit, female and male, the desire to be one and the desire to understand the truth of this unity supplies the constant motivating passion that characterizes the quest for understanding. But the only metaphysical truth to be found by Faust was the truth of change, not knowledge but a principle. Faust's damnation as well as his salvation lay in his striving, an unsatisfiable restlessness (as the great Germanist Erich Heller puts it[3]) that was to characterize a new age.

Faust had a musical analog in Beethoven's *Third*, *Fifth,* and *Ninth Symphonies*, all further examples of the transformation of art into a quasi-philosophical medium and based on our striving to produce unity out of conflict. Beethoven's music captured very general concepts such as Fate, Heroism, and Freedom conveying their essences through the organizational medium of the sonata form—a symbolic and dialectical representation of the unification of Spirit and Nature. These and other wonderful accomplishments in poetry and painting affected even philosophers. Hegel saw traditional philosophic disputes falling into patterns repeating themselves in flights of increasing complexity and comprehensiveness, actually capable of self-representation ('self-consciousness'). Like Goethe, Hegel also saw that art could actually represent these patterns with insights unavailable to the prose bound and invented a kind of philosophical-poetic language filled with images of growth and transformation to do that. But both Goethe and Hegel believed in compromise: the contingent transience of earth embodied the eternal.

In the second paragraph of the *Phenomenology of Spirit,* for example (published long before Goethe completed *Faust*), Hegel claims that traditional philosophy "does not comprehend the diversity of philosophical systems as the progressive unfolding of truth, but rather sees it in simple disagreement." In the very next sentence he inaugurates a radically new way of talking about truth: "The bud disappears in the bursting-forth of the blossom, and one may say that the former is refuted by the latter; similarly, when the fruit appears, the blossom is shown up in its turn as a false manifestation of the plant, and the fruit now emerges as the truth of it instead."[4] Here we see clearly the dramatic switch from mechanical to biological metaphors for truth, to the developmental character of truth rather than its timeless permanence. In fact, at the end of the *Phenomenology*, Hegel appeals to poetry in order to describe absolute knowledge or Spirit knowing itself as Spirit—a quotation from Schiller describing the dynamics of reality in the unmistakable imagery of a divine orgasm: "from the chalice of this realm of spirits/foams forth for Him his own infinitude." In so doing, he transformed the nature of rationality—reason was above all a *desire*; it could not be antithetical to passion because it could not exist without it.

One of the most instructive metaphors for the transformation of the self in the early nineteenth century, and one that evidently influenced Wagner, can be found in Hegel's story of master and slave in the chapter on self-consciousness in the *Phenomenology,* Section B. In this analogy there are no transcendent powers or values supplying meaning to life or structure to experience. Value and meaning emerge from the process of social interaction itself, they do not exist independently. The master, a being who initially exists completely "for himself," appears to be fully self-sufficient. But he enslaves another to serve him, to preserve his self-sufficiency. The slave's identity, in contrast, depends on his master, on what he would have the slave do. The slave's alienated identity therefore lies outside of himself: he is what the master tells him he is (farmer, horseman, cook, and bottle washer), he does what he is told to do. But as the analogy progresses to a higher form of consciousness, the master comes to depend more and more on the slave, who acts while the master merely desires (alienation in both directions). As a laboring being, the slave controls the environment through "work." The identities and values of both master and slave are therefore interdependent and fully determined by their interdefined roles. The slave, therefore, struggles for his identity too, for something that distinguishes him from the master. Hegel describes his parable as "a struggle to the death" (strikingly similar to Hobbes' view of nature in the *Leviathan* as a "war of all against all") in which one becomes master and the other slave. But Hegel did not believe in the state of nature. Man is *always* social.

Master and slave are thus not independent beings; they are not autonomous from the identities supplied by the miniature society they comprise. Self-consciousness for Hegel arises through the realization of this interdependence in the lives of the protagonists as they struggle with each other, one becoming dominant, the other subservient. An example of Hegelian self-consciousness comes out of the Master/Slave parable itself: in the end, the master depends on the slave and as soon as the slave realizes that, he has understood his relationship more deeply (he understands that mastery is dependence). Such a realization would be the basis for revolution as Marx later described the growth of self-consciousness in the slavish proletariat. Knowledge leads to power.

Self-consciousness results from a process that ties individuals together and to their world through progressively rational social activity (*Bildung*). Thus tied to moral progress, it requires the mutual recognition and acknowledgment of the participants. The self, therefore, is not 'given' and Descartes' symbolic exercise of closing himself off from the world, closing the drapes over his study windows in order to discover his essential nature, led to Hume's refutation. He could discover no such essence when he ironically tried to reduplicate Descartes' experiment. Isolated individuals, or even parts of individuals, do not possess the kind of identity required for self-consciousness. Essence is process, activity rather than substance. The self is made, not discovered, Kant argued. Hegel believed that self-consciousness must also be true of cultures: an individual's identity requires a society and culture; a culture's identity requires its realization of the history of Spirit, best captured in philosophy. He thereby transferred the unifying activities of Kant's transcendental ego to the cultural activities that make up civilization, in so doing, bringing Kant's two worlds of the noumenal and the phenomenal together. In fact, Hegel saw the history of philosophy as the theme of that process—overcoming dualism with unity. The unknowable becomes known.

For Hegel, Kant was right in holding that reality was reality *as understood*, as constituted, but wrong about the dualism of phenomenal reality and transcendent noumenon. This distinction also lies *within* reality, for Hegel, not between reality as we know it and what we cannot know. Phenomena and noumena are parts of the same process—the historical process of overcoming dualism. Kant overcame the dualism of mind and world by showing that we experience the world in accordance with the structure of the mind, the world was the world as we know it. Hegel argued that, once we view "experience" as an evolutionary dynamic rather than as an accurate pictorial representation of something different from us, the Phenomena/Noumena distinction falls away, to be replaced by the history of humanity coming to know "the world." This was, for him, the whole world and not just the phenomenal one. One knows the world better and better through interaction with it. Self-consciousness, the self-actualization of Spirit, emerges as the understanding of that process itself, analogous to the Master/Slave parable. This interaction took many forms: art, morality, religion, politics, but only philosophy, for Hegel, could grasp the point of all other activities because it deal with the history of spirit and was, therefore, the most rational form of activity. Noteworthy in this 'argument' is its emphasis on the determination of the individual by larger, constitutive processes: history and society through the interdependent activities of individuals express Spirit.

But of what do we individuals become conscious through this interaction? If knowers evolve too, then the mind and the world are interdependent not just in the way in which we know the world, but at every level of our interaction with it. Kant thought that morality was different from science since moral beliefs did not represent any *thing* (they depended on those unverifiable assumptions of freedom and universalization). Hegel pointed out that morality was a way of interacting with the world too and his large, difficult books showed how religion, morality, and politics, science, everything we do, put us into direct contact with the world in complex variations of the Master/Slave parable. To understand history as the story of the interdependence of humans and their world is to gain self-consciousness, to become spiritual. That divine orgasm is humanity itself.

3. Schopenhauer and Music

As we have seen Chapter 1, in his essay *Beethoven,* Wagner acknowledged Schopenhauer's *The World as Will and Idea* (published in 1818) as one of his most profound influences, causing him to make fundamental changes in his conception of music-drama. Schopenhauer vehemently rejected Hegel and Feuerbach's historicism, their view of the developmental progress in human conceptions of reality and truth, and he rejected their view that these changes could all be understood 'scientifically'. Instead, he took a 'back-to-Kant' reaffirmation of the dualistic Phenomena/Noumena distinction. But he also argued, contrary to Kant, that the noumenon could be *experienced*, not through the concept of causality and the other categories of the Understanding, but through ordinary life and ideally in art. The mood of the mid nineteenth-century German universities was definitely Hegelian. When Schopenhauer briefly pursued an academic career at the University of Berlin, he advertised his anti-Hegelianism and defiantly scheduled his lectures opposite Hegel's (whose courses were jammed). Hegel's famed obscurantism apparently thrilled students however, and few actually registered or showed up for Schopenhauer's lectures. He shortly retired from academic life (able to live comfortably on his family fortune). Outside the universities, however, Schopenhauer eventually met with a more favorable reception among artists and poets, including Wagner, and among nontraditional intellectuals such as Nietzsche. Later on, Wittgenstein's admiration of Schopenhauer has also been noted by many commentators.

There are several good discussions of Schopenhauer's metaphysics and his influence on Wagner and I will not repeat them here.[5] I will limit myself to making a few specific points about the character of Schopenhauer's metaphysics and the impact it had on *The Ring* and on Wagner's other works of this period (*Tristan* and *Die Meistersinger*). Fortunately, we do not have to go into great detail. The two main points of Schopenhauer's metaphysics Wagner took to heart were, first, that the universe consists not only of dynamic process rather than stable substance (something Wagner had already gotten from Hegel and Feuerbach), but that it was not a fully rational or historical process. This challenge to rationalism and historicism as modes of understanding constitutes a radical break from Hegel. Second, Schopenhauer writes at great and eloquent length, in vigorous and clear language, about how the processes of change in us and in the universe generally are always destructive, and that renunciation of the world of appearances stands as the central virtue of life. Appearances, Kant's phenomena, however, are the only rational part of the universe. We cannot, however, extend reason to the noumenon, even as Kantian speculation. Schopenhauer's pessimism thus contrasts sharply with Hegel's generally optimistic viewpoint.

Why renounce appearances? If we desire order and stability, that desire will always be defeated (a point understood by Faust). With Kant, Schopenhauer contended that what appears permanent and stable is not so. But instead of Hegel's progressive view of change leading to *higher* forms of civilization and selfhood (he tended to see Spirit anthropomorphically), Schopenhauer argues that the universe must be completely *arational*, lying beyond the objective categorizations typical of human experience as supplied by Kant's categories. The title of his *magnum opus*, *The World as Will and Representation* (or "Idea"), reflects the contrast between the world understood, the world as we represent it, and the world as pure desire—as Will. The by then old-fashioned parallel with Kant's Phenomena/Noumena distinction is explicitly intended by Schopenhauer (who saw himself as bringing consistency to Kant's dualism). In direct contrast to Hegel's conception of *Geist,* or Spirit, the Will has nothing to do with civilization, reason, progress or even individuals: *Can* the world be understood, even if reason "develops" in Hegel's way? When Schopenhauer—or Nietzsche for that matter—writes about reality as Will, they are not merely substituting process for permanence as its essence. They raise a fundamental question about the nature of reality. Hegel's process-theory claimed that all change must be rational and moving in some direction, even if we can only know where after the fact. Schopenhauer claimed that this begged the question: Does the mere organization of reality imply a *telos*? In order to experience ultimate reality we must understand the Will, both in us and generally. To do that we must renounce the importance of appearances, including human individuality. Human reality may be goal-directed, but we should not infer that the noumenon is too. Schopenhauer thereby connects renunciation and transcendence.

What is the Will? Although we 'will' every time we desire something, are motivated to do something, envisage a goal, and so on, all of these activities are directed at a specific end. They *seem* to be anyway: Schopenhauer denied that human acts of will, when properly understood, really have a point either. For Schopenhauer, the Will as the essence of reality is nonhuman because it lacks the fundamental character of practical reason possessed by individual acts of will: it lacks purposiveness. The Will, for Schopenhauer, like Kant's noumenon, cannot be directly characterized by the various categories of human knowledge. Yet, unlike Kant (who is not clear on this matter), he believed that we do in fact directly experience the noumenon. We are not limited to negative conceptions of transcendent reality (not spatio-temporal, not substantival), on the one hand, or to speculative assumptions on the other (the assumption, for example, that we must possess free will in order to conceive of ourselves as moral beings).

Besides experiencing the Will every time we desire something—and especially when those desires are frustrated—Schopenhauer argued that art was the best medium for representing the Will because it avoids the purposive characterization of everything else we do. It also gets behind the concepts that, as they did for Kant, controlled our objective representation of reality. Just as our wills individually determine us, so Will (as noumenon) determines the world (as phenomenon). Through the experience of willing, of desiring, we experience the nature of all reality. More than that, we can also represent the Will, indirectly at least, in art.

Schopenhauer claimed that the visual arts inadequately represented the essence of the world because they were endemically associated with images and particulars. He wanted to think of the Will as a pure dynamic force, as insatiable desire (but for nothing in particular) underlying all phenomenal activity (a point obviously influencing Wagner in *Beethoven* and in the music-drama *Tristan*, as I will show in the next section). In varying degrees, while all of the arts stood somewhere between phenomena and noumena as visible phenomenal representations, "objectifications" of the Will, music was as close to the noumenal as we can get. Music could represent the pure dynamic striving of the Will without images. He says that "music differs from all the other arts by the fact that it is not a copy of the phenomenon, or, more exactly, of the Will's adequate objectivity, but is directly a copy of the Will itself, and therefore expresses the metaphysical to everything physical in the world, the thing-in-itself to every phenomenon."[6] In the universe itself, striving (Will) is the force of change constituting the fundamental nature of the noumenon. For Schopenhauer, no desire can ever really be satisfied; it can only be replaced by another. Striving never *gets* us anywhere. This led Schopenhauer to his unique reversal of the Enlightenment: contrary to Leibniz, this is the *worst* of all possible worlds. Life is a cycle of dissatisfaction: the only proper attitude for the truly informed must be pessimism. As he puts it in his typically direct way:

> All *willing* springs from lack, from deficiency, and this from suffering. Fulfillment brings this to an end; yet for one wish that is fulfilled there remain at least ten that are denied. Further, desiring lasts a long time, demands and requests go on to infinity; fulfillment is short and meted out sparingly. But even the final satisfaction itself is only apparent; the wish fulfilled at once makes way for a new one; the former is a known delusion, the latter a delusion not as yet known. (*WWR*, Vol. I, p. 196)

In contrast to Hegel's Master/Slave analogy, the point of which was to describe the motivation implicit in the structure underlying self-consciousness, self-identity, and the emergence of civilization through conflict and change, Schopenhauer employs a classical example to underscore his pessimism. He refers us to Zeus's punishment of King Ixion, who abused the hospitality of the gods. Ixion was possessed of *pleonexia*—of wanting too much for his own good, of violating virtues such as *sôphrosunê*, the intelligent moderation and balance of action and desire essential to the conception of the competitive *agôn* or contest that made up life for the Greeks. Ixion was lashed to a fiery wheel in perpetual motion but going nowhere. A 'bad infinity' (because repetitive) perhaps even worse than the fate of Sisyphus (who at least had the illusion of progress to keep him pushing his rock up that mountain again and again). The survival of Hegel's master and slave depends on how well they understand their reliance to each other—the achievement of that understanding constitutes a 'good infinity' (evolution as increasing self-consciousness). For Hegel, this process shows how the seemingly disorganized part belongs to a rational whole, and the realization of this contextualization can lead towards a higher form of civilization, one that can keep on changing for the better. If the master and slave do not make that leap in understanding, their struggle will be, as Hegel says, to the death. (Marx, of course, took this aspect of Hegel seriously and saw the big picture as socio-economic history.)

Only by understanding the constitutive structure of conflict will it be possible for us to grasp the nature of both life and reality—in this Wagner agreed with Hegel. But Schopenhauer saw no progress in this because he could not accept Hegel's view of the convergence of rational behavior with the processes of the universe in the development of civilization (the highest manifestation of *Geist*). For Schopenhauer, these must be held apart: Spirit (humanistically conceived) can never be united with Nature—however rationally or scientifically described, it will always be "Idea" and never the Will itself. The unity of Spirit and Nature remains a fantasy, impossible to achieve because the universe, the Will, cannot be united with *human* spirituality. Although we can never get beyond conceptualizing our experiences for Schopenhauer, art can suggest other ways of understanding the world. Art can, as it does in tragedy, conjure images of alienation rather than unification, images that tell us human experience will never rise above the world of objects; but it can also suggest something about the Will in the unity and satisfaction that emerges out of dissonance and dissatisfaction in music. The Will consists of infinite lack, of infinite needs that can never be satisfied. It will always be dissonance out of which we try to achieve consonance. Schopenhauer believed that in music, consonance and harmony are impermanent illusions that cannot overcome their source: without dissonance we could not *have* a concept of harmony. Dissonance, the Will, has metaphysical priority (the Prelude to *Tristan* exemplifies this principle).

This profoundly changed Wagner's views about music. In *Beethoven,* for example, he characterized the world-view of the opening movement of Beethoven's C-sharp minor string quartet (op. 131, written between 1824 and 1827) in Schopenhauerian terms. Here music conveyed the basic character of a world of complete frustration; paraphrasing Goethe, he described it as the dawn of a day in which not one hope would be fulfilled (*Faust,* line 1555: "Ich möchte bittre Tränen weinen,/Den Tag zu sehen, der mir in seinem Lauf/Nicht einen Wunsch erfüllen wird, nicht einen"). This was an attempt to describe the character of the somber, introspective opening moments of the work, the *Stimmung* of its slow fugue. Wagner goes on to describe how op. 131 concludes with a "dance of the whole world itself: wild joy, the wail of pain, love's transport, utmost bliss, grief, frenzy, riot, suffering" and summarizing: "It is impossible to see Beethoven the man before us for an instant, without at once recalling Beethoven the wonderful musician to explain him." Music is the essence of the world, the "world-idea," as Wagner used Schopenhauer's connection between the Will and music to justify the conception of music in *Tristan* and later when he returned to *The Ring.* This idea, however, came to him much earlier in a Gothean dream about the watery origin of the world, an idea that led to the Prelude to *Das Rheingold.*

In nonmusical contexts *stimmen/Stimmung* is usually translated as "mood." Its literal meaning would be 'disposition' or 'frame of mind'. A mood may come and go, but one may also be predisposed to see the world in a certain way; it might be a permanent feature of one's personality. In music *Stimmung* means 'tone' in the sense of the harmonic atmosphere of a work. It also means 'tuning' or 'harmony', the connotation being that one's frame of mind or disposition possesses a kind of musical characteristic such as major or minor tonality. In his characterization Wagner avoided any appeal to specific descriptions arguing that music has the power to create an atmosphere, indeed an entire *Weltanschauung,* without the need for a specific text or specific programmatic references. In the case of the opening Beethoven's op. 131, we experience unrelieved depression, a world of resignation, of hope defeated—Schopenhauerian to the core. The lines from *Faust* might make that sense of defeat more precise, but its existence lies prior to any objectification. The rest of op. 131 must be experienced in the context of its opening fugue (also, because of its strict form, suggesting fate, pre-determination)—something wonderful, even joyful, can be created in the face of a depressingly uncreative world. But such creation must be seen in the light of the unanswerable question of op. 135: "Must it be?" (and its harmonic similarity to the Fate motif). Our only possible response must be that life must go on ("It must be!" Beethoven wrote above the optimistic, carefree final movement of op. 135: the will of the composer reigns supreme in the medium best suited for willing). But why be optimistic? Seemingly, only the desire to live would be reason enough; but where Hegel tried to rationalize this desire, to explain everything by it conceptually, for Schopenhauer desire transcends all imagery. Even the desire to live transcends individual life.

In *Beethoven,* Wagner used Schopenhauerian language in his description of Beethoven's *Ninth Symphony* as breaking through the "Veil of Maya," Schopenhauer's metaphor describing the illusory world of phenomenal experience, to the impersonal forces beyond. In the final movement the music finds expression in words, but words and concepts are not primary. The Will, musically represented, goes beyond concepts, manifesting itself in a vision of empathetic responsiveness. The 'idea' expressed in Schiller's poetic euphoria, with its visionary identification between humanity and nature, was also portrayed by Goethe at the end of *Faust.* For Wagner, in contrast, it pointed not to an harmonious society, but to the identity of all life in *Mitleid.* The joy expressed by the chorus symbolizes the boundless force of empathy transcending social boundaries—not the triumph of civilized, rational humanity but universal ecstasy (which Schopenhauer thought of as *sorrow* over the inability to rise above particularity).

For Schopenhauer, the experience of compassion stands as the highest form of the transcendence and actually expressed the renunciation of individuality within human experience. For him, the disposition of *Mitleid*, the desire shared by all life to transcend phenomenal pain expressed not the unity of Spirit and

Nature, but universal suffering, ultimate disunity. For Schopenhauer, *Mitleid* shows the illusoriness of autonomy and the things individuals take seriously. To continue Wagner's analogy, which it is important to understand in relation to his concept of Music-Drama, the final movement of the *Ninth* begins with an anguished tension rising out of the lower strings. The warmly human *adagio* third movement lay in stark contrast to the nonhuman, Will-centered natural world of the first two movements, and all three briefly reappear in the opening to the Finale, all inadequate expressions of something deeper. At that point the symphonic forces finally break into human voice, but even before the bass soloist summons us together in friendship, the lower strings seem desperately to be trying to tell us something in their prevocal enunciation of the motif that becomes *O Freunde*. Finally the entire chorus emerges out of the pure sound of the orchestra with the dramatic cry of *Freude!* expressing the essence of humanity and its deepest need—the unity between humanity and nature.

For Beethoven, however, great art cannot be a merely social achievement: the essence of the Revolution was freedom *from* oppression, freedom *from* the evils humans bring upon each other as social animals. Beethoven takes his aesthetic vision far beyond any kind of humanism conceivable during the Enlightenment—*Freude* and *Mitleid* are not so far apart. Thus Wagner rejected his earlier view in *Opera and Drama,* that music must give expression to the text, that music itself told us nothing. In *Beethoven,* the music conveys a "world idea." Music "speaks to us solely through quickening into articulate life the most universal concept of the inherently speechless feeling, in all imaginable gradations, can once and for all be judged by nothing but the category of the *sublime*; for, as soon as she engrosses us, she transports us to the highest ecstasy of consciousness of our infinitude." The end of *Tristan* could not have been far from Wagner's mind.

In *Opera and Drama* Wagner described the Beethoven of the *Ninth Symphony* as a fully realized social being. But in his later essay, the social does not enter into Wagner's account of music as "world idea." The assertiveness of Beethoven's genius cannot be contained by society; great art always lies just beyond comprehension. Even in his single opera, *Fidelio,* the pathos of the Prisoner's Chorus lies in their *hope* for a new a society, not in the actual achievement of that hope. For Beethoven, it was the *experience of liberation* that counted, not its results. In a way, *Fidelio* was a rejection of social hope: societies will always have prisons, and we will always struggle to free ourselves from oppression. Only love will prove strong enough to break these shackles, but not for long. True creators, like Beethoven, however, never abide by the conventions and mores of their time. The prison symbolized *society itself.* The tonal imagery of alienated genius, seeking its own world but alone on the heights, haunts Beethoven's later chamber music and piano sonatas. His nostalgia for the human world in the slow movement of the *Ninth* must be contrasted with his conviction that nature swallows up the phenomenal in the pure energy of the first movement. The ambiguous brotherhood of the final movement—are we united in *society*, or rather in our *passion* for transcendent sublimity?—expresses a passion that can be disturbingly inhuman. (Mahler used a virtually identical theme of the slow movement in *Der Abschied,* the last movement of *Das Lied von der Erde,* one of the most important expressions of alienated subjectivity in the early twentieth century.)

Wagner's views about music and drama differ from Schopenhauer's on a significant point. As I pointed out in Chapter 2, Wagner's leitmotifs assimilate the drama to the music. Music not only refers to the visible drama but also exemplifies the dramatic role and essence of the various events on the visible stage. Schopenhauer, however, held that the essence of music was totally independent of drama. For example, "if music tries to stick too closely to the words, and to mold itself according to the events, it is endeavoring to speak a language not its own" (*WWR*, Vol. I, p. 262). Music is not a "copy" of the world but is "directly a copy of the Will itself." But Wagner did not believe in "absolute" music, in the complete metaphysical independence of musical content. He held music and the world together in a way repudiated by Schopenhauer, for whom Will transcended representation. As Nietzsche was to characterize it in *The Birth of Tragedy,* music "expresses the metaphysical to everything physical in the world, the thing-in-itself to every phenomenon" (Section 16). This is a direct quote from *WWR,* Vol. I, p. 262. But Schopenhauer goes on to say, almost immediately, that

> ...individual pictures of human life, set to the universal language of music, are never bound to it or correspond to it with absolute necessity, but stand to it only in the relation of an example, chosen at random, to a universal concept. They express in the distinctness of reality what music asserts in the universality of mere form.

Wagner, however, thought that music conveyed the soul of the action on the stage. The musical "thing-in-itself" to the phenomenal world (the stage action) cannot be divorced from the dialogue but gives it a more profound, deeper sense. The relation cannot be that of an example "chosen at random." He thought that the essence of art must be grasped "without reflection" and that music conveyed that essence directly. It was not a copy of the Will in Schopenhauer's sense of the Will transcending the world as "mere form," rather music was more like the *meaning* of the phenomenal words and actions on the stage (as Schopenhauer himself characterized the relation in Vol. II, p. 449, quoted in the next section). By similarly thinking of the Will as part of the world of experience, Wagner established a closer connection between music and drama.

With the passing of romanticism we have lost much of the forcefulness and novelty of those wonderful images of the self and nature, creatively transcending the actual state of human affairs, leaving behind but yet vitally dependent on the tension between humanity and society. But the unity between Spirit and Nature dreamt of by Rousseau in his idealized image of pastoral and benevolent humanity, a universal vision described by Goethe and Hegel and Schiller, also seemed to threaten the nature of the self as a phenomenal, social being. The primary emotional ambiance of Beethoven's *Ninth* actually seems *anti*social! What is the connection between *Freude* or 'joy' and social existence as it was conceived in the Enlightenment? During the Enlightenment, human beings were conceived primarily as individuals realizing through natural instincts their true collective unity with Nature. In this context, after the Revolution, after Beethoven's (and everybody's) disillusionment with Napolean, is not the *Ninth Symphony* an impossible fantasy about the union of Spirit and Nature transcending human social existence altogether (Schopenhauer's point, after all)? Have we not then reached the vanishing point of the socially conceived self: the true joys of liberation extending from social repression to the world itself? Yet if one leaves the world behind, for what does one leave it? Whether with Hegel's *Geist* or with Schopenhauer's Will, we have given up individuality for universality, but at what price? Such is also the question facing us at the end of Brünnhilde and Siegfried's scene at the end of *Siegfried*. *Can* they be completely disengaged from the social world? The events of *Götterdämmerung* suggest otherwise. This question also lies at the heart of *Tristan,* but as I contend throughout this book, neither transcendence nor renunciation should be thought of as of Wagner's central categories even though they are his recurrent themes. Indeed, he is profoundly anti-Schopenhauerian in his refusal to transcend, Nietzsche refused to see this in Wagner.[7]

4. Schopenhauer and *Tristan*: Love *versus* Society

After breaking off work on *The Ring* in 1857 at the end of *Siegfried* II, Wagner created *Tristan und Isolde* (1857–59) and *Die Meistersinger* (1862–1867), each of these works as different from each other as they both are from *The Ring*. He had quit work on *The Ring* because he was unsure about what to do with its many threads and possibilities: Where did he want to go? The doctrines of *Opera and Drama* had begun to slip away in practice and *The Ring* now lacked a definite direction. During this period Wagner drastically rethought the role of music in his drama, a task reinforced by his discovery of Schopenhauer in 1854. Under his influence, the Appearance/Reality (Representation/Will) distinction became more prominent in *The Ring* when Wagner returned to it in 1869, and as a result so did the distinction between society and the dynamic forces of the universe (as he saw Schopenhauer's Will) with individuals falling precariously in between. As we have seen, music became "the essence of the world" (the "thing-in-itself to every phenomenon") for Wagner and the visible, phenomenal world in turn became the world of illusion and a representation of the Will. This contrast, with some important departures from Schopenhauer, lies at the heart of *Tristan, Die Meistersinger,* and *Parsifal* as well as the final version of *The Ring*.[8]

In *Tristan,* the lovers create through their intense mutual attraction an entire world, separate and opposed to their social existence. Their love expresses the Will in opposition social convention, even transcending their individuality as persons. Love changes the beliefs of Tristan and Isolde about who they are and about their highest values. Music rather than plot, mood rather than action, forms the center of this work. The entire work emerges slowly out of the first few measures of the Prelude: the opening motif on the cello (A, F, E, D–sharp) accompanies a G-sharp in the oboes against an F and B in the lower strings and woodwinds—the '*Tristan* chord'. This famous musical-psychological tension (also associated with the so-called Sorrow motif (because it symbolizes Schopenhauerian *Mitleid*)) immediately preceeds the rising motif of G–sharp, A, A–sharp and B, a motif associated with Isolde and her sensual desire to rise above mere individuality. The harmonic ambiguity of these motifs proceeds from desire to frustration to renewed but even more unsatisfiable desires. This music, through its continual avoidance of resolution, shapes every moment of the work, portraying the obliteration of the boundaries between the lovers as phenomenal beings as they dream of union with each other and with the universe itself.

Wagner's use of the orchestra parallels Schopenhauer's description in his Supplement to Book III of *WWR*, entitled "On the Metaphysics of Music." When music is composed with respect to drama, "it is, so to speak, the soul of this since, in its connection with the incidents, character, and words, it becomes the expression of the inner significance of all these incidents, and of their ultimate and secret necessity that rests on this significance" (*WWR,* Vol. II, p. 449: contrasting with the weaker connection asserted in the quotation near the end of the last section). By the middle of Act II, the world of Tristan and Isolde no longer consists of physical objects, social institutions and laws, or even distinct persons but almost entirely of their wills, merging with each other. Through Wagner's music we experience their world from the point of view of sexual desire; we feel/hear the Will working in them through the music which, to quote Schopenhauer again, "expresses [the] real and true nature [of the action of the opera] and makes us acquainted with the innermost soul of the events and occurrences, the mere cloak and body of which are presented on the stage" (p. 448).

The problem of the self and love had figured in Wagner's earlier works (Morse Peckham's *Beyond the Tragic Vision* has an excellent account of the search for the nature of the self in Wagner's earlier works), and most recently prior to *Tristan* in the first act of *Die Walküre* (1852). There Siegmund and Sieglinde approach the erotic ecstasy of Tristan and Isolde, but fall short because *Die Walküre* I has no suggestion of the metaphysical symbolism that underlies *Tristan*. The fact that their relationship is incestuous does, however, point directly to the power of love in its ability to eliminate the boundaries of social and moral conventions, everything Fricka symbolizes as the personification of Wotan's laws, how those laws had been mere expressions of a deeper desire. The fact that Wotan should condone natural instinct in opposition to his own laws indicates how far he saw himself to stand outside those laws. They became mere pretexts for the exercise of his will and, by appealing to its primitive force, he feels that nature in the form of Siegmund and Sieglinde's sexual drive, both literally expressions of Wotan's desire, will save him. In Schopenhauerian terms, he believes that there are more powerful forces at work in the formation of value than social convention.

At the end of Act I the lovers embrace with a passionate fervor necessitating a very hasty curtain, foreshadowing the almost explicit sex of the second act of *Tristan* five years later. Despite its powerful portrayal of sexual attraction, the transcendence of personhood was completely absent from *Die Walküre* I. While Siegmund and Sieglinde use traditional romantic imagery in their visions of each other ("You are the Spring," "The Spring's fair moon shines on you," etc.), they remain distinct persons throughout. When the more complex use of such symbolic language occurs in *Tristan,* however, it and the music explicitly take us beyond the idioms of conventional morality into the metaphysics of personal identity and the Death. When symbols of love, and even death, appear in *Siegfried* III, its music written after *Tristan,* they do not have those connotations. Siegfried and Brünnhilde have moved towards a more heroic than metaphysical love in their opposition to Wotan's world, more than that of Siegmund and Sieglinde's erotic attraction (although that relationship collides with political reality too), but none of them contemplates transcending their individuality. Siegfried and Brünnhilde's "laughing death" symbolizes the transcending power of love through the *affirmation* of individuality (the audience seeing their individuality and freedom over and against social oppression) rather than as the metaphysical discovery of the nature of the Will through sex. (Unknown to them, because Brünnhilde is really his aunt, their love breaks the rules too). Love in all its forms symbolizes the Will transformed into the principle of change that came to dominate *The Ring*.[9] In *Götterdämmerung,* love and death are associated not with transcendence but with redemption from destruction. Love redeems by reestablishing something human although fragile and unstable. In her last moments Brünnhilde, unlike Isolde, wishes to retain her individuality in death, to be reunited with Siegfried *as* Brünnhilde. This sense of personal identity, affirmed in Wagner's earlier works, has been drastically weakened by the time of *Tristan*.

Tristan is Wagner's most Schopenhauerian work not least of all because he conceived of it symphonically right from the start, the voices of the singers becoming part of the orchestra (as individuals are expressions of the Will). When more conventional dramatic events occur (for example, the discovery of the lovers at the end of Act II) they point up the extreme contrast between the dream world of the lovers and the real world from which they are isolated by their sensuous desire. In *Tristan,* Wagner intentionally used music to bypass the visual images on the stage and to take us behind the action into the Will and this conception of music was carried over into *The Ring* when he returned to in 1869. Music no longer simply supported the plot and provided emphasis for the text; it has become its most important part.

In their long Act II duet, Isolde and Tristan believe that they will be united as a single person through sexual experience—and Isolde later believes that she will in death outstrip her physical individuality for the spiritual union she almost shared with Tristan. They believe that, although their own identities as individual persons—their histories, memories, and social connections—vanish in this union, they become "tristanandisolde," and they will continue to exist together in some way. This belief in the transcendence of the self through sensual experience extends to the union of the self with some deeper sense of reality than that represented by the merely social daylight world. When Tristan sings "Selbst dann bin ich die Welt," for example, he identifies himself with the universe in the manner of the romantic spirituality, but the hope of transcendence also resembles the religious ecstasy of medieval Christian mysticism, the essence of which, for Schopenhauer, was loss of self. Throughout this scene the music continually surges toward a resolution eluding Tristan and Isolde in their phenomenal existence; but it also shows the division between dream and reality to be inherently indistinct. We see this culminating in Isolde's *Liebestod* at the very end of the work. Her greatest desire has become the "unconscious bliss" of her transcendent reunion with Tristan in death. Her sexual experience was but a metaphor for this transcendence, her desire for unity.

Wagner establishes this identification between transcendence and death musically as a reflection of the Will, and his text also recreates similar associations found in romantic poetry.[10] Wagner's own poetry, musically coupled with the continual avoidance of cadence, its emphasis on harmonic suspension, and a use of rhythm that often renders it invisible, reflects endless becoming with an unusual intensity. For Schopenhauer, however, the self cannot transcend its phenomenality in any sense involving the survival of death by the individual. The *principium individuationis,* the dominant metaphysical principle of phenomenal reality that produces the (apparently inescapable) illusion of individual selfhood, results from our representation of the world as discrete, spatio-temporal things (including ourselves). This is the *affirmation* of the Will for Schopenhauer: all affirmation centers on individuality. But once we discover the constitutive contingency of the phenomenal world, that we do not *perceive* it for what it is (whereas we can *feel* it for what it is) the question arises about the relationship between representation, or appearance, and reality. For Tristan and Isolde, the world of society (symbolized by the illusory objectivity of daytime, the world of visual perception) became the illusion and the night world of their love reality (as manifestation of the Will). For Schopenhauer, the *denial* of the Will led to the loss of individuality. In forsaking the phenomenal world of light with its emphasis on individuality, morality, and society for the dark dream world of pure Will, the world of feeling and emotion rather than sight, Tristan and Isolde not only seek the obliteration of the boundaries of the self but of phenomenal reality. If Kant was right, as Schopenhauer thought he was, why be content with the phenomenal world when the noumenon beckons?

In his essay on Schopenhauer, Thomas Mann writes about the impact on Wagner:

> The thing in Schopenhauer that worked on Wagner, and in which the latter recognized himself, was the explanation of the world in terms of "Will," the instinct, the erotic conception of the world (sex as "focus of the Will") by which the *Tristan* music and its cosmogony of yearning are conditioned. It has been denied that *Tristan* was influenced by the philosophy of Schopenhauer—correctly in so far as the "denial of the Will" comes in question: for it deals of course with a love-poem; and in love, in sex, the Will asserts itself the most strongly. But precisely as a love-mystery the work is to the last degree Schopenhauerian in its coloration. In it, as it were, the erotic honey, the intoxicating essence, is sucked out of Schopenhauer's philosophy but the wisdom left behind.[11]

That wisdom would show us how the lovers, in trying to deny the self, in fact indulge in its most individualistic desire. It would seem necessary that we humans must have bodies in order to satisfy sexual desires. Indeed, in order to have any desires at all. But in Volume II of *The World as Will and Representation* Schopenhauer discusses sex in a chapter entitled "The Metaphysics of Sexual Love." His legendary cynicism waxes full: lovers think they are creating a unique relationship between themselves as particular individuals, but in so doing they really satisfy a universal desire to perpetuate their species by trying to create more individuals like themselves. Noting that only a minute portion of our sexuality involves the sexual act itself, Schopenhauer argues that these interests have as their point the denial of individuality. Sexual love appears to be a unique bond between individuals, it appears to involve individuals attracted to each other, but their desire really forms part of the *general* will to live, a will that supercedes individuality. The *individual* ego desires to preserve its own life but we in fact procreate to perpetuate life *in general*. We therefore through this desire go beyond the limits of individuality through love for Schopenhauer and thereby understand how our own will manifests the Will itself by linking the particular to the universal. Love between individuals expresses that dependence and the desire to manifest it—the same universalized impulse expressed in the Finale of the *Ninth Symphony*.

Hence the world of representation becomes 'nothing' in a metaphysical sense for Schopenhauer. Now the rejection of the social world in *Tristan,* coupled with the symbolic experience of the Will through sexual love, seems to lead to the absolute experience of reality alluded to by Schopenhauer in his many references to Eastern thought as he attempted to describe at least the possibility of transcendent consciousness. On the one hand, he denies that such consciousness can be an experience of anything *in* the world. He argues that our only salvation from the turmoil of the Will in our own lives lies in the realization of the illusoriness of the objective world, including ourselves. The denial of the Will, through renunciation of phenomenal selfhood, rests on the realization of the illusoriness of individuality. But, on the other hand, Schopenhauer's characterization of ultimate reality as Will obviously leaves the door open to some form of transcending experience, even if it must always be indirect. As he says at the end of the first volume, "we freely acknowledge that what remains after the complete abolition of the Will is, for those still full of the Will, assuredly nothing. But also conversely, to those in whom the Will has turned and denied itself, this very real world of ours with all its suns and galaxies, is—nothing" (*WWR*, Vol. I, pp. 411–12). At this point subject and object no longer exist, the distinction no longer viable in the face of Schopenhauerian consciousness of the Will. The world can, then, at least figuratively, disappear for those who turn the Will away from its *principium individuationis*, who deny their own wills in order to dwell in inexpressible universality. In this way of describing the denial of the Will in the acceptance of the illusoriness of its particular personal manifestations, how metaphorical does Schopenhauer intend to be? Is this not, as Mann suggests, simply eroticism tinged with metaphysics?[12] Indeed, is that not the *point*—that erotic experience can also be metaphysical (just as religious experience can be erotic, as it is in *Parsifal*)?[13]

We saw in Section 3 how Schopenhauer based his concept of *Mitleid* on the realization of the shared essence of Being underlying all objective reality and personhood: suffering as the essence of life, the longing for transcendence of the Veil of Maya, the phenomenal world. To be alive means to be driven by desires that will never be satisfied. We spend most of our lives in frustration; pain, in one form or another, makes up a far more familiar part of life than does pleasure

(pleasure, for Schopenhauer, being simply the momentary absence of pain). Our understanding of the universe unified through suffering can be attained indirectly through art, but for the most part it still speaks the language of perception and objectivity. Music, however, allows us to represent the innermost, dynamic nature of all things (a way of putting it Wagner clearly borrowed from Schopenhauer in his distinction between the visible aspects of drama and music as the essence of the world).[14] As we saw in the last section, we can approach the essence of the Will itself through musical experience: in musical experience we can be conscious of the distinction between the phenomenal world and the Will and yet see their unity:

> Without the object, without the representation, I am not knowing subject, but mere, blind Will; in just the same way, without me as subject of knowledge, the thing known is not object, but mere Will, blind impulse. In itself, that is to say outside the representation, this Will is one and the same with mine; only in the world as representation, the form of which is always at least subject and object, are we separated out as known and knowing individual. As soon as knowledge, the world of representation, is abolished, nothing in general is left but mere Will, blind impulse. (*WWR*, Vol. I, p. 180)

Schopenhauer here writes as though the self can actually be identified with the Will (thus his anthropomorphic characterization of the noumenon as Will). In fact, he ends this section with a quotation from Byron's *Childe Harold* in which the poetically ecstatic persona affirms its identity with nature. Art and metaphysics are one. As Schopenhauer describes it: "he is the condition, and hence the supporter, of the world and of all objective existence." We have seen how the egoism and striving of the phenomenal self, however, are simply illusions for Schopenhauer. In sexual experience, as he symbolizes it, we rise above our particularity while still remaining particulars and thereby understand how our individual wills manifest the Will in general as an expression of the universal in the particular. *Mitleid* constitutes the experience of that connection, and the metaphysical basis of *Tristan's* music and sexuality.

Through the continually increasing tension of the music in *Tristan*, and the ambiguity of its resolutions, we see the mythology of romantic love through Schopenhauerian eyes of unsatisfied desire as the general nature of the universe—the essence of *Mitleid*. The avoidance of resolution throughout the Prelude, the tension, restlessly and relentlessly building throughout most of the work, conveys the essence of the desire, anticipation, and fantasy surrounding the lovers. Because this music so powerfully portrays the sexual attraction between the lovers, we are not the detached observers Schopenhauer describes in connection with non-musical representational art. We are uncomfortably active participants because the Will represents *our* desires as well! After dozens of false cadences throughout almost all of *Tristan,* we are finally led into the B–flat major chord at the very end of the work. This moment that should have a sense of infinite extension, the eternity sought in love and the only true resolution in the whole work. This final chord has the effect of the cessation of life itself—the conflict of existence has ended, the denial of the Will finally achieved, Isolde and Tristan are one. Their *Mitleid* has achieved their sexual unity, driving them both towards death as the mere symbol of their transcendence. (The ending of Act III should be understood in the context of its prelude and its premonition of disaster: see Chapter 3, Section 6.)

While Schopenhauer never identifies sex with the Will (it is simply a manifestation), Wagner *does*. His "slight modification" of the Will into the sexual love between men and women also transforms it into something quite different (as Mann suggests in the above quote): not withdrawal from phenomenal existence but the assertion of and preoccupation with our sensual humanity. In *Tristan* human individuals dream of escaping their individuality through sexual union and the work portrays the effect of this dream on its dreamers. Despite his debt to Schopenhauer, Wagner dwells on the human subjectivity of love in a way Schopenhauer himself cynically disparages. For him, we escape the illusion of individuality through the denial of the Will (in the form of the particular desires of individuals); for Wagner, the lovers see their individuality as an illusion, but they cannot escape it, even through transcendence. They want to escape the only thing that *can* be truly valuable for them. Hence, for Wagner, the denial of the Will in us, of our particularity, takes on the ironic aspect noted by Mann. Wagner in effect denies Schopenhauer and Kant's point about aesthetic beauty as universal disinterestedness. For Wagner, beauty always entails interest (see endnote 25).

The relationship between Tristan and Isolde can now be seen in its true light: they are individuals who want to transcend their individuality, but their attempt to do so is fatally ironic. In his eccentric but often insightful study of the nineteenth century, Morse Peckham summarizes this: *Tristan* not only portrays the metaphysical essence of romantic love but exposes the fundamental irony of transcendence:

> The lover...[exploits] the beloved; at the same time his dependency upon her denies the very thing his love is designed to achieve, a confirmation of his independent identity and selfhood. The pattern has the weakness of all forms of transcendentalism: it imagines that the not-self can in fact be redeemed into value by the activities of the self at the level of the social role. A dual violation takes place. The lover violates the be-

> loved by exploiting her as a symbol; and he violates himself by making his identity depend upon a symbol. If identity can be affirmed only by affirming another's identity, transcendental love is unable to turn the trick.[15]
>
> Erotic love...is a projection, a self created mask which the lover places over the face and the form of the beloved. Lovers do not see each other at all...they see only themselves. Thus Tristan reaches an emotional consummation of his love when Isolde is not with him, and he is dying; and Isolde reaches her ecstasy when Tristan is dead, through she is firmly convinced, to the moment of her own death, that he still lives. Further, the climax of her emotion is identical with her total loss of identity and her merging with nothingness. (p. 256)

In his "slight modification" of the Will, however, bringing the erotic directly into metaphysics, Wagner in effect rejected the ambiguous transcendence and universalization implied by Schopenhauer's denial of the Will. The desire for transcendence has been part of the romantic conception of love for centuries, but it has sometimes led to the *denial* of our humanity. Because sex is the primary motivating force in life, for Wagner, it can lead to the denial of the significance of individuality. Along with Tanner, however, I think that we experience this differently than Peckham suggests: *Tristan* does not analytically, or clinically, unmask our illusions of transcendence—it puts us right into that illusion. We share it. The work ends with the stark contrast between our now deceased hero and heroine and their/our unfulfilled dream of transcendence. As Tanner points out, we are sympathetically *involved in* this contrast rather than detached observers witnessing the metaphysical self-destructiveness of an antiquated mythology. The myth remains *our* myth, its redemptiveness—and love *is* redemptive for Wagner—must therefore be understood not as the metaphysical/ecstatic outstripping of individuality but its inescapability. Therefore, Peckham's "dual violation" exposes not only the failure of transcendental redemption but also the inevitability of symbols for redemption in our lives—the *inescapability* of illusion.[16]

5. *Die Meistersinger* and the Art of Illusion

With its combination of lightness and message, *Die Meistersinger* (1867) resembles a Shakespearean comedy, all of which also have deeper plots. Underneath the superficial story of the Knight Walther's courting of Eva, the daughter of a prominent citizen and competing in the mastersinger competition, lies the story of the unifying social interrelations of the reformation town of Nuremberg, held together by its crafts (celebrated in the procession and festival of Act III) and its devotion to art (the guild of Mastersingers). But a deeper philosophical level, involving the relation between illusion and reality, also emerges to explain why that society—and why Wagner—took art so seriously. This work practices what it preaches: in this town, art and society reinforce each other.

In Scene 1 of Die Meistersinger III, Hans Sachs, that epitome of bourgeois sensibility and artistic creativity decries the delusions of his fellow citizens and their inability to see beyond their own selfish vanity. He uses the word Wahn: "Wahn! Wahn! Überall Wahn!":"Illusion; illusion! Everywhere illusion!" We can see here the influence of Schopenhauer even in this most un*Tristan*-like work as Wagner focuses our attention on the illusory nature of the phenomenal. Indeed the conception of *Wahn* stands at the center of all of Wagner's mature works. All belief involves *Wahn* and Sachs implies that the most dangerous form of illusion in his society is delusion (*Wahnsinn*), something destructive, a limitation of vision and a failure of understanding. The verb *wähnen* means to imagine, to believe erroneously. But *Wahn* can also be a creative transformation of experience and value, something that might have positive results under the right kind of control.[17]

The Prelude to Act III begins with the so-called motif of "Regret" and casts a contemplative light on the opening scene, a reflection of Sachs' own character and far more serious than the rest of what has happened up to that point. The mood contrasts with the preceeding, brilliantly conceived Act II, with its continuous action and humor. The Prelude indicates Sachs's deeper concerns about the social and moral function of art as well as the nature of society. We find Sachs sitting alone in his workshop, a metaphor for the artist's studio, reading. In the Seattle production I attended in the summer of 1989, for example, the workshop in Act II is surrounded by the town of Nuremberg, while in Act III it seemed to be floating in space against a backdrop of the purest sky-blue. When Sachs refers to Nuremberg at the end of the *Wahn* aria, he sings:

> But now has come Midsummer Day!
> Let's look now at what Hans Sachs can do,
> trying to guide that vain deceit
> to do some nobler deeds....

But when he gestures towards the town at "right here in Nuremberg," it has disappeared! His beloved community is itself an illusion. Despite its apparent solidity and firmness, it too has been the result of the collective activities, hopes, and traditions of its members. Sachs accepts the contingency of his community. For him, its values are inventions that must be sustained by its the efforts of its citizens. The music surrounding the end of the monologue includes the Nuremberg motif, with its Reformation, Lutheran connotations of responsible individuality and progress through community. There is also the Shakespearean theme of Midsummer Magic indicating Sachs's potential as an artist, a controller of illusion for the noble end of preserving community through individual creativity. This deeper theme of creative illusion justifies the seriousness of the Prelude to Act III. As Sachs puts it: "Let's look now at what Hans Sachs can do,/trying to guide that vain Deceit to do some nobler deeds." In the aria, the '*Wahn*' motif, combined with the Meistersinger and Nuremberg motifs indicates the force of illusion in Sachs's society. Because it involves *Wahn*, society must be a construct; but if social activity requires some shared beliefs, the question is: How do we come to have and to share beliefs that lead to the best possible society, to its most constructive form?

Sachs tries to guide the "vain deceits" and unacknowledged delusions of his society into more socially positive as well as artistically creative achievements. I have tried to show how this aspect of nineteenth-century German art intersects with the philosophical debate about the nature of reality contemporaneous with it. We live as beings who see ourselves as (relatively) stable and fixed, but we can also see that those features are the results of deeper, underlying processes, of larger contexts. The unity of experience is not the experience of unity. We can understand ourselves as illusions in this sense, thus recognizing the contingency of selfhood and community, but the worst illusion must be the one that does not or cannot recognize itself for what it is—that is a *de*lusion.

The procession of the guild members in Act III symbolizes the connection between community and creativity. Against this background, the *Wahn* aria and the Prelude to Act III indicate a more complex level of perception than might be suggested by the comedic events that give the work its superficial structure. The complex social interplay between Sachs, Walther, Eva, Beckmesser (Wagner's comment on uncreative critics such as, he thought, Edward Hanslick who failed to see the point[18]), and the rest of the community rests on values such as love, German history and art, craft and its dependence on sense of community. But all of these, as well as the community formed from them, are seen to be inventions depending on the shared, critically held beliefs of their participants. The events that take place in Sachs's workshop show art as the creation of value metaphorically on the grand scale of society. For Nietzsche and Wagner, only through art that can we understand the nature of illusion and its control—as Peckham describes it: "the power of art…introduces value into the world by creating in the hearts of men the experience of order and meaning" (p. 260). This "orientative drive" describes exactly what Sachs sets out to do in the remainder of Act III and what he does reverses Schopenhauer's view of everyday life and phenomenal reality. Instead of allowing the discovery of life and value as illusions leading to the conclusion that they must be evil, we turn instead to the creation of illusions with more interest than ever before.

Pessimist though Sachs clearly is, seeing so many harmful beliefs and attitudes around him, he nevertheless sees the control of illusion as a positive value. Even negative beliefs can be turned to noble ends. Nietzsche also argued—it is the focal point of all his works—that even negative values are better than no values at all. Our only categorical imperative lies in the creation of value in life and what greater challenge can there be but to do so in a world that may be uncongenial for creativity of any sort—positivity needs negativity. The message of *Die Meistersinger* at its deepest level must be that where art shows us how creation works—Sach's involvement in Walther's Prize Song, his "John the Baptist" role—the principle is the same in all human endeavors.[19] So we come to have and share beliefs *together*, not as isolated individuals but as members of a community. The theme of aesthetically creative individual and collective tradition—Walther and Sachs—exemplfies this Wagnerian point.

For Sachs, advocate of socially responsible bourgeois individualism through artistic innovation, our beliefs must be under control—if not ones own control then under the non-oppressive control of someone, or a community, that can draw the proper distinctions between appearance and reality relevant to a life of moral value and social innovation. In helping Walther to write his prize-winning song, Sachs metaphorically uses his "craftsman" approach to art and society (in his humble role as village cobbler he has everyone's respect as a great tune-smith) to set an example of civilized and creative control. He appeals to the accepted standards of composition that forms his tradition. He thus sets out to convince others to understand their own traditions and to use them to create something new.[20]

The problem of self-control stands at the center of Wagner's music-dramas. If, as Peckham puts it, "illusion is the mode in which man exists" (p. 259), from where does the authority originate to establish order within society and value for its citizens? What makes one illusion better, more productive, than another? How do we separate constructive illusion from destructive delusion? If we can find no absolute standards that will help us to answer these questions, a certain resignation and pessimism might well seem attractive; but to say there are no absolute standards that cut across culture and tradition, time and place is not to say there are no standards at all. Nor should we see ourselves toppling into hopeless relativism and cynicism about our traditions once we see them as inventions rather than discoveries. It would seem that the only general guideline for distinguishing illusion from delusion is 'creativity'. Constructive *illusions* enhance society even though they may change it. *Delusions* are destructive and do not; they make us "less human" as Nietzsche puts it. But "creativity" is just as troublesome a word as "illusion": When are we truly creative and when, while we might *think* we are, are we instead being destructive? We will be unable to answer this question except by continuing the activity in question and seeing what happens—by taking our everyday reality to be the most significant.

For nineteenth-century artists and philosophers as different in their conclusions as Hegel, Schopenhauer, Goethe, Nietzsche, and Wagner, we are, for all of them, continually interpreting. Reality, in the transcendent sense of God's point of view, must be unavailable to us (it cannot be a "point of view" anyway as Nietzsche said in *The Genealogy of Morals* (Essay III, Section 12)). In effect, Nietzsche argues, such a reality does not exist since there can be no interaction with it. I have described how Schopenhauer approaches the Will through the realization of the interpretive nature of experience. But beyond that we can only conceive of the world as Will without purpose. Peckham argues that Wagner rejects transcendence and severely attenuates Schopenhauer's conception of the Will into the concept of the Self (represented by Wagner's orchestra), thus preserving some sense of noumenal interaction. Wagner's music then depicts the contrast between illusion and delusion in the persons of the drama, universalizing the self as Will-generated illusion. I have argued against this by suggesting that the only will for Wagner is the human will. For his character Sachs, the only values are the ones defined by our activities as self-actualizing expressions of our interests within the world of ordinary social experience, but that experience includes not only making shoes and creating art but sustaining community. There can be, for Wagner, no purpose-free, autonomous self. *The Ring's* orchestra summarizes power and love *in* life, not transcending it.

Wagner's conception of human reality—what we believe to be real, good, beautiful, rational and wise—depends on the myths that express and control our efforts at self-creation. If he was sensitive to the Eastern view (brought to him by at least in part by Schopenhauer's frequent use of Buddhist and Hindu metaphores and analogies), he still saw the self as active rather than passive and he saw how fraught with danger the activity of self-creation can be. We cannot escape these dangers, these threats to stability. We are always in the world as individuals when we experience anything at all and the denial of the Will, the denial of our creations because of their impermanence, cannot take us beyond that world—as we see in Wotan's and Brünnhilde's failed attempts at forestalling change. The mythology of love in *Tristan* portrays the dream of that kind of transcendence and Siegfried III depicts a less metaphysically charged view of love transcending politics, but we can only witness such dreams of permanence from the phenomenal world of change and their significance lies only within the roles they play in that world. This contrast between illusion and value seems to be the point of connection between the very different worlds of *Tristan* and *Die Meistersinger*.[21] Instead of moving from the phenomenal to the noumenal, and contrary to Peckham himself who overgeneralizes this point, it seems to me that Wagner abandons the distinction: nothing lies beyond the human world.

However, images of sight, eyes, and vision fill *The Ring* with contrasts between appearance and reality. All of the characters are limited in sight actually and symbolically. A great deal happens on the stage in the course of the cycle and there are many things to see while *Tristan*, on the other hand, remains for long stretches almost motionless and suspended. In *Tristan* the action becomes entirely inward and the eye sees very little in this work—even if it were possible to be more sexually explicit during the duet, the point of the music would be lost because of the visual distraction! In *Tristan*, the kind of understanding sought by the lovers cannot be objectively represented, it exists only in their minds and, despite its far more visual orientation, the emphasis on belief and desire carries over to *The Ring* after Wagner returned to it. The early stages of *The Ring* center on Wotan's striving against what appear to be external threats. His efforts at saving his society are symbolized by his vision of the sword at the end of *Das Rheingold* (symbolizing his dream of heroic redemption). But in his monologue during *Die Walküre* IIii, the emphasis begins to shift towards the conflict between Wotan's hopes and fears, his inner-life, and the world he has created—a world that has taken on a life of its own. The entire third act of *Siegfried*, despite its ample visual imagery, also points toward the transforming and redemptive power of love in opposition to the external world of power. Although *Götterdämmerung* contains a good deal of action, it too centers the dynamic tensions within and between the beliefs of the characters.

In both *Tristan* and *The Ring,* the desire for transcendence remains unsatisfied. The music expresses the frustration of this desire in *Tristan* through the many transformations of the seventh chord derived from the Prelude. As Carl Dahlhaus points out in the *New Grove Dictionary of Music*, the tonic of that chord never directly appears. In *The Ring,* Dahlhaus notes again, the harmonically ambiguous Tarnhelm motif symbolizes the "allegory of alienation": through its vision-distorting power. The tarnhelm prevents Brünnhilde and Siegfried from achieving their goal of identity in love—by the very actions of the magically controlled Siegfried himself at the end of *Götterdämmerung* I. *Die Meistersinger* and *The Ring* are, in contrast to *Tristan*, firmly diatonic in conception. However, Dahlhaus points to the precarious harmonic stability of *Die Meistersinger*: "it is like a thin, fragile layer of ice over a ground swell of chromaticism. It is memory rather than corporeal presence, and there is a strand of reflection in its artless nostalgia; but it owes its emotional effect precisely to the listener's sense that it is endangered" (p. 120). *Tristan,* on the other hand, relies on a direct and continual awareness of harmonic deviance, on the explicit rejection of diatonic firmness and stability.

To understand the point of the *Die Meistersinger*, we must realize the solidity and harmonic firmness of its music to be an illusion (and Sachs refers directly to the contingency of society in his *Wahn* aria). In *Tristan*, completed just three years before, Wagner had used radical innovations in harmony to convey the sexual fantasy world of doomed lovers who contrasted their private 'night-world' with the public 'day-world' of society and conventional morality. Like Brünnhilde in *The Ring,* Tristan and Isolde believed their world of love to be more real than the social world of public activity. As one more clue to the illusion of stability in *Die Meistersinger,* Wagner injects *Tristan's* harmonic and metaphysical ambivalence directly into *Die Meistersinger.* This occurs when the motif of Tristan's longing appears as Sachs cautions Eva about the power of love by referring to the Tristan legend and to the fate of King Mark near the middle of Act III. This moment, although it passes quickly, conveys to the discerning a slightly uneasy feeling because of the shift between two—seemingly opposite—harmonic (and sexual) worlds. In the *Wahn* aria at the beginning of the act the reference to "old Nuremberg" and the sense of recollection and the added significance given to earlier motifs not associated with illusion gets to the heart of the nature of *Wahn* in *Die Meistersinger.* The reference to *Tristan* in a work apparently resting so firmly on stable harmonic ground shows by example what illusions can do to people.

Dahlhaus argues that the apparently 'old German' simplicity of *Die Meistersinger* must be sentimental rather than naive (in Schiller's sense): that is, it expresses nostalgia for a simpler life (that never existed) but also includes a higher reflective consciousness about the very stability one seeks. His point is that:

> [t]he impression that diatonicism has been reinvested with its old, classical rights is completely illusory: what is denied is always present, even through unexpressed.... The diatonicism of *Die Meistersinger* is somehow dreamlike, not quite real in the 1860's; the style of the work is less a restoration than a reconstruction.... (p. 158)

6. Nietzsche's Metaphysical Perspectivism

In *The Gay Science,* Nietzsche speaks of the capacity of art to show us the structure of appearance, of the world as it seems to be (Book II, #107). He writes: "as an aesthetic phenomenon existence is still *bearable* for us, and art furnishes us with eyes and above all the good conscience to be *able* to turn ourselves into such a phenomenon." In part he means that we should stop thinking of ourselves as determinate essences (such as Descartes' characterization of the mind as pure thinking substance or as Plato's affinity between the immaterial soul and the eternal Forms). He wants us to see that we are malleable, open to different characterizations. Ten years earlier, in *The Birth of Tragedy,* his first major work (published in 1872),[22] he had said that it was only "as an *aesthetic phenomenon* that existence and the world are eternally *justified.*" His point, in part at least, was that we know art to be "false" in the literal sense of the word.

Art does not objectively *describe* the world, it *interprets*; but art's very artificiality can convey an insight into the character of reality as we understand it.

Still pursuing this theme in his last, unfinished work he wrote, "we possess *art* lest we *perish of the truth*" (*The Will to Power,* #822). Like Hans Sachs in *Die Meistersinger*, he meant that art shows us how our conception of reality came to be—our society, our way of understanding the world, has been invented rather than discovered and we can understand this insight by studying the creative processes of artists such as Goethe. The "cult of the untrue" (art) enables us to study the formation of illusion in itself—by creating something we know to be an illusion. If, hoping for eternal verities, we were to discover how "delusion and untruth" are the conditions of life without our being able to control at least some of it, "the truth" (the constituted nature of reality) would be unbearable to us. If we live under the delusion (the uncritical illusion) that there are absolute values then, were we somehow to discover that there were none, this discovery would be unbearable. We cannot easily live with only relative values if we really want absolutes. This would be "nihilism" as Nietzsche understands it: the inability to sustain moral principles. But even if there are absolutes, Nietzsche asks, *why* would it be better for us to appeal to them? If we realize that we are creators of illusion and that this power of creativity sustains us in the face of the recognition that everything in life depends on it, then we will have understood life in terms of art.

In Section 18 of *The Birth of Tragedy,* Nietzsche ironically praises Kant and Schopenhauer for having defeated the *optimism* of Western civilization, its chief characteristic since Socrates "murdered" Sophoclean tragedy.[23] Socrates' (really Plato's) optimism rested on his belief in the existence of eternal truths and our ability to appeal to them for solutions to the riddles of the universe. This optimism depended most of all on the viability of rationalism, on the power of reason to generalize its historical moment through knowledge of the universal. But "Kant showed that these really served only to elevate the mere phenomenon, the work of *maya* [illusion], to the position of the sole and highest reality, as if it were the innermost and true essence of things, thus making impossible any knowledge of this essence or, in Schopenhauer's words, lulling the dreamer still more soundly asleep." That is, for Kant, the structure of experience ("our" law) has nothing to do with whatever lies beyond it, with the noumenon. We believe that the real is the rational, but the rational is limited to the phenomenal (the "Veil of Maya"). Kant thereby reintroduced mystery back into the universe when he said he criticized reason to make room for faith. By showing us that knowledge and truth could not be validated from outside of our experience by appealing to God's veracity and benevolence (as Descartes, Leibniz, and Locke had argued). The noumenon lies beyond reason and cognition, at best the object of faith and speculation.

Arguing that Kant's noumenon must be thought of as the *opposite* of the objective, represented world, Schopenhauer, as we have seen, characterized it as "the Will" (endless conflict as opposed to static substantiality) and we have seen the effect of this on Wagner's conception of music. Although it is not an object of scientific inquiry, we can experience the Will in art and in willing itself. Nietzsche too was obviously influenced by Schopenhauer in his emphasis on aesthetic interpretation rather than science as an insight into the nature of reality. The insight would be that whatever we say or believe about the world depends on the 'perspective' of interests, a point of view that establishes our fundamental truths and values.

In *The Birth of Tragedy* Nietzsche first drew his distinction between Apollo and Dionysus to point up the difference between science (understood as the search for absolutes) and art. This dichotomy generally stands for Schopenhauer's distinction between objective reality and the Will. Apollo was the patron spirit of reason and representation, of order and stability, of civilization driven by intellectual contemplation as the highest virtue. Dionysus, on the other hand, was the patron of wine (*in vino veritas*), ineffability, danger, magic, the music Plato banned from his republic, uninhibited sex, willfulness and desire, the transcendence of the *principium individuationis* and, above all, tragedy. Nietzsche argued that the spirit of Ancient Greece was not characterized by the search for permanence (where "Beauty is truth, truth beauty,—that is all/Ye know on earth, and all ye need to know" as Keats said of his Grecian urn) until Socrates, Euripides, and Plato. Before them, the Greeks were positively Dionysian in their metaphysics of tragedy. To use Thomas Mann's image, tragedy shows us the skull beneath the cultivated outer skin of civilization. This was for Nietzsche the Sophoclean view of life and reality, "reborn" in Wagner: through the conflicts of creation and destruction we see the ephemeral nature of human value and understanding.

Some sixteen years later, Nietzsche wrote in *The Twilight of the Idols* (*Götzen-Dämmerung*, 1888—his last year of sanity) that Goethe, and presumably others such as Keats, who praised the Greeks only for its Apollinianism, did not understand them because he denied the fundamentally Dionysian mystery of the universe and of the "will to life" (see #4, "What I Owe to the Ancients"). Instead of the harmonies of reason leading to an idealized conception of beauty rising above the turmoil of experience, Nietzsche saw it as a dangerous psychological force paradoxically deriving absoluteness from the urge for domination rather than dispassionate insight into timeless truths. For him the early romantics followed Socrates (and Euripides he thought) by eliminating the Dionysian essence of tragedy in their attempt to aesthetically idealize the universe in contrast to their alienating society. Even in *Faust*, Goethe seems to identify Mephistopheles with Dionysus so that the redemption of Faust in the last scene incorporates a contrasting Apollinian fantasy of order emerging out of the *eros* of Dionysian ecstasy.

The last scene of *Faust* contrasts the transient with the eternal, earth with heaven, the contingent and the divine. Goethe wanted to find a *direction* for human striving: How can we live in a world of contingency without a guiding beacon of universality? Hence the "ewig Weibliche," the 'eternal' feminine, elusive ideal for which Faust lusted. For Nietzsche, however, in our desire to find the eternal within the contingent, Western civilization has tried to stabilize experience and reality through art, religion, science, philosophy, and ethics. We have appealed to principles of reason and objectivity as the fundamental values of our culture. For Goethe, the point of *Faust* lies in the universality of striving, to create stability within the contingencies of life. How to do this: Through universal truths or creative illusion? For Nietzsche, the eternal and the contingent cannot cohabitate: the 'eternal' feminine and the 'momentary' masculine. The contrast ensures that men and women cannot be happy together.

Despite his praise of the erotic, Apollo and Dionysus are, for Nietzsche, *both* essential to Western experience: the maxims of Apollo are "know thyself," "Man is the rational animal," and "nothing in excess." They are principles employed in the attempt at overcoming the ineffability of existence, in making human life endurable (see *The Birth of Tragedy*, #4). For Nietzsche, the Buddhist withdrawal from 'striving' that characterizes Schopenhauerian resignation *ought not* follow from our comprehension of the essence of struggle, desire, and *eros* in life. As he notes in several places, if Schopenhauer believed that striving was truly irrelevant, why did he bother to write such eloquent books? Why did he not just withdraw? Why the evangelical zeal? For Nietzsche, we learn from the tragedies of Sophocles and the music-dramas of Wagner that art justifies life because it establishes the purpose of living as active creation against the knowledge of an otherwise fundamentally valueless nature. We strive not to know what we truly are in the abstract but to create interesting solutions to our immediate problems (which often have features of generality). Great art drives us—compels us—to reaffirm life, to live it anew.

While creation sometimes, perhaps *always* for Nietzsche, violates social conventions, he saw the nature of life as the balancing of creation and destruction, as the interdependence of Dionysus and Apollo and not the diminishment or rejection of social life. That, for him, was also a form of nihilism. We must reject detachment for engagement; we cannot eliminate the indifference of the universe to human striving but we can try to control the myths that make striving possible. In this Nietzsche, along with Wagner, rejected Schopenhauer's dualism of Will and representation. They rejected the inference that since the essence of reality is destructive of individuals, resignation can be the only rational alternative in an arational universe ('*arational*', again, in the sense that its structure may not coincide with that of human rationality or objectivity). To assume that the universe is *irrational* would commit the same mistake as to assume that it is rational. Whether the universe is for or against humanity does not matter for Nietzsche, because we can never know it. *We*, however, *have* to be for or against *something.*

In *The Birth of Tragedy* Nietzsche saw the relation of Greek culture to nineteenth-century Europe as an inversion. His own era, he suggested, was moving through Greek history in reverse: instead of beginning with Dionysian directness and evolving towards detached rationalism and Socratic demythologization, the nineteenth century moved from the rationalism of the Enlightenment and Kant—the classicism of Haydn, the early Mozart, and Italian opera—towards the later Mozart, Beethoven, Schopenhauer, and ultimately, Wagner. The *rebirth* of tragedy was supposed to defeat the decadence of later European civilization by overthrowing its outmoded forms of expression and thought. Western civilization had become rigid, abstract and self-defeating in its search for permanence. That is, absolute values became irrelevant to life (God was 'dead', or at best no longer able to sustain and exemplify civilized values). Wagner and Schopenhauer broke through this rigidity in their Dionysian view of art and reality.

Soon after *The Birth,* however, Nietzsche accused both his heroes of giving up on their revolutionary insights in their pessimism and in their transcendence of human existence for the universalistic eroticism of Eastern religion and escapist music. Nietzsche saw himself as reversing this decline by projecting the Daytime world of Italian opera and southern "dancing" as the antidote to the gloomy Teutonic night—as he was to put it later in *The Case of Wagner* (1888): *Carmen* over *Tristan*. Wagner had become too 'serious'; he could not get beyond Schopenhauer. *Tristan* don't swing.

Despite Nietzsche's disillusionment with Wagner, it was their mutually emphasized activism toward life and value that put them both in opposition to Schopenhauer (in "The Total Work of Art," Tanner calls this their "moral vitalism." Tragedy did not lead to the denial of the Will or to mysticism for the Greeks but to renewed energy—to achieve, however temporarily, that elusive union between Apollo and Dionysus. As he writes near the end of *The Twilight of the Idols*:

> Tragedy is so far from proving anything about the pessimism of the Greeks, in Schopenhauer's sense, that it may be considered a decisive refutation and counter-instance of what he says. Saying Yes to life, even in its strangest and hardest problems, the will to life rejoicing over its own inexhaustibility even in the very sacrifice of its highest examples—*that* is what I call Dionysian, *that* is what I guessed to be the bridge to the psychology of the *tragic* poet. *Not* in order to be liberated from

> terror and pity, not in order to purge oneself of a dangerous affect of its vehement discharge—Aristotle's understanding of tragedy—but in order to be oneself in the eternal joy of becoming, beyond all terror and pity—that joy which included even joy in destroying.

One should add to this the last sentences of the *Genealogy of Morals* (published in 1887, fifteen years after *The Birth*) in which Nietzsche ends the *Genealogy* with a criticism of conventional (Christian-Kantian) morality. The "ascetic ideal," the otherworldliness of Christianity, forces us to deny human desires and to forsake our bodies (as Paul and, to a lesser degree, Augustine admonish us), to see morality as suffering through guilt over one's human instincts:

> This horror of the senses, of reason itself, this fear of happiness and beauty, this longing to get away from appearance, change, becoming, death, wishing, from longing itself—all this means—lest us dare to grasp it—*a will to nothingness*, an aversion to life, a rebellion against the most fundamental presuppositions of life; but it is and remains a *will!* And, to repeat in conclusion what I said at the beginning: man would rather will *nothingness* than not *will*.

Indeed, Schopenhauer ultimately denies the Will to the point of treating "sexuality as a personal enemy (including its tool, woman, that '*instrumentum diaboli*')." Wagner's *Parsifal* epitomized for Nietzsche precisely this "aversion to life." He characterizes this urge for transcendence and denial as the self-contradiction of "life against life" motivated in the ascetic ideal "that springs from the protective instinct of a degenerating life which tries by all means to sustain itself and to fight for its existence." In other words, it takes an act of will to deny the Will, this being the ultimate inconsistency for escape artists like Wagner and Schopenhauer.

Ironically, however, Nietzsche's anti-Wagnerianism emphasizes the very theme essential to our understanding of *The Ring*. His rejection of the Schopenhauerian connection between pessimism and the denial of the Will (and his misunderstanding of Wagner as a pure Schopenhauerian) rested on what he took to be the most fundamental metaphysical mistake—that reality has a determinant nature (Plato's fundamental question-begging assumption). For Nietzsche, Wagner, like Schopenhauer, escapes tragedy through the diminishment of appearance in the denial of the Will whereas real tragedy, takes us into life. It *affirms* the Will. Instead of Schopenhauer's and Wagner's transcendence of conflict through *Mitleid* or Dionysian sensuality confused with religious ecstasy, we should concentrate on life itself. This life-affirming individualism became the basis for what Nietzsche called "the will to power" whereby he transforms the Will back into life through the creation of value in the world of conflict. This is the core of Nietzsche's moral vitalism.

The German word for power is *Macht*. The verb, *machen*, means 'to make' in the sense of acting or doing something. The will to *machen* implies the will to produce or create, to bring something about.[24] While we should be careful not to see Nietzsche's will to power *either* anthropomorphically (connected to a specific historical image of human action) *or* mechanistically (mere biological drives or instincts), his concept has more definition in its attachment to historical human projection and orientation than it does with Schopenhauer who thought of the Will as noumenal, as transcending human interest and value. Nietzsche, in contrast, saw the will to power as an extended metaphor applied to humans as active creatures bent on domination, 'striving' of one kind or another, and who define or create their world through their actions. For Nietzsche what we do, desire, hope for and fear ultimately result in action (even the 'activity' of doing nothing—choosing to opt out).

Both Nietzsche and Wagner, I contend, transform Schopenhauer's Will into activity completely *within* the phenomenal world (thus making it the *only* world) and they use the model of the creative artist as their metaphor. Both Nietzsche and Wagner understood the Will as the capacity for change and transformation in civilization through the evolution of the kind of awareness and comprehension symbolized by Hans Sachs. But while they rejected Schopenhauer's pessimistic escapism, they also rejected Hegel's metaphysical optimism. Striving may go fatally wrong and we have no way of knowing which path we are on except to keep on with it, to keep living within it. Power is a two-edged sword.

In *Beyond Good and Evil* (#259), Nietzsche sums up his characterization of life as the will to power (notice the striking similarity to Faust's striving):

> Life itself is essentially appropriation, injury, overpowering of what is alien and weaker; suppression, hardness, imposition of one's own forms, incorporation and at least, at its mildest, exploitation.... "Exploitation"...belongs to the essence of what lives, as a basic organic function; it is a consequence of the will to power, which is after all the will to life.

We must also see the will to life as the will to truth. But the will to truth has led to realism, to the world "in itself," and then to "asceticism" or the self-contradictory opposition of one part of life to the other, of reason to emotion, of the Apollinian to the Dionysian. In Nietzsche's terms, to see the will to life as the will to truth provides the only ultimate perspective of our awareness on the constitution of life, the source of our life-giving and life-destroying interpretations. The exploitation characterizing life is therefore central to our understanding of truth. Truth is always *for* something, for some purpose. For Nietzsche, unlike Goethe, striving happens with nothing at the end of the road, no absolute eternal feminine, no universal waterfall/ocean metaphor, no imagery other than what we supply.

The famous last section of *The Will to Power* provides a good summary of the points I have been making. The general sentiment, I suggest, also fits the ending of *The Ring*:

> And do you know what "the world" is to me? ...This, *Dionysian* world of the eternally self-creating, the eternally self-destroying, this mystery world of the twofold voluptuous delight, my "beyond good and evil," without goal, unless the joy of the circle is itself a goal; without will, unless a ring feels good will toward itself—do you want a *name* for this world? A *solution* for all its riddles? A *light* for you, too, you best concealed, strongest, most intrepid, most midnightly men"—*This world is the will to power—and nothing besides!* And you yourselves are also this will to power—and nothing besides. (*The Will to Power*, #1067)

Schopenhauer's account of the Will, for Nietzsche, flawed but prescient, makes more apparent to us the insight that objective uniformity does not make up 'the truth' about the world. Within the limits of our possible experience, based on the interpretations or perspectives we construct relative to historical interests and contexts, the world and its values are established through such ("Dionysian") 'striving' activities as coping with specific situations—but ("Apollinian") creation and preservation, organization and control, generalization and universalization are also forms of coping. His point is that all order, and all disorder, happens relative to our interests and abilities rather than by discovering the world's most abstract underlying principles of organization. For Nietzsche, the world in itself has no such principle; and even if it did, what need it have to do with human knowledge and interests? Perspectivism, his term for this view, opposed to absolutism, is 'the truth'—the truth as we see it, to be sure, but truth as it emerges from coping—truth relative to purpose, in relation to solving problems. The contingent, contextual character of coping will always be forgotten or generalized away when our commitment has become the standard and hence the basis for an entrenched system of judgment. For Nietzsche, the "will to truth" carries with it the danger of *moral* entrenchment. His general point seems to be that the difference between 'the truth' and 'the truth as we see it' must be a matter of degree and not of kind since it only exemplifies the distinction between *my* interests and *our* interests, or between short-term and long-term interests. The difference between illusion and reality will likewise be dependent on the relative stability of given practices and beliefs, on experience relative to everything we believe. He denies that there are facts; there are only interpretations (*Will to Power*, #481). The stability of belief depends on shared values. God's eye view from no perspective in particular entails total disinterestedness, but for Nietzsche there can be no truth without interest and no interests without values. True/False thus becomes Better for us/Worse for us.

Again turning Schopenhauer around, understanding the Will as coping in life rather than transcendence to absolutes, Nietzsche argues that any understanding of the world can only be a function of whatever systems of organization we have constructed (as Schopenhauer and Kant said too but, for them, these are systems permanently implicit in the structure of the mind rather than historical artifacts). Hence, our fundamental values and interests remain oriented towards the world. Transcending phenomenal life simply reflects a desire to change the world. For Nietzsche, 'the world' and 'life' come down to the world and life as we interpret it, thus realizing their interdependence, plus the understanding that any such relationships are interpretations, perspectives, ways of coping with cognitive dissonance. But our ability to cope/succeed and thus interpret should not be identified with the ability to accurately represent reality once and for all, apart from all interests. The will to power sums up the forces responsible for the formation of the traditions of interpretation that establish human values while they continue to evolve in conflict internally and with one another. So, again, the difference between the world and our understanding of the world cannot be a difference in kind since there will be no characterization of the world in itself *except* as we understand it to be, except as we *hope* it will be, and so on. In this, Schopenhauer was right but his conception of the Will was then abstracted away from its human origin as an expression of alienated rationality rather than Kantian justification for reason—both, however, question-begging in their relevance to truth as coping.[25]

For Nietzsche, and this was the only good part of Hegel, concepts, interpretations, perspectives develop and change. Coping is *historical*. Once that anti-Platonic point sinks in, Kant's Scheme/Content and Phenomena/Noumena distinctions vanish because there can be nothing for interpretive schemes or concepts to grab onto, no *independent* characterization of the noumenal—except by extension of *our* understanding, *our* interpretation. What has the fact that knowledge depends on interpretation have to do with what really exists? We might never *know* what really exists, but our ignorance is perfectly consistent with a reality transcending our cognitive abilities. This is "metaphysical realism." Nietzsche contends in the first section of *Beyond Good and Evil*, that truth in the metaphysical realist's sense might well *not* be good for us under our current self-understanding (assuming that we can know what this truth is). But the question of what it is good for us to do or to believe will arise for *any* metaphysics, idealist or realist (see #4 and *The Gay Science*, #121 and 354). His point is that if there *are* absolute truths, something *untrue* in that absolute sense may actually be better for us as human beings because a transcendent reality might not provide anything relevant to human interests. In any case, we will never know because there is no characterization of reality that could settle the question of absolute truth for Nietzsche. We only have the truths we produce, we cannot dispense with them in favor of some *other* truths since we can have no conception of what they could possibly be without comparing them to what we already have. If we *understand* another set of values or life style, an alien language or civilization, we have understood it in terms of concepts we already have. He says, for example, in *Beyond Good and Evil,* #211:

> *Genuine philosophers...are commanders and legislators:* they say, *"thus it shall be!"* They first determine the Whither and For What of man, and in so doing have at their disposal the preliminary labor of all philosophical laborers, all who have overcome the past. With a creative hand they reach for the future, and all that is and has been becomes a means for them, an instrument, a hammer. Their "knowing" is *creating,* their creating is a legislation, their will to truth is—*a will to power.* (See also *The Will to Power,* #972)

For Nietzsche, as for William James, truth is normative; it concerns the recommendation of beliefs and their suitability. Truth as 'representation', in this view, reflects the consistency and compatibility of one belief with others. It evaluates how well a belief fits in with other beliefs, estimating its future usefulness. As Willard Van Orman Quine put it, "...our statements about the ...world face the tribunal of sense experience not individually but as a corporate body" (see endnote 26 below). Hence metaphysical realism has the same status as theology—both are matters of *faith* and not *knowledge.* Nietzsche and James challenge the *value* of this belief in an independent reality. If it cannot be connected to any human coping activity, what role *does* it play, what is its "cash value" (as James puts it)? What *use* is it (understanding "use" broadly)? Hence the operative content of truth lies in coping plus evaluation. These are the activities that settle questions about representation. The important point that the pragmatists shared with Nietzsche concerns the cognitive dissonance of belief: some beliefs will be in conflict with others, they will never as a group be completely consistent or even well-defined. 'Truth' is a success word, therefore, having to do with the goal of our process of justification. 'The World' is what the sum total of our successful beliefs tell us it is.

Under perspectivism, therefore, the difference between 'true for me' and 'true for us' and 'true in general' turns out to be one of degree, not kind. These distinctions are based on generalizations of coping activities and the justificatory process, connecting beliefs together to form a coherent whole (as much as we can get). There can be no way to compare 'our truths' with the truth in general. 'True in general' simply means 'our truths' in a broader historical context, our truths universalized. What could the standard of comparison be except a generalization of the historical standards of rationality we implicitly or explicitly already have through centuries of trial and error? 'Truth in general', then, would be *not* Nietzsche's "perspectiveless perspective" but simply 'ours' in the sense of all humanity. In *The Will to Power* he includes the interpreter in this too:

> 'Everything is subjective', you say; but even this is interpretation. The 'subject' is not something given, it is something added and invented and projected behind what there is— Finally, is it necessary to posit an interpreter behind the interpretation? Even this is invention, hypothesis. In so far as the word 'knowledge' has any meaning, the world is knowable; but it is *interpretable* otherwise [i.e., as unknowable], it has no meaning behind it, but countless meanings—'Perspectivism'." (#481)

Nietzsche did not believe, however, that the rejection of metaphysical realism (the perspectiveless perspective) leads to pessimism and to the diminishment of striving for truth (in fact he just does not care about metaphysical realism since it cannot be connected to his view of truth at all). For him, reality does not have a preferred way of being represented (to use Richard Rorty's phrase) because, relative to truth as interpretation, it does not have a determinate nature.[26] Will to power, on the other hand, will certainly prefer representing the world one way to others. The concept of Reality-in-Itself, the world, simply holds open a space for the results of potentially infinite activities of interpretation. No one interpretation in science, art, even religion, can be *the* truth except by o*ur deciding*, explicitly or tacitly, that it should be so: no discoveries we could ever make will eliminate that aspect of decision from the concept of Truth. While, as perspectivists, we continue to distinguish between interpretation and reality, we cannot claim to have achieved a complete or final interpretation of reality, one that takes precedence over all others on the basis of its ability to represent its structure more accurately, better than any other interpretation. The truth of an interpretation cannot be determined by finding out how accurately it represents Reality-in-Itself because 'accuracy', 'coherence', 'simplicity', and so on (to take some of the standard terminology) will themselves also be a matter of interest and perspective. No truth can ultimately be determined by correspondence between representation and reality, for how could the standards of accurate correspondence be determined apart from *another* interpretation, a theory about the correspondence relation? What gives a particular interpretation or representation precedence over others—what gives it the laurel of truth—cannot be primitive, pre-belief correspondence to reality but a privilege established through the will to power in the form of agreement that bestows upon it the status of correspondence. Hence correspondence must be essentially evaluative and this seems to me to be the core of Nietzsche's perspectivism.

Must we then simply give up the straightforward sense of "truth" that connects our beliefs to the world, the sense of truth as correspondence? The sentence, "It is raining," uttered under appropriate meteorological conditions is *true*. Alasdair MacIntyre, to take a prominent contemporary critic of Nietzsche, argues in two books that the perspectivist

> fails to recognize how integral the [realist] conception of truth is to tradition-constituted forms of inquiry. It is this which leads perspectivists to suppose that one could temporarily adopt the standpoint of a tradition and then exchange it for another, as one might wear first one costume and then another, or as one might act one part in one play and then a quite different part in quite a different play.[27]

This description does not fit Nietzsche at all, however, whose concern about the development of Western civilization and its creative/destructive potential precludes him from arbitrarily adopting an interpretation, of switching from one to another, without justification. He argues that the desire for absolute truth has been the most creative—and destructive—characteristic of the West. But he also argues that justification has nothing to do with truth in an absolute sense. It concerns the invention and development of societal roles that MacIntyre takes to be purely optional and even accidental. Such roles are indeed historically contingent, but our choices between them are not arbitrary for Nietzsche.

Life-style changes, for example, are not *random* or casual exchanges of personal identity, for Nietzsche; they are stages in the development of a person's self-conception relative to an evolving sense of social identity, the stages of which may well be incoherent or in opposition. They do not rest on isolated subjectivity. The resolution of such conflicts of identity through the unification of character—*Bildung*—requires acculturation. A change in perspective, such as a life style or a new work of art, or a new civilization, will be due to the internal incoherence that comprises the current state of affairs. Changes in ones life and in ones culture occur through social interaction as much as through abstract, purely principled attempts to resolve internal ('personal') difficulties. Nietzsche may sometimes encourage constrained arbitrariness in this process, and he may even be committed to it. Just because our traditions are contingent, however, does not mean we have no reason to hold onto them, or to hold onto one role rather than another, and to prefer some to others for good reason. Justification has to do with giving good reasons for changing, not with comparisons to absolute standards. Any standard has to be *accepted* whether implicitly or explicitely. Contingent standards can play the same role as absolutes in this process. Nietzsche argues, however, that even if we recognize a standard as absolute, that cannot be a *reason* to accept it as absolute other than its universal acceptance.

The problem with perspectivism lies in its central metaphor: Should aesthetic creation be a model for scientific inquiry, moral decision, and political activity? The aesthetic model stresses individuality, a good thing, but it also stresses community. The problem, however, seems to rest on the fact that art needs no contact with anything that determines truth. However good or bad, interesting or uninteresting, art is not true or false. We saw, in Chapter 3, that Adorno and others criticized Wagner for treating his audience passively, "transmitting" his surreptitious denials of rationality and civilization. He avoids real people, real politics. But the aesthetic model explicitly denies exactly that passivity. Such a view implies that the audience, or Sach's community, is incapable of independent judgment, passively intimidated, dictated to, by the Artist-Philosopher. In *Die Meistersinger,* Walther must struggle with his inspirations, he must adapt his talent to the rules in order to express himself coherently. That requires inventiveness and rationality on his part and Sachs gives him examples of how something might be done. There can be no absolutely 'best work of art' or 'best art-song' to which Walther's efforts lead him. Good art has to engage its community, but there are no absolute standards governing engagement either. There is no such external standard in art because art depends on community. Art and its standards of evaluation always exist in the context of a culture. Nietzsche extends this analogously to science: there is no final, ultimate scientific truth either since truth must be produced in relation to interests, traditions and practices that retain their vitality through change rather than through correspondence with independently characterized reality. What counts as 'correspondence to reality' changes along with our conception of truth, along with science and the nature of scientific law. Indeed, for Nietzsche, it is the artists who seem to know more about the world than the philosophers or the scientists because they live with illusion.[28]

The real question concerns the nature of truth itself. The aesthetic model does not take truth to be basic, explaining it relative to other concepts such as coping, problem solving, exploiting, compromising (all versions of the will to power). Is that sufficient? Can Nietzsche preserve the function of truth in his appeal, quoted earlier, that "we possess *art* lest we *perish of the truth*"? (An adequate answer to this question takes us into the history of twentieth-century philosophy. (Martin Heidegger and the pragmatists, especially John Dewey, deal explicitly with this question, both of whom are discussed by Rorty in *Philosophy and the Mirror of Nature* and elsewhere.) A parallel question concerns moral justification: What are justifying reasons in morality? If Nietzsche wishes to create analogies that draw interpretation, creation, desire, and the will to power together in the way I have outlined, has he in effect denied that there *are* reasons that can justify one moral point of view over another? Nietzsche's point about truth as perspective assimilates truth to morality so that truth is conceived as an evaluative concept and rests on justification, on giving reasons for adopting one perspective over another.[29]

What then are *good* reasons? How do we know when we have coped successfully? In Nietzsche's view, we naturally tend to prefer *our* creations, our values, and our interpretations because they express commitments directly connected with our identity. We value our values not just because they are ours but because we have constructed them, we have found them to be successful by the best standards available. Because of our "internal oppositions," our beliefs will change, whether or not we believe we have discovered the true meanings of "virtue" or "humanity" or even "atom" or "gene."

MacIntyre himself, for example, makes the case that the tradition of Biblical interpretation has virtually nothing to do with truth in the transcendent, metaphysical realist sense. Biblical scholarship relies on the test of coherence and contrast between readings rather than correspondence to a fixed meaning: the meaning of the text emerges as the most historically inclusive interpretation. Answering the question: "What did this text mean to Peter, or a generation later to Paul?" does not depend on finding out what Peter and Paul's beliefs were (after all they tell us in their writings what they believed) but perhaps on something like projecting from *our* reconstructed view of the texts which of *our* beliefs might have had counterparts in their minds. This may help us understand what they have written. Peter's beliefs about Jesus could not possibly have been the same as Paul's, nor could either's have been the same as Augustine's. But what they were *must* depend on inferences, projections, based on our standards of inferential adequacy, on our beliefs about how best to cope with these texts relative to their very different historical contexts. To live within a tradition for Nietzsche means to believe in it, to think of it as true because it represents (corresponds to) reality better than any other we can see from that perspective. In part this means that a tradition of practice meets the needs of its participants better than others. They are the best ways of coping—for now. Seeing representation dependent on coping, as historical rather than absolute, engenders a healthy conception of change.

Why, asks Nietzsche, should "better" *ever* mean better *absolutely better*, better from God's point of view rather than the best for us or the best for now or the best we can do? A perspective will always constitute the truth through some process of justification, and justification is always an entrenched social process. Such a truth stands as the sum total of what has convinced us so far that the world is the way we think it is. It will be the perspective that survives only if it is at some point widely shared, but popularity alone does not determine truth. Justification remains essential. Justifications require reasons, evidence, and arguments that exhibit the explanatory power of an interpretation or perspective through the amalgamation of disparate beliefs rather than establishing a correspondence relation between belief and reality. Neither "true" nor "good" have ultimate definitions for Nietzsche; they are summaries of successful attempts at bringing beliefs together, at integration. Justification and truth differ as conditions of application and commendation or recommendation: while conditions of applying or using "true" vary historically and culturally, the word itself confers a certain status, perhaps the same status in all cultures. But to connect the status of being true with a state of the world "in itself" simply does not follow. Nor, for Nietzsche and James, is it necessary. We have ways of justifying *this* belief or *this* theory, but not all belief, or theory in general as the path to the true representation of reality except by established comparisons between beliefs and between theories.

Nietzsche takes persons themselves as perspectives, constructs emerging through coping. But just as art does not rest on arbitrariness, so persons are self-creations for Nietzsche even when they express "herd values." I think he would hold that we cannot completely occupy a deconstructionist stance towards ourselves, however, without giving up the identities within the traditions of value and belief that supply the basis of identity. To do so would be, as MacIntyre says, to see oneself paradoxically as an "assemblage," an arbitrary construct; but that would be different from seeing oneself as changing, growing, or evolving with emerging identity—which is certainly closer to Nietzsche's actual view of the matter. He underscores development through conflict as the core of justification. That representations of the world are constituted through interpretations does not mean that we should not believe in them or think of them representationally (so long as we remember what that means). After all, they are the outcomes of an evolutionary process akin to natural selection, for Nietzsche, tempered with the sense of an artist.

Turning finally to Nietzsche's view of value, the difficulty, as Nehamas has put it, centers on the apparent inconsistency in denying that conventional moral values have any foundation in God's commandments, or in human nature, and nevertheless claiming one culture or one set of values to be more creative and life-enhancing than another (as he does by invidiously comparing nineteenth-century Europe to the good old days of heroic aggressiveness: Homeric Greece, early Rome, and Shogun Japan). In recommending *his* view about what constitutes healthy civilization, does Nietzsche not appeal to a very traditional distinction between good and evil, between representing reality correctly and getting it wrong, that is, the very distinction he wants to abandon? Does he merely substitute creativity for truth with his own (absolutized) standards of creativity? If he wants to undermine the moral and metaphysical traditions of

Western civilization by reminding us of its shortcomings, he can be rejected as a sour-grapes nihilist by those who wish to preserve those traditions (a poor thing, perhaps, but our own, and the best so far). But if he claims to have invented a different and more interesting view of values, then what is it and, because it is *true,* does it not amount to realism after all, a realism that appeals to natural desires and instincts as implicit metaphysical structures—human nature naturalized? I will argue that Nietzsche does not surreptitiously defend a realist system of values, yet another final definition for "good" to be preferred to all the others because it is 'truer' than they are. He offers instead a new perspective on values in general, in relation to the model of the creative artist and his historically changing society.

For Nietzsche, it does not follow that a culture's survival, or a belief's pervasive persistence, implies that it is better able to represent the real nature of reality, or that its values are better grounded in nature. Perhaps, as happens in tragedy, the surviving culture will collapse even more spectacularly—as Nietzsche claims Christianity has now in fact done after two thousand very successful years during which its believers understood justification as representation of reality. Survival and domination as traits of human nature, on the one hand, are for Nietzsche value-free—beyond good and evil in the sense of an absolute distinction. Value emerges out of survival but survival can also stultify value. This is what distinguishes his theory of values from that of Kant, for example. But, on the other hand, the instinct for survival, for domination, for control—the will to power—can lead to all kinds of incompatible values or destructive ways of life. So appealing to survival or domination cannot justify one belief over another except as *part of* the domination or success of one interpretation over another. But, again, success does not depend on the truth of one and the falsity of the other. For Nietzsche, the Master/Slave analogy as he applies it to the genealogy of moral values captures the dialectic of this scenario.

"Survival" for Nietzsche does not mean simply biological durability. He means the ability to sustain values created within a perspective, a way of life. Perspectivism implies evaluative principles, and evaluation for Nietzsche means simplification. While we live in "illusions" in the sense that there are no absolutes that justify one evaluative principle over another, the "will" for him comprises the active selection of some things, some experiences, as more important than others. As Nehamas says:

> To recognize that illusion is inevitable is to recognize that the views and values we accept wholeheartedly and without which our life may not even be possible depend on simplifications, on needs and desires which we may at the moment be able to locate specifically. It is also to realize that though these simplifications are necessary for us and for those like us, they are

> *not* necessary for everyone. (*Nietzsche: Life as Literature,* p. 61)

So one of the main functions of any perspective should be organization, proposing a sorting-principle by means of which 'the real' emerges as 'the most significant' for us, for our community. Life means selection: life is interest, interest involves choice, and choice takes us back to principles. Where, asks Nietzsche, do principles come from?

Advocates of any principle will see their survival, individually or collectively, as significant to the content of their views. What we believe ought somehow somewhere to make a difference in what we do. Because of the historical fluidity of our self-conception, values for Nietzsche have been achieved through the struggle for survival. We cannot say in advance what specific content the distinction between good and bad will have, or what values will survive and what will not, just as we cannot predict what the next great work or art will be (without actually creating it). Advances often require breaking rules, but they might also happen by following them. The only condition Nietzsche places on the process involves the generation of unity, as in a literary text. "To be beyond good and evil is to combine all of one's features and qualities, whatever their traditional moral value, into a controlled and coherent whole" (as Nehamas puts it, p. 227). But in so doing we move "beyond good and evil" by not looking for absolute content in value. While "bad" means a poor choice relative to some goal, "evil" characterizes the disruption of the *status quo*, the destruction of tradition and its internal options. But for that reason "evil" characteristics should sometimes be encouraged for their creative impetus through their ability to overturn stagnating values. Nietzsche distinguishes between 'Good/Evil' and 'Good/Bad' as the difference between the appeal to absolutes or perspectives taken absolutely (and what opposes those absolutes), on the one hand, and between what we prefer and what we do not, on the other.[30]

For these reasons, Nietzsche describes morality as creative on the analogy of art. Such a creator overturns received values, accepted conventions (*WP* #1026, see Nehamas' discussion, pp. 223–234). Just as we cannot know in advance what the next great work of art will be without creating it, so we cannot know in advance what "good" will mean in the next wrinkle of our civilization except that it will be part of an interpretation that supports survival. As Nehamas characterizes it, Nietzschean creativity can be evaluated "only in the light of [its] contribution to a complete person, a complete life, or, as he would doubtless prefer to put it himself, a complete *work* (cf. *Zarathustra*, IV, 1, 20)" (p. 229). I would add to this Nietzsche's point that creative individuals are also measured in relation to their culture, by the effect that they have on it. Principles therefore arise as mechanisms of perpetuation. But they can run dry, encounter adverse environmental conditions, or new ideas with which they cannot successfully cope.

In *The Will to Power* (#490), he uses a political analogy for selfhood: the self is not a democracy of cells but an aristocracy (although an "aristocracy of equals") driven by the predominant goals and interests of each of us (see also Nehamas p. 177). Nietzsche's individualism entails that these goals always involve a succession of choices to accept or reject surrounding traditions. But choice requires standards and standards imply justification. These standards and traditions are not imposed on us by God—or by nature—but arise out of the process of self-creativity, or cultural-creativity, relative to an image, a dream, a tradition about the best way to live. Biology may have something to do with this process for Nietzsche, but it will ultimately rest on evaluation, which again depends on participation in a culture. But if the unity of the self rests on this constructive account, the value of such persons to society (like Hans Sachs) cannot merely lie in how well they maintain the *status quo*. Ceative individuals are "masters of chaos" (*Will to Power* #842), what Sachs saw the self and society ultimately to be in the allegory of his education of Walther's raw talent.[31]

7. A Nietzschean Reading of *The Ring*

In *The Case of Wagner* (1888), Nietzsche recalls Wagner's switch from revolutionary optimism to Schopenhauerian pessimism as part of his solution to the problem of creation *versus* destruction in *The Ring*. How can destruction be creation too? In #4 (some of which I quoted in chapter 3, Section 9) he imagines Wagner's state of mind in trying to explain how the "misfortunes of the world" arise—they come about through old "customs, laws, moralities, institutions, from everything on which the old world, the old society rests." How to abolish the old society? Declare war on contracts, on tradition—to set oneself beyond the good and evil of conventional society. And, Nietzsche writes, "that is what Siegfried does...his very genesis is a declaration of war against morality—he comes into this world through adultery, through incest. Siegfried continues as he has begun: he merely follows his first impulse, he overthrows everything traditional, all reverence, all *fear*." Nietzsche then describes Wagner's radical shift of emphasis in *The Ring* after reading Schopenhauer: when he quit working on *Siegfried* in 1857, Wagner was "stranded on a reef" unable to find another set of values to substitute for the old ones. His Feuerbachian-Hegelian optimism had become sterile in the face of a new conception of reality. Something was missing from his account of society and the self. So he took the destructiveness of Siegfried and made *that* into his goal: he "translated *The Ring* in Schopenhauerian terms. Everything goes wrong, everything perishes, the new world is as bad as the old: the *nothing*, the Indian Circe beckons." Instead of Brünnhilde welcoming a new era of socialist utopia, she has to "study Schopenhauer." At the end of this section Nietzsche writes: "In all seriousness, this *was* a redemption. The benefit Schopenhauer conferred on Wagner is immeasurable. Only the *philosopher of decadence* gave to the artist of decadence—*himself.*"[32]

Like Adorno's Wagner-critique, this is perfectly accurate up to a point, except that Nietzsche believed it was Wagner's *intention* (or subconscious desire) to substitute sensuality for responsibility as the new morality, his eroticized metaphysics. His Schopenhauerian understanding of *The Ring* led him to believe that Wagner accepted entirely the doctrine of resignation and the view of transcendence implicit in the denial of the Will. Without denying for a moment the "seductive force" of his music, Nietzsche saw it as corrupting, decadent sensualistic irrationalism, a loss of control over dangerous emotions. Such music should be against the law! Yet, as Hollinrake points out, Nietzsche's early and middle periods are also influenced by Wagner despite his growing sense of independence (which he described as the unmasking and rejection of Wagner's decadence). While Schopenhauer's effect on Nietzsche during this early period was similarly profound, he did not remain a Schopenhauerian in his views on tragedy. In Section 6 of *The Birth,* for example, he denies that the Greeks were pessimists in their tragedies because they ultimately "say Yes to life even in its strangest and hardest problems" (as he later put it in *Twilight of the Idols,* Section 5 of "What I Owe the Ancients"). His 'Dionysian' view: "in order to be oneself the eternal joy of becoming, beyond all terror and pity—that joy which included even joy in destroying"—the deepest truth of tragedy.

Thus, although Nietzsche's early infatuation with Dionysus-Wagner sprang from his Schopenhauerian pessimism, he did not remain a pessimist. In later remarks such as: "[t]he price of fruitfulness is to be rich in internal opposition" (*Twilight*, Section 3 of "Morality as Anti-Nature") he means to characterize tragedy as the antithesis of the Buddhist negation of the Will he had come to see in *The Ring*.[33] The joys of becoming include the joy of destruction: in both cases we desire 'life', striving, the assertion of value. Even when we want to leave it, we do so for something better (we hope). But because life consists of oppositions and opposite things, we must try to keep the formative process of individual creation alive rather than denying the Will in its individual manifestations. Are not those manifestations the most important things to us? Why should we deny them because of the constructed nature of their existence?

But *The Ring* did not become the purely Schopenhauerian work Nietzsche thought it was. It reaffirms life, not just life in general, but life under an interpretation, life defined by an image (like Sachs' Nuremberg or Wotan's Valhalla). At the end of *Götterdämmerung* we are presented neither with the promise of a new society better than the old, nor with the antihuman denial of the Will, but with the prospect of new life encountering its own problems of conflict and authority, confronting its own "internal oppositions" in the will to power. Along with Peckham and Tanner, I have argued that in *Tristan,* the dream of love fails to take the lovers beyond life in any literal sense. It is about the power of an il-

Philosophical Contexts and Applications 217

lusion. In *The Ring* we also see how conflict and change cannot be transcended. The value of phenomenal life rests on its potential for creativity and destructiveness, on its response to conflict.

Nietzsche explored the philosophical difficulties of creating and destroying order—what he described as the problem of bringing Apollo and Dionysus together—in ways Wagner did not, eventually becoming much more of (but not entirely) a deconstructionist about the self than Wagner. The self became ever more an illusion for Nietzsche as he explored the will to power in his last, unfinished work of that title. But however much self-identity rests on the forces of the creation and destruction that characterize the will to power, individualism remains at the center of his account of value (rather than abstract forces rising above individuals such as 'society', 'economic history', 'class consciousness', or 'language'). However "grammatical" in form, individuals gain their identities in conflict, so they are never isolated for very long. His conception of the will to power connects up with perspectivism in his attempt at showing how personhood changes relative to its *interactive* relationships. He does not try to eliminate persons as features of the world, although the concept of Motivation receives a new interpretation. Furthermore, because of their creative/destructive potential, values are always personal rather than absolute for Nietzsche. Values define our personalities. He thus never completely abandoned his fixation on the striving, idiosyncratic, romantic conception of the artist—Goethe, Beethoven, and—yes—Wagner (at least at the beginning). They did not 'withdraw' in their *own* self-creative activities. *They* did not deny the will; indeed, they changed our conception of what it is. What if Nietzsche did *not* believe *The Ring* to be 'Schopenhauerian'? How might a more positive account be given *via* perspectivism?

Wagner's Schopenhauerian rhetoric certainly seems to persist in his later view of *The Ring*. In 1872 (while working on *Götterdämmerung*) Wagner told Cosima that Wotan finally "recognized the guilt of existence and atone[d] for the error of creation," his destruction of the World Ash Tree in order to build his society. Much earlier, in 1854 (around the ending of *Das Rheingold* and the beginning of *Die Walküre*—and before *Tristan*), he wrote to Liszt that we should "treat the world only with contempt; this is all it deserves: but place no hope in it, no deception for our hearts. It is evil, evil, *fundamentally evil*.... It belongs to Alberich, to no one else. Let it perish!" Wagner was already in Schopenhauer's grasp. Wotan's 'atonement' was his renunciation of power, his denial of the Will—but it was not enough to prevent the destruction of his society. By the end of the cycle (and looking at *The Ring* from the intervening context of *Tristan* and *Die Meistersinger*) the Schopenhauerian recognition of the evil of individualistic desires must be taken along with Wagner's refusal to transcend the phenomenal world and his abandonment of Schopenhauer's doctrine of the

Will. Renunciation is not an option since it does nothing to stop the struggle for power.

To put a Nietzschean rather than Schopenhauerian interpretation on this quotation, the world is 'evil' in the sense that our quest for permanence will always fail. We cannot escape the change and decay of what we value. But we are not by contrast 'good' because we can know what is absolutely of value (for Schopenhauer, this was the denial of the Will in us as individuals, a disparagement of life). Wotan's atonement, however, makes way for redemptive action, but not the kind of redemption he hoped for. Wagner's Schopenhauerian moral must be that life cannot be transcended *in* life except by chaning our beliefs about life. This was Nietzsche's conclusion as well. They disagreed, however, with Schopenhauer's view that life itself was therefore pointless and we ought to metaphysically transcend by refocussing our values away from individuality. For Nietzsche, furthermore, good and evil are part of the same world: the "evil" world cannot be transcended for something better. There is nothing else to compare it to, except what we imagine. Ultimately we cannot free ourselves from the forces of conflict; as living beings we cannot escape our will to power, we can only find different forms for its manifestation. But we can try to rechannel this very understanding of the Will into some kind of control of these forces, just as we have done throughout our history. When we discover that we are not as free as we think, we try to become free in some higher sense—not to abandon the concept of freedom through the denial of the Will.

Nietzsche's perspectivism sometimes conflicts with his theory of the will to power. Where the perspectivist self has to make do with the lessons of history applied to the contingency of the present and hopes for the future, to describe that as an *activity* of the will to power implies that there might be something *more* than contingency, something new and different that flows unendingly from the Will. That, unfortunately, seems too metaphysical, too much like what he rejects. It may be, however, that perspectivism and the will to power should not be seen as latent doctrines, waiting for full articulation. At his edifying best, Nietzsche would prefer open-endedness to endings. Now it seems to me quite wrong to describe music-drama as an attempt to "respiritualize" the world. At their best, they too seem to concentrate on contingency, including the contingency of metaphysical hope.

As Warren Darcy claims, Wagner's mature works "explore various methods of renouncing the Will: love between man and woman…in *Tristan*; art in *Die Meistersinger*; and compassion (in many ways the best solution) in *Parsifal*."[34] In *The Ring,* moreover, we see that love holds no infallible solution to the problem of congenital instability in morality and politics. If *Götterdämmerung* ends in resignation about achieving something absolute, its vitality does *not* encourage us to "leave the world to Alberich" because it shows how there can be no escape from the flux of existence except by ceasing to exist. Reality just *is* the flux of development—always becoming rather than being. Even Brünnhilde's life ends with an act of will, a final expression of her individuality, and not an act of resignation. She tries to achieve her impossible dream as Siegfried's funeral pyre destroys Valhalla through the transforming power of her love. I have argued that if victory implies destruction, the end of *The Ring* does not establish the victory of love over power through Brünnhilde's transcendence of politics; neither does it reveal the destructiveness of our illusions about *eros* by showing the primacy of the Will over individuality. It concerns the destructive/creative force of *both* love and politics: it shows how love does not take us away from the world but places us even more firmly within it in the way Nietzsche tried to describe. Whether we like it or not, we cannot leave the world to Alberich because Alberich remains part of us in whatever we do—the joy of creation and the joy of destruction go together to make us what we are.

At the end of *The Ring,* Wagner does not moderate the destructiveness of conflict through Brünnhilde's pacification of the Will. She does not establish a new moral order based on love, any further actions would have to come from the spectators, from us. Rather, the forces of creation and destruction are seen (finally by Brünnhilde herself) to be the condition of all Being. Indeed, the universe continues to be characterized by that tension even after Wotan's world has collapsed. However, in *Parsifal* or in *Die Meistersinger* Wagner did not to take the next Schopenhauerian step: the metaphysical depreciation of the phenomenal self and the activities of civilization.[35] Schopenhauer's transcendence of the self through the denial of the Will destroys the empirical self that Wagner reaffirms.

Tristan certainly does contain this self-destructive Schopenhauerian element when the lovers push their personhood to the limit of comprehensibility. If their love cannot be called a "psychosis" in its rejection of Western individuality (as Peckham and Raphael suggest), it still constitutes a powerful force in the creation and alteration of self-imagery and value. Their social *personae* are uprooted and radically altered into sensual, boundless identity with the universe through the symbolism of death in love (at least that seems to describe their belief). But we do not get near that point in *The Ring,* despite the ardor of its own lovers. Wagner rejected the explicit Buddhist ending that worried Nietzsche (and which obviously did not satisfy Wagner either) and the problem of tipping the balance towards creation rather than destruction remains central to the hope of redemption in *The Ring* even in its concluding moments. But there can be no redemption (of the transcendent kind anyway) because the dynamic of *The Ring*—its politics and its view of love—*requires* a transcendent authority, an absolute of some kind to ground value. As a story about the death of God, *The Ring* shows us the impossibility of that kind of redemption. But while *Tristan* implies that we cannot transform love into a substitute for God either, *Parsifal* and *Die Meistersinger* show us how value and stability can result from creativity and love.

In this Wagner can certainly be described as a pessimist, and the conclusions of all Wagner's later works do not suggest that we can somehow find a way to get beyond the fundamental conflict and tension of existence. Like Cooke, Peckham says that *The Ring* does not aim for the "reconciliation of opposites but their full exposure" (p. 252). The story of *The Ring* concerns the presence of transforming conflict within our highest ideals. Wotan's failure to compromise does not cause his destruction; because his universe precludes the possibility of compromise, his destruction is inevitable. He tries to cope with change, but does so by involving Brünnhilde in his dream of regaining stability. Indeed, Wotan *does* try to compromise: he tries to get redemption from outside rather than achieving it himself; but even his indirect approach encounters the dynamics of conflict between power and love. If we think of compromise as the fundamental mechanism of Enlightenment rationality, *The Ring* shows us that this too remains one of our illusions—and one that can be very destructive.

In her vision, Brünnhilde sees what must be some very specific truths about power and love through her grief for Wotan and Siegfried; but her *Mitleid* does not lead to the transcendence of her individuality for a higher form of existence (as Isolde dreamt). After all, she wishes to rejoin Siegfried, not the Will. She does not, as Tristan fantasizes, become identical with the universe. Where Isolde wishes for the bliss of unconsciousness as the core of unification, Brünnhilde seeks awareness through understanding—her problem in *Götterdämmerung*, as she realizes, rests on her diminished grasp of what is really going on. Her compassion takes in her love for Siegfried as well as her realization that she is the destructive force of the Gods, that she as much as Alberich and Hagen has been the causal agent of Valhalla's destruction. But *The Ring* ultimately reverses the emphasis of Schopenhauer's metaphysics: instead of taking us *beyond* life, we are forced *back into* it. A good example of this very point occurs in Joseph Conrad's *Lord Jim*: to redeem himself, Jim must immerse himself "in the destructive Process" itself. The narrator, Stein, summarizes the process (reminiscent of Nietzsche but perhaps also Hans Sachs):

> "A man that is born falls into a dream like a man who falls into the sea if he tries to climb out into the air as inexperienced people endeavor do to he drowns—*nicht wahr*? No! I tell you! The way is to the destructive element submit yourself, and with the exertions of your hands and feet in the water make the deep, deep sea keep you up. So if you ask me—how to be?" ... "And yet it is true—it is true. In the destructive element immerse." He spoke in a subdued tone, without looking at me, one hand on each side of his face. "That was the way. To follow the dream, and again to follow the dream—and so—*ewig—usque ad finem*." ...That was the way, no doubt.

Yet for all that the great plain on which men wander amongst graves and pitfalls remained very desolate under the impalpable poesy of its crepuscular light, overshadowed in the center, circled with a bright edge as if surrounded by an abyss full of flames. When at last I broke the silence it was to express the opinion that no one could be more romantic than himself.[36]

Out of conflict comes value (at least sometimes) and, for Conrad, Nietzsche, and Wagner, value would not have come into existence were it not because of conflict (although for Conrad, perhaps more of a Schopenhauerian, the outcome seems to be reflective awareness rather than active assertion). *The Ring* can have a morally bracing effect: instead of reflective resignation, let us remember that reflection implies action. As Tanner summarizes *Götterdämmerung*:

> *The Ring* is best seen, despite the Rhinemaiden's ill-advised claims on its behalf, as the image of what almost everyone seeks but either fails to find, or regrets it if they do. It is a focus, in the cycle, for extensive plotting, intrigue and deceit, but the only worthwhile states we see anyone in are the ones which are quite unrelated to it. If that was what Wagner was "instinctively" trying to express, then he was overwhelmingly successful. But he was trying to express much more than that.... The resulting dislocations are among the chief reasons for the work's perennial appeal. A promise of wholeness is held out by one part of it, and denied by another. It is difficult to envisage a time when we shall no longer want to explore the conflicts within it, for that would suggest that we no longer had them in ourselves. (*Wagner*, pp. 182–3)

Looking so intensely at the limits and fault lines of our self-image, as *The Ring* does, helps us to understand better why we are what we are through the conflicts that shape us. The world may be an evil place relative to one or another of these self-images, as Wagner seems to thought, but evil requires comparison with its opposite, whether dream or actuality. It is only through a *conception* of life and value, an *interpretation* of the world, that this comparison can occur. The effect for Nietzsche has been a deconstruction of the distinction between absolute conceptions of Good and Evil into one centered on the creation of new forms of life, new interpretations based on his aesthetic model. The distinction between Good and Evil emerges through his dialectic of internalization and social opposition. Nietzsche, seeing only the celebration of destructiveness in *The Ring* however, saw only the Schopenhauerian aspect of the work. But *The Ring* cannot be completely pessimistic since it has no implied irony about

Brünnhilde's 'foolish' belief in her illusion of redemption through love. Even the irony attending Siegfried's failure seems diminished by that love. Given what I have said about the interdependence of love and power, that conflict and change are essential for human life, we have no choice but to live within the limitations of creation and destruction, illusion and delusion. Even our desire to escape that world must be seen as an aspect of life within it.

Notes

1 Kant separated space and time off from the twelve categories arguing that all experiences are temporal, and all objective experiences spatial, while we use the categories only sometimes in analysing experience.

2 All quotations from: J.W. von Goethe, *Faust*. Original German, translation and introduction by Walter Kaufmann. (New York: Doubleday and Co., Anchor Books, 1963).

3 Erich Heller, "Goethe and Tragedy," in *The Disinherited Mind* (New York: Meridian Books, 1959), p. 61. To experience the full power of the last scene of *Faust*, listen to a good performance of the second part of Mahler's *Eighth Symphony*. A century earlier, in his *Damnation of Faust*, Berlioz clearly saw the relevance of music to striving.

4 G.W.F. Hegel, *Phenomenology of Spirit,* trans. A.V. Miller (Oxford: Clarendon Press, 1977), p. 2.

5 See, for example: Roger Hollinrake's book, cited in endnote 32, and Bryan Magee, *The Philosophy of Schopenhauer* (New York: Oxford University Press, 1983) for two discussions especially relevant to Wagner. See also Ronald Gray, "The German Intellectual Background," in Burbidge and Sutton, *The Wagner Companion*.

6 Arthur Schopenhauer, *The World as Will and Representation,* trans. E.F.J. Payne (New York: Dover, 1969), Volume I, p. 263. Hereafter *WWR*.

7 For a detailed comparison of Nietzsche, Schopenhauer, and Wagner's views on the relation between music and drama, see Dieter Borchmeyer, *Richard Wagner: Theory and Theatre*, trans. Steward Spencer (Oxford; Clarendon Press, 1991), Chapter 12.

8   There is a story about Wagner sending Schopenhauer a copy of *The Ring*, but since Rossini was Schopenhauer's ideal musician, he seems not to have understood what Wagner's fuss was all about.

9   Wotan's frustration thus exemplifies Schopenhauer's point about the Will. Wotan's laboring giants are dissatisfied with their payment and threaten to ravish Freia, the symbol of love that sustained Valhalla. His son and daughter fail to satisfy his desire for a redeeming hero, his other daughter Brünnhilde defiantly turns against him, and then when he makes peace with her, his grandson carries her off and destroys what little power he has left.

10 Byron, for example, in *The Dream*, writes of sleep as "A boundry between the things misnamed/Death and existence" in a way that establishes the loss of self as the object of love. This loss shows the connection between the things misnamed "persons" and Schopenhauer's description of Kant's noumenon as the Will.

11 Thomas Mann, "Schopenhauer," in Thomas Mann, *Essays of Three Decades*, trans. H.T. Lowe-Porter (New York: Alfred A. Knopf, 1948), pp. 396–7. This collection also contains "The Sufferings and Greatness of Richard Wagner." Both of these essays, while not exactly 'introductory', because they are as much about Mann himself as about Wagner or Schopenhauer, are essential reading. See also Lucy Beckett's discussion of Mann in "Wagner and His Critics," in Burbidge and Sutton, *The Wagner Companion*.

12 His early best-seller *Buddenbrooks* stands as a case in point: the hero, Thomas Buddenbrook, appropriately discovers Schopenhauer as his marriage and business collapse around him and fantasizes about living on as part of the universal Will—a life of sensual directness rather than reserved propriety.

13 The historical connections between love, religion, and society, including an important discussion of the Tristan legend, is explored in Denis De Rougemont, *Love in the Western World* (New York: Pantheon, 1958).

14 See especially the chapter "On the Inner Nature of Art," *WWR*, Vol. II, p 406.

15 Morse Peckham, *Beyond the Tragic Vision*, p. 257. See also Peckham's discussion of Beethoven's op. 135. Also see a similar treatment of Wagner

in Robert Raphael, *Richard Wagner* (New York: Twayne Author Series, 1969). Raphael describes the world of Tristan and Isolde as a "psychosis": "Not only does love destroy reality and identity; it cannot, as Wagner shows, redeem anyone, simply because it cannot function as a genuine basis for empathy between human beings, not to mention society as a whole" (p. 65).

16 Michael Tanner, "The Total Work of Art," p. 179–186.

17 In English, "illusion" means the ascription of truth or reality to what only seems real or true. "Delusion" is usually associated with being misled into false belief. To delude means to lead from truth to error, to be misled with perhaps destructive results. The deluded have fixed, difficult to remove misconceptions, often specifically about the self. Persons are deluded about the world, themselves, their intelligence, their friends, etc. "Illusion," as I am using it throughout this book, has a more philosophically specialized sense: what appears to be real from one point of view is not so from another. Yet in this sense illusion may be impossible to escape entirely. Nietzsche suggests that we simply trade one illusion for another rather than transcending them altogether.

18 The dispute between them centers on Hanslick's book, *On Beauty in Music*. He tries to argue that only absolute music can be beautiful, untainted by poetry and programs, because there are uniquely musical attributes independent of literary or visual or thespian allusions. But the line between absolute and program music remains notoriously hard to draw (admitting that there are obvious cases of each at the extremes). What, for example, constitutes an 'intrinsic' characteristic of musical beauty? For a discussion of Hanslick, see Malcolm Budd, "The Repudiation of Emotion: Hanslick on Music," *The British Journal of Aesthetics,* XX, 1 (1980). Also, again, Lucy Beckett, "Wagner and His Critics."

19 See Tanner's "Richard Wagner and Hans Sachs," p. 95, cited in Note 21 below.

20 See Raphael's discussion of *Die Meistersinger*. Sachs never asserts moral authority for controlling illusion in his society but rather holds art to be the only way of truly freeing ourselves from deception because "the artist is able to view experiential reality as symbolic" (*Richard Wagner,* pp. 81–82). We can never be sure which of our beliefs embodies some delusion about ourselves; the point is not to escape illusion as such, however, but to use it to

gain deeper understanding of the creative process since our personhood depends on that process both individually and collectively.

21 Tanner discusses *Die Meistersinger* in both "The Total Work of Art" and in *Wagner*. John Warrack's collection, *Richard Wagner: Die Meistersinger von Nürnberg* (Cambridge: Cambridge Opera Handbooks, 1994) contains an essay by Tanner entitled "Richard Wagner and Hans Sachs" as well as several other good pieces.

22 Wagner and Nietzsche met in 1868; Wagner published *Beethoven* in 1870.

23 *The Birth of Tragedy out of the Spirit of Music* was originally published in 1872 (Nietzsche was 27) but sections 16–25 were added in 1878 and show Nietzsche's rush of enthusiasm for Schopenhauer and Wagner. In 1886 Nietzsche changed the title to *The Birth of Tragedy or Hellenism and Pessimism,* and added a new Preface, the "Attempt at a Self-Criticism," wherein he regrets his youthful enthusiasm. But, as I will show, the influence of Wagner's music never left him, even if Wagner the man was a disappointment.

24 See Richard Schacht, *Nietzsche* (London: Routledge and Kegan Paul, 1983), p. 225.

25 See, for example, *The Genealogy of Morals* Essay III, # 5 and 6 for Nietzsche's extremely pointed discussion of Schopenhauer's aesthetics.

26 See Alexander Nehamas, *Nietzsche: Life as Literature* (Cambridge, Mass.: Harvard University Press, 1985), pp. 63–67. See Also Richard Rorty, *Philosophy and the Mirror of Nature*, pp. 300 f., and Chapters 7 and 8. Rorty discusses the Good/True analogy on pp. 306 f. The quotation from Quine is from his "Two Dogmas of Empiricism" (1951); see also Rorty's extensive discussion of Quine and metaphysical realism in *Philosophy and the Mirror of Nature.*

27 Alasdair MacIntyre, *Whose Justice? Which Rationality?* (Notre Dame, Indiana: University of Notre Dame Press, 1988), p. 367, and see the rest of Chapters 18, 19, and 20. This book is the sequel to his *After Virtue: A Study in Moral Theory* Second Edition (Notre Dame, Indiana: University of Notre Dame Press, 1984) where MacIntyre first made this point (see Chapter 9).

28 As I understand him, to simply note the contrary position, Steven Hawking seems to believe that there is a God's point of view when he ends his Introduction to *A Brief History of Time* expressing his hope to "know the mind of God." Steven Hawking, *A Brief History of Time* (Toronto and New York: Bantam Books, 1988).

29 MacIntyre's criticism of perspectivism resembles that of critics of coherentist theories of truth: if beliefs are 'true' simply on the basis of consistency with other beliefs, then the truth will change as belief-changes reflect differing criteria of acceptable inconsistency. If truth merely reflects the way beliefs hook onto each other (rather than the way they hook onto the world), nothing governs coherence except tradition. But Nietzsche rejects this relativism in his perspectivism, as I attempt to indicate in what follows. I do admit, gladly, that more must be said on this matter.

30 Nietzsche discusses this set of distinctions in *Beyond Good and Evil* and *The Genealogy of Morals*. See also Chapter 2, Section 6 for another discussion of Good/Bad *versus* Good/Evil.

31 Nehamas discusses self-creativity and in connection with his theme of aesthetic "style" (see Nehamas, pp. 192 f.) but see Tanner's comments on Nehamas in his *Nietzsche* (London and New York: Oxford, 1994), pp. 44–45.

32 In *Nietzsche, Wagner, and the Philosophy of Pessimism* (London: George Allen and Unwin, 1982), Roger Hollinrake shows how the interactive relation between Nietzsche and Wagner directly influenced the early and middle works of the former. It seems clear that Nietzsche's understanding of Wagner's later works remained largely Schopenhauerian (see p. 70).

33 See Walter Kaufmann, *Tragedy and Philosophy* (Princeton: Princeton University Press, 1968), pp. 346–350 for a more detailed discussion of this point. As Mann points out in "The Sufferings and Greatness of Richard Wagner," "Buddhist drama" must be an oxymoron.

34 Warren Darcy, "The Pessimism of *The Ring*," p. 28. See also Warren Darcy, "'The World Belongs to Alberich!' Wagner's changing Attitude towards *The Ring*" in *Ring of the Nibelung: A Companion. The Full German Text with a New Translation* by Steward Spencer and commentaries by Barry Millington, Elizabeth Magee, Roger Hollinrake, and Warren Darcy (London: Thames and Hudson, 1993).

35 Both of these works are about civilization. I agree with Tanner that just as *Die Meistersinger* as well as being a work or art itself, is a work about society and art, whereas *Parsifal* is a work about religion rather than a religious work (like the *Missa Solemnis* or the *B–Minor Mass*).

36 Nehamas also quotes part of this passage at the beginning of his Chapter 7.

Bibliography

Some of the entries on this list also have extensive bibliographies (designated by *).

Adorno, Theodore. *Philosophy of Modern Music.* Anne G. Mitchell and Wesley V. Blomster, trans. New York: NLB, 1973.

———. *Negative Dialectics.* E.B. Ashton, trans. New York: Seabury Press, 1973.

———. *Minima Moralia: Reflections from Damaged Life.* E.F.N. Jephcott, trans. London: NLB, 1974.

———. "On the Social Situation of Music," *Telos*, XXXV (1978).

———. *In Search of Wagner.* Rodney Livingstone, trans. Manchester: NLB and Schocken, 1981.

Bailey, Robert. "The Structure of *The Ring* and its Evolution," *Nineteenth-Century Music,* I (July, 1977).

Beckett, Lucy. "Wagner and His Critics," in Burbidge and Sutton, *The Wagner Companion.*

Borchmeyer, Dieter. *Richard Wagner: Theory and Theatre.* Steward Spencer, trans. Oxford: Clarendon Press, 1991.*

Boulez, Pierre. "Time Re-Explored," in the book accompanying the 1981 release of the 1976 Bayreuth *Ring* by Philips records, reprinted from the 1976 concert program published by the Verlag der Festspeilleitung Bayreuth.

Budd, Malcolm. "The Repudiation of Emotion: Hanslick on Music," *The British Journal of Aesthetics*, XX, 1 (1980).

Burbidge, Peter and Richard Sutton (eds.). *The Wagner Companion.* New York: Cambridge University Press, 1979.*

Burbidge, Peter. "The German Intellectual Tradition," in Burbidge and Sutton, *The Wagner Companion.*

Cooke, Deryck. *An Introduction to Der Ring des Nibelungen,* prepared for the Solti/Vienna *Ring* on Decca/London (RDN–1), 1969. (Shorted to *Introduction to Wagner's Ring.*)

———. *I Saw the World End.* New York: Oxford University Press, 1979.*

———. "Wagner's Musical Language," in Burbidge and Sutton, *The Wagner Companion.*

Cormack, David. "Thomas Mann, Hanns Eisler and the 'New Bayreuth'," *Wagner,* II, 2 (May 1981).

Cord, William. *An Introduction to Richard Wagner's Ring des Nibelungen: A Handbook.* Columbus, Ohio: Ohio University Press, 1983 (revised and enlarged 1995).

Corse, Sandra. *Wagner and the New Consciousness: Language and Love in The Ring.* London and Toronto: Associated University Presses, 1990.

Dahlhaus, Carl. "Soziologishe Dechiffrierung von Music: Zu Theodor W. Adornos Wagnerkritik," *International Review of Music, Aesthetics, and Sociology,* I, 2 (1970).

———. "Über den Schluss der *Götterdämmerung*" *Richard Wagner: Werk und Wirkung.* Ed. Carl Dahlhaus. Regensburg, 1971.

———. *Richard Wagner's Music-Dramas.* Mary Whittall, trans. New York: Cambridge University Press, 1979.*

Darcy, Warren. "The Pessimism of *The Ring,*" *Opera Quarterly,* IV (Summer 1986).

———. "'The World Belongs to Alberich!' Wagner's changing Attitude towards *The Ring,*" in *Ring of the Nibelung: A Companion. The Full German Text with a New Translation* by Steward Spencer and commentaries by Barry Millington, Warren Darcy, Elizabeth Magee, and Roger Hollinrake. London: Thames and Hudson, 1993.

De Rougemont, Denis. *Love and the Western World.* New York: Pantheon, 1958.

DiGaetani, J.L. (ed.). *Penetrating Wagner's Ring.* Teaneck, New Jersey: Fairleigh Dickinson University Press, 1978. Reprinted by Da Capo Press: New York, 1991.

Deathridge, John and Carl Dahlhaus. *The New Grove Wagner.* New York and London: Norton, 1984.*

Donington, Robert. *Wagner's Ring and its Symbols.* London: Faber and Faber, 1963.*

Ewans, Michael. *Wagner and Aeschylus: The Ring and The Orestia.* London: Faber and Faber, 1982.*

Goethe, J.W. von. *Faust.* Original German; translation, and introduction by Walter Kaufmann. New York: Doubleday and Co., Anchor Books, 1963.

Gray, Ronald. "The German Intellectual Background," in Burbidge and Sutton, *The Wagner Companion.*

Grey, Thomas. *Wagner's Musical Prose: Texts and Contexts.* Cambridge: Cambridge University Press, 1995.*

Gutman, R.W. *Richard Wagner: The Man, his Mind, and his Music.* New York: Harcourt, Brace and World, 1968.*

Hauser, Arnold. *The Social History of Art*, Volume III. London: Routledge and Kegan Paul, 1951.

Hegel, G.W.F. *Lectures on Aesthetics.* Bernard Bosanquet, trans. In *The Introduction to Hegel's Philosophy of Fine Art.* London: Routledge and Kegan Paul, 1905. Reprinted in J. Glenn Gray (ed.), *G.W.F. Hegel: On Art, Relgion, Philosophy.* New York: Harper and Row, Harper Torchbooks, 1970.

———. *Phenomenology of Spirit.* A.V. Miller, trans. Oxford: Clarendon Press, 1977.

Heller, Erich. "Goethe and the Avoidance of Tragedy," in Erich Heller, *The Disinherited Mind.* New York: Meridian, 1959.

———. "Nietzsche and Goethe," in *The Disinherited Mind*.

———. "The Artist's Journey into the Interior," in Erich Heller, *The Artist's Journey into the Interior*. New York: Harcourt Brace Jovanovich, 1976.

Hobbes, Thomas. *Leviathan*. Ed. C.B. Macpherson. London: Penguin Books, 1968.

Hollinrake, Roger. "Carl Dahlhaus and *The Ring*," *Wagner 1976: A Celebration of the Bayreuth Festival*. Ed. Steward Spencer. London: Wagner Society, 1976.

———. Holman, J.K. *Wagner's Ring: A Listener's Companion and Concordance*. Portland, Oregon: Amadeus Books, 1996.

———. *Nietzsche, Wagner, and the Philosophy of Pessimism*. London: George Allen and Unwin, 1982.

Jacobs, Robert L. "A Freudian View of *The Ring*," *The Music Review*, XXVI, 3 (1965). Reprinted in J.L. DiGaetani, *Penetrating Wagner's Ring*.

Jay, Martin. *Adorno*. Cambridge, Massachusetts: Harvard University Press, 1984.

Kaufmann, Walter. *Tragedy and Philosophy*. Princeton: Princeton University Press, 1968.

Kerman, Joseph. *Opera as Drama*. New York: Vintage/Knopf/Random House, 1956.

———. *Listen*. New York: Worth Publishers, 1987.

Land, S.K. "The Rise of Intellect in Wagner's *Ring*," *Comparative Drama*, V, 1 (Spring, 1971).

MacIntyre, Alasdair. *After Virtue*, Second Edition. Notre Dame, Indiana: University of Notre Dame Press, 1984.

———. *Whose Justice? Which Rationality?* Notre Dame, Indiana: University of Notre Dame Press, 1988.

Magee, Bryan. *Aspects of Wagner*. New York: Stein and Day, 1968.

Bibliography

———. *The Philosophy of Schopenhauer*. New York: Oxford University Press, 1983.

Mann, Thomas. "Schopenhauer," in Thomas Mann, *Essays of Three Decades*. H.T. Lowe-Porter, trans. New York: Alfred A. Knopf, 1948.

———. "Richard Wagner and *The Ring*," in Mann, *Essays of Three Decades*.

———. "The Sufferings and Greatness of Richard Wagner," in *Essays by Thomas Mann*. H.T. Lowe-Porter, trans. New York: Random House, 1957.

Marx, Karl. *Writings of the Young Marx on Philosophy and Society*. Ed. Loyd Easton and Kurt Guddat. New York: Doubleday and Co., Anchor Books, 1967.

Miller, J. Hillis. "Some Implications of Nietzsche's Thought about Marzism," *Telos,* XXXVII (1978).

Millington, Barry. *Wagner*. London: J.M. Dent and Princeton, New Jersey: Princeton University Press, 1984.

———. "Nuremberg Trial: Is There Antisemitism in *Die Meistersinger*?" *Cambridge Opera Journal,* III, 3 (1991).

———. *The Wagner Companion: A Guide to Wagner's Life and Music*. New York: Schirmer, 1992.*

Nehamas, Alexander. *Nietzsche: Life as Literature*. Cambridge, Massachusetts.: Harvard, 1985.

Newman, Ernst. *The Wagner Operas*. New York: Harper, 1983. Originally published as *Wagner Nights.* New York:Alfred Knopf, 1949.

———. *A Study of Wagner*. New York: G.P. Putnam and Sons, 1899.

———. *Wagner as Man and Artist.* London: John Lane, 1925.

———. *The Life of Richard Wagner.* 4 vols. London and New York: Cassell and Company, and Alfred Knopf, 1933.

Nietzsche, Friederich. *Beyond Good and Evil.*, Walter Kaufmann, trans. New York: Random House/Vintage, 1966.

———. *The Birth of Tragedy* and *The Case of Wagner*. Walter Kaufmann, trans. New York: Vintage, 1967.

———. *The Will to Power*. Walter Kaufmann and R.J. Hollingdale, trans. Ed. Walter Kaufmann. New York: Random House, 1968.

———. *The Genealogy of Morals* and *Ecce Homo.* Walter Kaufmann and R.J. Hollingdale, trans. New York: Random House/Vintage, 1969.

———. *The Portable Nietzsche.* Walter Kaufmann, trans. New York: Viking/Penguin, 1982.

———. *Untimely Meditations: Richard Wagner in Bayreuth*. R.J. Hollingdale, trans. Cambridge: Cambridge University Press, 1983.

———. *Human, All Too Human*. R.J. Hollingdale, trans. Cambridge: Cambridge University Press, 1986.

Nussbaum, Martha. *The Fragility of Goodness: Luck and Ethics in Greek Tragedy and Philosophy.* New York and Cambridge: Cambridge University Press, 1986.

Peckham, Morse. *Beyond the Tragic Vision*. New York: George Braziller, 1962.

Raphael, Robert. *Richard Wagner*. New York: Twayne Author Series, 1969.

Rappl, Erich. "Insights into the Creation of a Musical World," in *Wagner 1976: A Celebration of the Bayreuth Festival.* London: Wagner Society, 1976.

Rather, L.J. *The Dream of Self-Destruction: Wagner's Ring and the Modern World*. Baton Rouge, Louisiana and London: Louisiana State University Press, 1979.

Rorty, Richard. *Philosophy and the Mirror of Nature*. Princeton: Princeton University Press, 1979.

———. *Contingency, Irony, and Solidarity.* Cambridge: Cambridge University Press, 1989.

Rose, Lawrence Paul. *Wagner: Race and Revolution.* London: Faber and Faber. 1992.

Rosen, Charles. *The Classical Style: Haydn, Mozart, Beethoven.* New York: Norton, 1972.

Schacht, Richard. *Nietzsche.* London: Routledge and Kegan Paul, 1983.

Schopenhauer, Arthur. *The World as Will and Representation.* 2 Volumes. E.F.J. Payne, trans. New York: Dover, 1969.

Schoenberg, Arnold. "Brahms the Progressive," in Arnold Schoenberg, *Style and Idea.* Leo Black, trans. Ed. Leonard Stein. New York: St. Martin's Press, 1975.

Shaw, George Bernard. *The Perfect Wagnerite.* New York: Dover, 1967; first published 1898.

Solomon, Maynard. "Beethoven, Sonata, and Utopia," *Telos,* VI (1971).

———. "Beethoven and the Enlightenment," *Telos,* VII (1972).

Solomon, Robert. "Beethoven and the Sonata Form," *Telos,* VII (1972).

———. *History and Human Nature.* New York: Harcourt Brace Jovanovich, 1979. Republished as *The Bully Culture: Enlightenment, Romanticism, and the Transcendental Pretense.* New York: Rowan and Littlefield, 1992.

Staiger, Emil. *Musik und Dichtung.* Zurich and Freiburg: Atlantis Musikbuch-Verlag, 1947 & 1980.

Stein, Jack M. *Richard Wagner and the Synthesis of the Arts.* Westport, Connecticut: Greenwood Press, 1960.*

Stein, Leon. *The Racial Thinking of Richard Wagner.* New York: Philosophical Library, 1950.

Tanner, Michael. "The Total Work of Art," in Burbidge and Sutton, *The Wagner Companion.*

———. Introduction to R.J. Hollingdale's translation of Friederich Nietzsche's *Daybreak: Thoughts on the Prejudices of Morality.* New York: Cambridge University Press, 1982.

———. "Wagner's *Ring,*" *Classical CD,* (November 1990).

———. "Richard Wagner and Hans Sachs," in *Richard Wagner: Die Meistersinger von Nürnberg.* Ed. John Warrack. Cambridge: Cambridge University Press, 1994.

———. *Nietzsche.* London and New York: Oxford University Press, 1994.

———. *Wagner.* Princeton, New Jersey: Princeton University Press, 1996.

Wagner, Richard. *Beethoven..* William Ashton Ellis, trans. New York: Broude Brothers, 1960.

———. *Opera and Drama..* William Ashton Ellis, trans. New York: Broude Brothers, 1960.

———. *The Ring of the Nibelung.* Andrew Porter, trans. New York: W.W. Norton, 1977.

Weiner, Mark. *Wagner and the Anti-Semitic Imagination.* London and Lincoln, Nebraska: University of Nebraska, 1995.

von Westernhagen, Curt. *The Forging of The Ring: Richard Wagner's Composition Sketches for Der Ring des Nibelungen.* Arnold and Mary Whittall, trans. Cambridge: Cambridge University Press, 1976.*

Windell, George. "Hegel, Feuerbach, and Wagner's *Ring.*" *Central European History,* IX, 1 (March 1976).

———. "Hitler, National Socialism, and Richard Wagner," in DiGaetani, *Penetrating Wagner's Ring.*

Zuckermann, Elliot. *The First Hundred Years of Tristan.* New York: Columbia University Press, 1964.

Musical References

I include below the principal motifs to which I refer. I have modeled most of them from the following sources (see Bibliography) where further discussion can also be found: Deryck Cooke, "Wagner's Musical Language" (WML); Deryck Cooke, *I Saw the World End* (WE); Deryck Cooke, *Introduction to Wagner's Ring* (IR); Robert Donnington, *Wagner's Ring and its Symbols* (D).

Alberich's Curse: D

Beethoven op. 135: WML

Muss es sein?

Brünnhilde's Awakening:

Brünnhilde's Holy Love: D

Brünnhilde's Reproach: WE

Brünnhilde's Womanhood: D

Dragon: D

Dawn of Hagen's Day: IR

Musical References

Erda: D, IR

Fate: WML

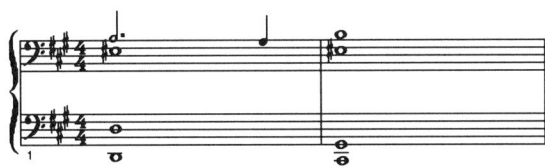

Freia I and II: WE

Gold: D, IR

Golden Apples and Ring: *Das Rheingold,* scene ii:

Gutrune: WML

Hagen:

Musical References

Love's Greeting: IR

Love (Freia I): IR

Love's Greeting and Friea II: IR

Love's Redemption: D, WML

Magic Fire: IR

Nature: D, IR

Need of the Gods and Wotan's Frustration: D, IR

Power of the Ring: WE

Purpose of the Sword: IR

Renunciation: D, IR

Reproach: WML

Musical References

Rhine: D, IR

Rhinegold: IR

Rhinemaiden's Innocence: D

Ring: D

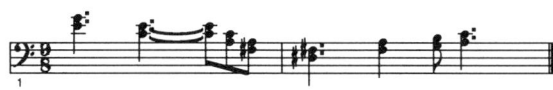

Seduction of Siegfried: IR

Servitude or Bondage: IR

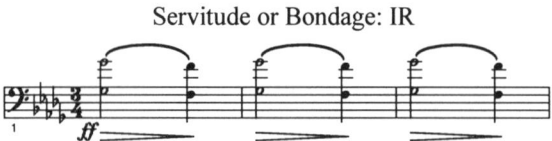

Siegfried:

Siegfried's Heroism: D

Siegfried's Horn-Call: D, IR

Siegfried's Mission: IR

Siegfried's Yearning for Love: IR

Siegfried's Youthful Exuberance: D

Siegmund/Sieglinde: D

Sleeping Brunnhilde:

Sword: D, IR

Tarnhelm: IR

Twilight (Decline) of the Gods: D, IR

Valhalla: IR

Volsung Race: WML

Wotan's Frustration: D

Wotan's Spear: IR

Wunshmädchen (*Die Walküre* II, iv): IR

Index

This is primarily a subject index. Because of the large number of proper names and titles, it would otherwise be filled with useless information. I try to identify those items and names directly relevant to the development of my thesis. The Table of Contents also serves as an outline of my discussion.

A

Adorno, Theodor 3, 157-158
    aesthetics 122-129
    on Schopenhauer 107-109, 124
    leitmotifs 105-107, 138 (n. 29)
    on Wagner 103-109
    sonata form 115-116
    The Ring 123-124
    Tristan 107-109

B

Beckett, Lucy 223 (n. 11)
Beethoven, Ludwig van 77-78, 174
    Fidelio 127, 182
    Ninth Symphony 30-31, 181-182, 184
    op. 131 Quartet 180-181
    op. 135 Quartet 22, 65, 181
    op. 47 Violin Sonata 144
Borchmeyer, Dieter 222 (n. 7)

C

Conrad, Joseph 220
Cooke, Deryck 8, 9, 55-56, 65, 91, 102, 110, 127, 149, 155, 220, 27 (n. 10), 28 (n. 11)
Cord, William 8
Corse, Sandra 2, 139 (n. 36)

D

Dahlhaus, Carl 7, 197-198
    on Adorno 117-120
    optimistic *Ring* 88-93, 153
Darcy, Warren 9, 218, 82 (n. 18), 83 (n. 21), 226 (n. 34)
Deathridge, John 7
Donnington, Robert 2, 8, 9, 135 (n. 5)

E

Eisler, Hans 109
Evil, concept of
    Christianity 67-70
    Goethe 69-71
    Goethe's *Faust* 71, 77
    Mozart's *Don Giovani* 71
    Nietzsche 72-73
    Paul 70
    Plato 68
    Wagner 217-218
        The Ring (Hagen) 72-77
Ewans, Michael 82 (n. 20)

F

Feuerbach, Ludwig 34-39, 142, 151

G

German terms discussed
    aufheben/Aufhebung 90, 91, 95
    Bildung 5, 150, 171, 175, 209
    Einfühlung 107
    machen/Macht 204
    Mitleid 59, 63, 181, 189-191
    Wahn 193-195
Goethe, J. 180
    Faust 172-173, 200-201
Gray, Ronald 222 (n. 5)
Grey, Thomas 8, 81 (n. 17), 137 (n. 21), 138-139 (n. 29 & 30)

H
Hauser, Arnold 116-117
Hegel, G.W.F. 78, 171-172, 178
  Master/Slave analogy 38, 55, 102, 174-176
  philosophy 174
Heller, Erich 68-69, 77, 173
Hobbes, Thomas 98
Hollinrake, Roger 89, 216
Hume, David 165-168

J
James, William 207
Jay, Martin 137 (n. 21), 139-140 (n. 37)

K
Kant, Immanuel 175, 177, 199
  knowledge 165-169
  morality 169-170, 171
  sublimity 173

L
Land, S.K. 161 (n. 4)
Love and Power 18-19, 38, 127-128, 145-148
  conflict 41-43, 147, 151, 217
  redemption 52, 58-66
    Mitleid/compassion 61, 62-64, 181
  renunciation 53-58, 146

M
MacIntyre, Alasdair 209-212
Magee, Bryan 7
  Edward Dent 126
  music-drama 125-126
Mann, Thomas 29, 76, 188, 85 (n. 33), 160 (n. 1), 223 (n. 11 & 12)
Millington, Barry 7, 9
moral vitalism 157-159, 202, see also Nietzsche: perspectivism/coping, see also Conrad

Mozart, W.A. 172

N
Nehamas, Alexander 212-214
Newman, Ernst 7, 55
Nietzsche, Friedrich 1, 3, 157
  creativity 153-154, 196, 201
  on Schopenhauer 203-205, 215-216
  on tragedy 202, 203
  on Wagner 5, 103, 130-134, 215-216, 140 (n. 38)
  perspectivism 4, 205-215
    coping 206
  philosophy and art 198-205
  will to power 4, 204-207, 208, 210, 213, 216

P
Peckham, Morse 5, 8, 41, 56, 131-133, 150, 186, 191-192, 195

Q
Quine, W.V.O 207

R
Raphael, Robert 5, 8, 223-4 (n. 15 & 20)
Rather, L.J. 26-27 (n. 4), 84 (n. 30 & 32)
  Sophocles 67
Röckel, August
  Wagner's letters 29, 103, 154, 78-79 (n. 2), 81 (n. 15)
Rorty, Richard 208, 210, 28 (n. 12), 162 (n. 13)
Rosen, Charles 139 (n. 33)
  musical form 119-122

S
Schopenhauer, Arthur 4, 29, 176-177
  Mitleid 181
  music 178, 183, 185, 190

Index

the Will 31, 152, 177-180
   and sex 188-189
Shaw, George B. 2, 9
Solomon, Maynard 138 (n. 25)
Solomon, Robert 138 (n. 25)
Staiger, Emil 33, 100
Stein, Jack
   leitmotifs 111

T

Tanner, Michael 8, 41, 147-148, 159, 192, 202, 221, 26-27 (n. 4), 140 (n. 40), 225 (n. 21)

W

Wagner, Richard 217
   Anti-Semitism 7, 26 (n. 4)
   Die Meistersinger 192-195, 210
      illusion/delusion and *DieMeistersinger* 193-195, 198
   leitmotifs, general 10, 106
   music-drama 6, 30-35, 155, 180-183
   musical form 118-122
   refusal to transcend 5, 19, 41, 132-133, 152, 196, 204, 219-220
   sex and the Will 89, 152, 191-192, see also: Schopenhauer, the Will and sex
   The Ring
      conflict, four levels 41-43
      endings of the four parts of *The Ring* 44-52, 148-150
      Götterdämmerung endings 39-41, 141-148, 160-161 (n. 1)
      Götterdämmerung Prolog 16, 25, 45
      principal leitmotifs discussed: 20-25, 110-115, 155-157

Fate 22, 44, 65
Freia motifs 59-61
Redemption Through Love 18, 47, 48, 93-95, 119, 146-148
Renunciation 10-11, 21, 53-58, 146, 149
monologues 36-38, 62, 100-102
tragedy 73, 158
Wotan and politics 96
Tristan 185-188, 198, 219
Will as essence of the world 31, 103, see also Schopenhauer: the Will, music
Windell, George 79-80 (n. 8)

This series of monographs, translations, and critical editions covers comparative and interdisciplinary topics of significance from the early eighteenth century to the present. Volumes, both published and projected, include a collection of essays on German drama, a study of the Künstlerroman, and a study on the aesthetics of the double talent of Kubin and Herzmanovsky-Orlando.

For additional information about this series or for the submission of manuscripts, please contact:

>Peter Lang Publishing
>Acquisitions Dept.
>516 N. Charles St., 2nd Floor
>Baltimore, MD 21201

To order other books in this series, please contact our Customer Service Department at:

>800-770-LANG (within the U.S.)
>(212) 647-7706 (outside the U.S.)
>(212) 647-7707 FAX

or browse online by series at:

>www.peterlang.com